Wild Men

New Narratives in American History

Series Editors
James West Davidson
Michael B. Stoff

Colonial

Richard Godbeer — Escaping Salem:
The Other Witch Hunt of 1692

Southern

James E. Crisp — Sleuthing the Alamo:
Davy Crockett's Last Stand and Other
Mysteries of the Texas Revolution

William L. Barney — The Making of a Confederate:
Walter Lenoir's Civil War

Civil War and Reconstruction

John Hope Franklin
and Loren Schweninger — In Search of the Promised Land:
A Slave Family and the Old South

William L. Barney — The Making of a Confederate:
Walter Lenoir's Civil War

Twentieth-Century Environmental

Mark H. Lytle — The Gentle Subversive:
Rachel Carson, Silent Spring, and the Rise of
the American Environmental Movement

African American

James West Davidson — 'They Say': Ida B. Wells and the
Reconstruction of Race

John Hope Franklin
and Loren Schweninger — In Search of the Promised Land:
A Slave Family and the Old South

Twentieth-Century U.S. History

James West Davidson — 'They Say':
Ida B. Wells and the Reconstruction of Race

John Hope Franklin and
Loren Schweninger — In Search of the Promised Land:
A Slave Family and the Old South

Allan M. Winkler — "To Everything There Is a Season":
Pete Seeger and the Power of Song

Wild Men

Ishi and Kroeber in the Wilderness of Modern America

Douglas Cazaux Sackman

UNIVERSITY PRESS

2010

OXFORD

UNIVERSITY PRESS

Oxford University Press, Inc., publishes works
that further Oxford University's objective of excellence
in research, scholarship, and education.

Oxford   New York

Auckland   Cape Town   Dar es Salaam   Hong Kong   Karachi
Kuala Lumpur   Madrid   Melbourne   Mexico City   Nairobi
New Delhi   Shanghai   Taipei   Toronto

With offices in

Argentina   Austria   Brazil   Chile   Czech Republic   France   Greece
Guatemala   Hungary   Italy   Japan   Poland   Portugal   Singapore
South Korea   Switzerland   Thailand   Turkey   Ukraine   Vietnam

Copyright © 2010 by Oxford University Press, Inc.

Published by Oxford University Press, Inc.
198 Madison Avenue, New York, New York 10016

www.oup.com

Library of Congress Cataloging-in-Publication Data
Sackman, Douglas Cazaux, 1968–
Wild men : Ishi and Kroeber in the wilderness of modern
America / Douglas Cazaux Sackman.
p.   cm. — (New narratives in American history)
Includes index.
ISBN 978-0-19-517852-4; 978-0-19-517853-1 (pbk.)
1. Ishi, d. 1916.   2. Yana Indians—Biography.
3. Kroeber, A. L. (Alfred Louis), 1876–1960   4. Kroeber, A. L. (Alfred Louis),
1876–1960—Relations with Yana Indians.   5. Anthropologists—United
States—Biography.   I. Title.
E99.Y23S235 2009
301.2092—dc22   2009020660

1 3 5 7 9 8 6 4 2

Printed in the United States of America
on acid-free paper

For the children

CONTENTS

Contents

ACKNOWLEDGMENTS

T HIS BOOK WAS WRITTEN IN A HUNDRED LANDSCAPES, IT SEEMS. The trusty laptop came with me on various journeys: down the road to the public pool, to the home in which I grew up in Sacramento, and across the country to New York. Notes were written along the streams of Mount Lassen and the streets of San Francisco. Words made their way onto the page while I was parked at the waterfront at Tramp Harbor, at my wife's office, at my temporary office while on sabbatical in the library tower, on my porch, in a café in Oakland, and on a ferry in Puget Sound.

As much as place was a Clio for this project (and Apple my Hermes), the book could not have been written without the help and encouragement of fellow scholars, friends, and family. Any work on the meeting of Ishi and Alfred Kroeber owes a great debt to the original participants and their stories and writings, principally Thomas T. Waterman, Saxton Pope, Edward Sapir, and Kroeber and Ishi themselves. My indebtedness to the scores of scholars and writers who have furthered our knowledge and understanding of Ishi and Kroeber and their world is conveyed in the endnotes, but I would like to acknowledge up front what I think of as "the big six": the book that rekindled interest in Ishi, Theodora Kroeber's beautifully written *Ishi in Two Worlds* (1962); Theodora's revealing biography of he husband, *Alfred Kroeber: A Personal Configuration* (1970); the sourcebook of documents Theodora put together with Robert Heizer, *Ishi the Last Yahi* (1979); Jed Riffe's probing film documentary, *Ishi, the Last Yahi* (1994); the vital volume containing a wealth of new scholarship edited by Alfred's sons, Karl and Clifton, *Ishi in Three Centuries* (2003); and Orin Starn's brilliant exploration of Ishi's life and legacy, *Ishi's Brain* (2004).

I began this project just before Starn's work was published, and when I found out that it was in the works, I almost gave it up. I knew Starn would be looking again at the entire story partly in the light of newer approaches to the history of anthropology and Indians, as I was planning to do. Fortunately my editors at Oxford encouraged me to go forward. Ultimately the book I wrote shares similarities with parts of all of the big six, but in another respect it is an entirely new narrative exploring different aspects of our shared American history that the meeting of these two men illuminate. I can only hope that readers, whether or not the story of Ishi and Kroeber is familiar to them, will enjoy the narrative, and through it see themselves and their history at least partially in a new light.

Initial research for this book was supported by the Graves Award in the Humanities. Though some of the research was done in situ—along Deer and Mill Creeks, in San Francisco and Berkeley, and in New York City—most was done through reading published sources and poring over archival records at the California State University at Chico and, principally, the Bancroft Library at Berkeley, which houses the papers of Alfred and Theodora Kroeber as well as the Berkeley Anthropology Department. My thanks to the staffs of both institutions. For help with the photographs and images I am indebted to Jed Riffe, Herb Puffer, David Carlson, David Dewey at the Butte County Pioneer Museum, and the staffs at the Phoebe Hearst Museum of Anthropology, the Bancroft Library, the California State Library, and the San Francisco Public Library. I thank the University of Puget Sound for subsidizing the publication of the images.

I am grateful to my colleagues at Puget Sound for creating a stimulating and collegial environment in which to be a scholar. Students in my Frontiers of Native America course also helped me broaden my understanding of how we might today reckon with the actions of the legacies of Ishi and Kroeber. I benefited greatly by the knowledgeable, perceptive, and challenging reviews of the proposal and the manuscript by Colin Fisher, Sam Truett, John Lear, William Bauer, George Cornell, Brian DeLay, Kathy Morse, and the anonymous readers for the Press. I thank them all for the seriousness with which they took my project and this history; they helped me make it a much better book.

My experience working with the editors at Oxford has been wonderful. I thank Peter Coveney for his early support and Brian Wheel for shepherding the project to completion. I would also like to thank Judith Hoover for her expert copyediting and Christine Dahlin for taking the manuscript through the production and design process. It has been a great privilege to write under the encouraging and sure guidance of James West Davidson and Mike Stoff, the series' editors. As I was reviewing a book proposal for their series, it popped into my mind that it was time to take up the Ishi and Kroeber story again. The notion grew out of an old idea that suddenly found a new outlet for expression. In an anthropology class as an undergraduate at Reed taught by Gail Kelly, I had first studied Kroeber's writings about Native Californians; I had long thought I would like to turn the anthropological gaze around and try to recover how Kroeber had appeared to the people he studied. That idea was reborn in a new form as I put together a book proposal. I'm grateful that Mike and Jim thought it had promise and decided to include it in their remarkable series. Mike did an astounding job incisively and insightfully editing the manuscript, helping me to see on every page ways to strengthen the narrative.

My family also made this book possible, and imaginable. Karin stepped up when I was away, and her support of her favorite son-in-law has always been a feather in my cap. Bill always had faith in the book and helped keep me going. Last summer, after I anxiously read the reviews of the first draft poolside in Pennsylvania, it was great to be able to talk it all over with Bill and Harry. Harry provided the sage advice, though it must be said that Bill taught him pretty much everything he knows.

My wife, Sonja, has been an amazing sounding board, and much more. John Steinbeck once said of *The Grapes of Wrath* that there are five levels in the book, but that readers would discover only as many as they had in themselves. I don't know how many levels are in this book—or how many are in me—but I do know that Sonja has them all. She sounded out the greater depths of the history and the relationship I was exploring.

Maybe it's true that you can never go home again, just as you can never stand in the same river twice. But there was a part of writing this book that was very much like going back to the

Acknowledgments

landscapes of my childhood with my brother, Kurt, along the American River. I am eternally grateful to my mom and dad, who gave me a home base for this book back when I was growing up and again when I was writing it. Just as I was completing the book and a chapter in my career, they gave me more gifts of music and poetry. I will pass these on to the next generation.

My daughters, Zoë and Iris, have heard verses of this story in progress. I hope that they will enjoy reading it one day and see something more of their father in its pages. Alfred, too, loved his children deeply, and in a way left to them this story as well. Clifton, Karl, and Ursula have borne the legacy of their father's involvement with Ishi gracefully. I hope, if they read this, that my version does justice to the man they knew. We do not know if Ishi had any children of his own, but we do know that he loved children. We also know that Indians of his day, against all odds, had children and taught them to carry on in an increasingly hostile world. If any of their children, or their children's children, read this book, I hope that my version honors the history they know.

This book is dedicated to the children.

Wild Men

"Ih si" flash card. Alfred Kroeber, "Ishi Reading Lessons," A. L. Kroeber Papers, BANC FILM 2049. Courtesy of the Bancroft Library, University of California, Berkeley.

· Prologue ·

ONE SMALL STEP

✴

HIS FEET, BROAD AND THICKLY SOLED THROUGH USE, PRESSED
down evenly on the pale stone of the city. He took short steps,
sliding his feet along carefully, as he always did. Walking, he knew,
is about finding the right way along the earth, the trail. Walking
is living. His stories were about walking, about when He stepped
along the trail. But here it was different, he could already sense.
Walking was something the *saltu* did on the side. And they made
night into day with their lights. This was a ghost world, and now
he was stepping right into it.

After another packed day of work at the museum, Alfred
Kroeber sat at home across the city, waiting. He had been waiting for him a long time, dreaming about this man; before he
ever saw him for himself, Kroeber believed in him and his
people, telling the world about "a totally wild and independent
tribe of Indians, without firearms, fleeing at the approach of
the white man, hidden away for more than forty years in one
of the longest settled and most densely populated States of the
West." Doubters scoffed that this tribe was imaginary, nothing more than an Old West legend. But the young, bearded

anthropologist insisted that they were real, that their existence was an "incontrovertible fact."[1]

Now the fact was on his way to him. What was this man experiencing, he wondered. This was what Kroeber did, his profession: he studied man to discover his origins and nature, to find out what made him tick. The wild sensations of the scene seized him, a cacophony of sounds and expectations. The man's first step into the city was a giant leap into the unknown; it was as if Kroeber himself "were to visit the moon," he mused. Though he wasn't actually there to see the man arrive in the city, Kroeber recorded the momentous encounter, the last of its kind, for posterity: "There stepped off the ferry boat into the glare of electric lights, into the shouting of hotel runners, and the clanging of trolley cars on Market Street, San Francisco, Ishi, the last wild Indian in the United States."[2]

San Francisco was a place to behold in 1911. It was a modern and beautiful city, risen like Phoenix from the ashes of the Great Earthquake and Fire of 1906. Five years earlier, at 5:12 in the morning of April 18, the San Andreas fault had ruptured, the earth rumbled. Brick and mortar shook, buildings fell or dropped into liquefied earth, streets twisted, and chasms wrenched open, swallowing debris and people. Gas lines broke and fires erupted. There wasn't enough water in the city to put them out. Desperately, firefighters dynamited buildings to create firebreaks.

Thousands fled to the Ferry Building, which somehow withstood the shock, though rods buckled and rivets sheered off. In the days that followed, you could look out from the Ferry Building tower and behold the devastated city, smoldering, buildings bombed out and black along the city's arteries; a half-dozen trolley cars that had survived were lined up on a section of intact track, the only order in a street scene strewn with horses, donkeys, and carts, a few of the new horseless carriages, two bicycles, and people, up and down and around the great Market Street, once the Champs Elysées of San Francisco, wearing their black bowler hats, trying to recover but moving about aimless and dazed like newcomers to Purgatory, or like men caught in a Magritte painting.

Kroeber was out in this crowd. After the shaking stopped that morning, he left his hotel apartment on Eddy Street in downtown San Francisco and looked for a trolley on Market Street. He had to get to the other side of the city, but trolleys were out of commission. He took a small step forward and resolved to walk. He passed upstream through the shell-shocked throngs wandering about the surreal scene, making his way over the rubble and buckled cobbles of the city, compelled on to Parnassus Heights, where his responsibilities lay. That was where the Museum of Anthropology, with its irreplaceable collection of art and artifacts from Greece and Egypt and the Indians of North America, stood. He hoped it still stood. It was just three miles, but the journey seemed immeasurably long.

When at last the museum came into view, he was relieved. A chimney had toppled, a front stoop was crooked, but the building had withstood the quake. Venturing inside, he heard a familiar sound that was strange now: the tapping of a typewriter. Upstairs he found the museum secretary, despite the uproar in the city at large, going about her work. Kroeber got to work, too. Cataloguing the damage, he found that the collections had come

Market Street after the Great Earthquake of 1906, as viewed from the Ferry Building.

through well. A small quake months before had inspired him to use copper wire to secure shelving and artifacts. The precautions paid off, and he could write Phoebe Hearst, the patron of the museum, that "the damage sustained was very light under the circumstances." He gave his report a silver lining: "We all feel that the outcome will be not only a greater San Francisco but a greater University."[3]

He found a place to stay nearby for the next few days as the city burned, and helped protect the museum and its belongings from wind-borne embers. Smoke filled the air; day had been turned into night. Tens of thousands of refugees camped out at the nearby Golden Gate Park, set apart from urban growth in the 1870s; now it became a safe haven for the homeless San Franciscans in 1906. Like so many others, Kroeber's hotel apartment had burned to the ground. He lost all of his personal belongings, including the only copy of his handwritten master's thesis on the English heroic play. But that hardly mattered. The museum had survived the Big One.[4]

Kroeber was back in the field soon, collecting more material, curious about how Indians had viewed earthquakes through the years, since they must know this land in all of its geologic permutations. He went to see an old Yurok man named Stone who lived along the Klamath River, three hundred miles north of San Francisco. "Chy-kee," Kroeber said, greeting the man and shaking his hand. Stone looked him up and down, making sure he wasn't a ghost. "I never think you arrive again." Kroeber's interpreter explained: "He sure been thinking you be killed that time you got shaking down below." "Down below" meant down the river and down the coast, to Arcata or Eureka, or all the way to San

Francisco. When the Yurok say someone "has been taken below," they mean taken to San Francisco, usually to be put on trial by white men or put in prison at San Quentin. Kroeber told Stone, "I was a little too tough to be killed that quick, but tell me, what did the old people tell you about earthquakes?"[5]

Stone said the Yurok believed that the earth was tilting, and that the failure to keep doing the traditional dances, the jump dance and the deerskin dance, contributed to the declination. If the earth tilted too far, it would fall off completely. "The earthquakes are therefore a warning," a warning that had always been heeded in the past, the anthropologist noted. "All the Indians of California have a name for the earthquake, and most of them personify it," Kroeber reported. The Wintu—Ishi knew these downstream neighbors as the Ya'wi—believed that the earth was once small, but as Indians became more numerous Coyote, the trickster, stretched the earth to make room. Each time he did so, the earth quaked and the valleys and mountains formed. The Wintu were divided about what had happened in 1906. Some thought that, as the Indians were nearly extinct, this was the beginning of the great transformation of the world that would make it flat, like the abode of the dead. But one shaman thought that rumors of the Indians' passing were greatly exaggerated and that the earthquake was just a sign that Coyote was stretching the world again, this time to make room for the teeming whites.

Kroeber later interviewed another Yurok Indian man named Re'mik about the quake. "Now Earthquake is angry," Re'mik said, "because the Americans have brought up Indian treasures and formulas and taken them away to San Francisco to keep. He knew that, so he tore up the ground there." This explanation of the supernatural forces at work in this place was written down and published in a book called *Yurok Myths.*[6]

Undeterred, Kroeber went on with his work of collecting artifacts and knowledge from California Indians. Meanwhile San Franciscans filled in the fissures, made new land along the bay, and generally covered up the effects of the quake. They even suppressed knowledge about how many people had been lost in the disaster, losing them a second time so that the city could get on with the business of growth. The newspapers proclaimed, "SAN FRANCISCO WILL RISE FROM THE ASHES, A GREATER AND MORE BEAUTIFUL CITY THAN EVER." The *Examiner* depicted the city as a grizzly bear, shot with arrows labeled "Earthquake," "Fire," and "Famine." But the Bear was "UNDAUNTED." A more magnificent city was built on the smoldering ashes of the old. By the time Ishi arrived in San Francisco, the city had been reclaimed, and it was growing taller.[7]

That September night in 1911, Ishi stepped onto a street lined with fifteen-story buildings, billboards for the newest products, and electric lights; he was assaulted by the clamor of the streetcar traffic and the thousands of people; fifty thousand others came through the Ferry Building that day, and the street ahead was alive with activity, even at this late hour. Market Street was a Grand Canyon of commerce, a wonder of the modern world.

City leaders were planning a world's fair—the Panama Pacific International Exposition, they called it—to celebrate progress and expansion. A great sign would go up on the Ferry Building, and the tower would bear the numbers of the year in which the fair was to be held: 1915. The earth divided on its own accord in 1906, but the fair would celebrate the parting of land by American engineers in Panama to connect the Atlantic and the Pacific. A new stage for world commerce would open up, and the exposition would show the world that San Francisco was the queen city of the Pacific, the site where westward expansion culminated and where new expansion across the ocean would commence. Charged with electricity and lighting up the sky, San Francisco positioned itself as the beacon of American progress.

A hundred years before the earthquake reminded San Franciscans of the power of nature, Thomas Jefferson envisioned America as an Empire of Liberty that would stretch across the continent, and dispatched Lewis and Clark to survey the land. As their expedition was leaving the Mandan Indian village along the Missouri River, Lewis breathlessly wrote in his journal, "We were now about to penetrate a country at least two thousand miles in width, on which the foot of civilized man had never trodden."

Ishi's was not the first foot of "uncivilized man" to tread the streets of San Francisco. The Chutchui, Amuctac, Tubsinte, and Petlenuc had walked the site of the city for generations before Spanish colonialists turned it into a pueblo in their empire and called the place Yerba Buena. But the city took on a new character after the United States wrested California from Mexico in 1848. In 1849 San Francisco boomed as people from around the world rushed to California looking for gold; the earth was pried open, this time by human hands, and social fissures cracked across the state. In just five years San Francisco's population grew to fifty thousand; it was an instant city, and Americans wanted to make the most of that fact to speed expansion.

Far to the north, in the Puget Sound of what would become Washington Territory, Indians far outnumbered white

Americans in the 1850s. And their rough towns were not impressive. A S'Klallam leader named Chetzomoka was strategically invited to visit San Francisco. He went onboard a "colossal canoe with two masts" and sailed down the coast. In San Francisco he walked the city and took in the sights and sounds, the buildings and the masses of people. He came back home with a photograph of himself in San Francisco and "very enlarged views of the number and power of the white man." Whites believed that transporting individual Indians to San Francisco would awe them, and shock them a little, too. After setting foot in the city, Indians would find it harder to stand their ground in their homelands, whites reasoned.[8]

Ishi took only a few steps of his own in the city that first night. Escorted by Thomas Waterman and Sam Batwi, Ishi boarded an electric trolley in front of the ferry terminal. It took him up Market Street toward his ultimate destination, Kroeber's Museum of Anthropology on San Francisco's Mount Parnassus, 909 feet above sea level. The museum had been named after the mountain above Delphi in Greece, 8,062 feet high, the fabled home of the Muses and thus the seat of poetry, music, and learning. One time, it was said, Zeus, angered by the behavior of people who murdered their brothers more readily than they worshiped their gods, "let loose a great flood on earth, meaning to wipe out the whole race of man." But Deucalion built an ark and went aboard with his wife, Pyrrha. The floods came quickly and violently, submerging the whole world except the mountaintops; all other mortals were lost beneath the waves, but these two, the last of their tribe, floated for nine days until the water began to recede and their ark came to rest on Mount Parnassus. This explanation of the supernatural forces at work in this place was written down and published in a book called *The Greek Myths*.

Ishi ascended Mount Parnassus and became an American myth. Americans from across the country clamored to find out more about this mysterious stranger. But when they wondered about him, they were also wondering about themselves and the new world they inhabited. They were thrilled to walk the streets of modern America, or be whisked along by rail or automobile. But they were also anxious about this new world, and the world they had left behind. Many believed that a unique American identity had been born in the wilderness. Was that wilderness altogether gone now? And what of the Indians—had they tragically vanished? Were they responsible? For them, Ishi became an American idol, a larger-than-life figure against whom to measure their own sense of self, a hero of sorts in their myth of where they had come from and where they were going. They wanted him to be *wild*, absolutely. Because they thought of themselves as *civilized*, ambivalently. Though they stood on the streets of the city, they wanted nonetheless to reach out and touch a man and a land that were still wild. Alfred Kroeber wanted to do the same thing, for reasons that were close to but also far removed from those of his countrymen. When Kroeber and Ishi came face to face it was a momentous event, not only for each man, but for the cultures they represented. Each stood on the brink: one was in danger of losing something vital; the other was in danger of disappearing altogether.

Now Ishi was in Kroeber's museum on Parnassus, and the anthropologist would have to begin to take responsibility for him, both the man and the myth. Ishi spent the first night in a square room, refusing to take off his new clothes to go to bed. Anxiousness must have kept him awake, though certainly he must have been tired from his journey by train, ferry, and trolley car. He never got tired traveling by foot. Kroeber and Saxton Pope, the university physician who would treat Ishi and become his friend, marveled at Ishi's natural body, at his feet made for walking. Pope measured them, making casts, noting, "The longitudinal and transverse arches are marvelously well preserved." The shod men admired Ishi's straight and "unspoiled toes." Pope

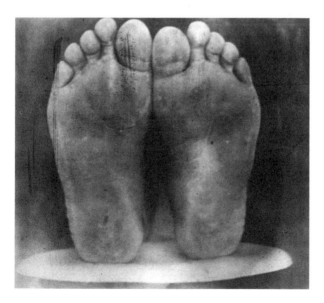

Ishi's feet. Photograph by University of California Hospital, 15-6094. Courtesy of the Phoebe A. Hearst Museum of Anthropology and the Regents of the University of California.

wrote, "[His] foot is a beautiful example of what the human foot should be." Kroeber offered Ishi shoes, or moccasins, if he preferred. But Ishi rejected them at first. "I see the ground is stone here," he explained. "Walking on that all the time, I would wear out shoes, but my feet will never wear out."[9]

He was accustomed to walking, but he would soon adjust himself, and his body, to new means of travel. "He speedily assimilated civilized ways," Kroeber observed. Ishi soon fell in love with trolley cars; he found their warning gong delightful. He preferred trolleys to cars. Going around too much in automobiles, he once told Dr. Pope, might be responsible for all the sickness among the *saltu*. That first night in the city lit up by electric lights, Ishi gave his feet a rest and got onboard, for the people here walked on the side but took trolleys down the middle of Market and the other streets of San Francisco. Some of the streetcars pulled themselves up the steep slopes on ropes, like Rabbit rappelling over the mountains or Grizzly Bear climbing up to the hole in the sky.[10]

· *One* ·

THE YAHI IN THREE WORLDS

❋

Genesis: The First World

It was dark there, long ago. Dark, in the mornings. Cottontail Rabbit wasn't doing anything. The people back then, the story people, told Rabbit they had a job for him. "You be the one to pack up Sun and take it to the East." So Rabbit whirled it around in his hands, dust flew up, he let it fly all around, from place to place, down to the river in the East, across the water in the river. He dribbled it east, all the way to the edge of the world, the place where Sky touched Earth. Sky was a blue dome over the circle of land on which the People lived. Rabbit told Sun, "You shall go up the wall of the dome, you shall come up from the East in the Sky." All done, he whirled himself into the air— he became a whirlwind flying back from the river. He grabbed the rope in the mountains to the west, the rope of quartz. He pulled the mountains together, and rappelled back home at night. It all worked out pretty good. The People were pleased. The Sun came up in the East in the morning. In the middle of the day, it shined overhead. "The sunrise will always be like this," those story people said.[1]

The sun was still coming up from the East when Ishi was born. It was a miracle: they stood watching every morning with their hands over their hearts, like a pledge. The stories of the first-time people were still unfolding, all around, the same as they had done since the place that they knew came into being. But now more than the sun was coming from the East. There were the ones digging out the ropes in the mountains, the ones who were not Cottontail but who made a great whirlwind nonetheless.

Young Ishi grew up close to the women. He learned to speak the women's tongue, went with them collecting seeds and reeds. He saw how everything was made, baskets and all they held. For a while he lived along the *ga'me'si,* a small stream that flowed into Deer Creek.

Growing older, he spent more and more time with the men, going out to hunt or fish, learning their tongue. He learned to chip arrowheads, to keep watch, to sing the language of the birds, the animals. All the world was alive. All the world was watchful. You had to respect it. He had to learn how to pay respect, and he did. There was a way to hunt deer. You became a deer to hunt deer. Antlers of a buck were split at the bottom, and the pith removed. Now they were light enough for you to carry them on your head. He would wear deerskin over his body and go out to find a herd. In brush nearby he would thrust his head up and around, browsing like a buck. Deer would look up, curious, staring transfixed at their strange kin. Ishi would let his arrows fly. The fallen deer had to be respected: there was a way to prepare and eat it. Do it right and the spirit of the deer would be released. There was a hole on the top of a rock above the stream, hollow and surrounded by a ring of quartz, like a rope. That was where the deer's spirit went after you killed it—if you treated it correctly. There was also a way to take a salmon out of the streams, and a way to cook and eat it. If you failed to follow the way, that could come back to haunt you, and everything about you. Your environment, the nature that encircles you, would shrivel. Pay attention. Pay respect. It was all your life. All of this Ishi learned.

They all went up the slopes of the mountain Wahganupa in summertime, men and women, boys and girls. The heat down below was great, but berries and nuts and deer and coolness awaited up on the mountain, Little Shasta, they called it. To the mountain it was four days walking on well-known paths, stopping along the way to gather what the spring had offered, bulbs and clover and fish from the river. Below, Mill Creek and Deer Creek spread miles apart, and the trails between them were rugged and difficult; above, the streams nearly converged at Bopmayu'wi, so the people would gather in the high mountain meadows. The people from far and wide gathered, shared their stories and lives and landscapes with each other, and gathered more of the world around them.

On its high slopes, Ishi could look back from above, and see the lands on which they lived, the cañons around the streams flowing westward off of Wahganupa. As he walked and looked and worked he came to know these lands. There were stories for all these places they moved through. By going and listening, he learned the land and its movements. He learned the stories of places. He could reach out and touch the stories and grasp the goods they carried for the people. For the stories showed you what Earth had to offer. From experience and memory, from story and song, and from what he could see from Wahganupa, Ishi could map the whole world, the circle of land on which people lived along the streams. He could see a lot of the world from these slopes, but he did not stand outside of it when he gained the heights of the mountain. You called for deer. You filled the baskets.

The Yahi world was a woven basket, reeds and words and dreams woven tight into a vessel of creation. The basket could hold fire, and had. To cook acorn soup, you placed stones heated in a fire into the basket and stirred. The basket held all the people. But now its strands were being pulled out, one by one. You could see the sun through it; water washed right out. Repairs were made every day to the basket, but they were always undone by the next day. It could still just hold you, if you were careful. Women kept weaving. Lizard kept on making arrows. Ishi and the others saw to it.

In the sometime-houses of the cow-men, they found once or twice stone-hard black baskets. They were good for cooking acorn soup: you could put them right in fire and they would not burn up. And they found once or twice in those sometime-houses a thick brown liquid in baskets of metal. It was good, sweet beyond belief: "log cabin" syrup.[2]

Genocide: The Second World

The world of the Yahi was nearly washed away by a dream. This dangerous dream had many manifestations. Columbus had it; he dreamed of spices and riches in the New World. Cortes had it; he dreamed of gold and power. The Russians had it; they searched for the soft gold of otter skins in Alaska and all the way down to California. Presidents Jefferson, Jackson, and Polk had it; they dreamed of a nation moving westward, sweeping over lands, discovering its wealth, and turning gold into freedom. This was

Yahi country.

the great alchemy of manifest destiny: the lands Americans reached out for and grasped would turn to gold, making everyone happier, freer, more full of life.

In 1849 the dream seized ordinary Americans, infecting them with "California fever." The California Dream was the American Dream concentrated on the landscape, like water pushed at great speed through a nozzle. Concentrate water through a nozzle, miners found, and you could bring whole mountains down. Concentrate the dream, and you could also bring whole mountains down, and the people and animals with them. The gold rushers thought dislodging all of them from their set places on the land would set them free.

In 1849 Goldsborough Bruff led a wagon train west, dreams of gold filling his head. Geology brought him to California, and geology nearly killed him. His company of argonauts took Peter Lassen's trail, blazed by the Danish American in 1847 through the volcanic mountains of northeastern California. Lassen had dreams of building an agricultural empire; he'd be the emperor. He laid out a town-to-be and called it Benton City, named after the expansionist senator Thomas Hart Benton. Westward movement was to Benton "the course of the heavenly bodies, of the human race, and of science, civilization, and rational power following in their train." His daughter Jessie married John C. Frémont, an American explorer nicknamed "the Pathfinder," who is also credited with jumpstarting the American conquest of Mexican California in 1846.

Goldsborough was an ordinary American traveling the paths toward gold and empire opened up by the likes of Polk, Benton, and Lassen. But the actual trail was rough-going back in 1849. Sick and unable to carry his belongings, Goldsborough stayed behind in the mountains as the rest of his company forged on. Scores of other emigrants passed by his rude camp, and Goldsborough offered shelter and food when he had it. But no one offered to take him along to Lassen's ranch, just thirty miles away. Hunkered down with his possessions, Goldsborough waited and watched the Yahi fires from his camp. After barely making it through the winter, he poured his thoughts into his diary in April 1850, beginning with weather observations: "Thank God! 'tis day!—commences (sun rise) clear." The sun came up in the East, and the Yahi Indians around him surely saw it, too, and welcomed the warmth. Weak from hunger, Goldsborough found "fresh tracks of an Indian." The footprints led him to a wild place in his own mind. "Oh! If I can only over take him! Then will I have a hearty meal! A good broil!"

Goldsborough decided to walk out of the wilderness that day, spurred on by cannibal fantasies. "My mouth fairly watered, for a piece of Indian to broil!" He stumbled on under the heavy burden of his backpack. The next day he rested it on a shriveled carcass of an abandoned ox, his dog tearing at the putrid flesh. Despairing and delirious, Goldsborough wrote, "Feet quite sore, shoulders very sore, and would fail altogether, but for the hope of shooting an indian, to eat."

But when he did meet an Indian—probably a Yahi—his desire for human flesh vanished. Instead he begged the man for food. Later he got directions from Indians who worked for Peter Lassen, and discovered that, even without a wagon, he could make his way through this rugged country with a little help from the people his mind had turned into sumptuous beasts.[3]

Dame Shirley saw Indians through a different lens. Originally from New England, she traveled in 1851 with her husband to the gold mining camp of Rich Bar, on the Feather River in the territory of the Yahi's southern neighbors, the Konkow or Mountain Maidu. When Shirley first decided to leave her adopted home of San Francisco for the gold camp, her friends thought she was crazy; that was no land for a lady, they warned, adding that she would be killed and eaten by Indians. But she was determined to go. After promptly getting lost, she and her husband camped out one night; she wrote to her sister that Indians "generally take women captive": "Who knows how narrowly I escaped becoming an Indian chieftainess, and feeding for the rest of my life upon roasted grasshoppers, acorns, and flowerseeds?" She and her husband later passed by a group of Indian women harvesting seeds from flowers, bearing conical baskets on their back. She took in the scene from a distance: "These poor creatures were entirely naked, with the exception of a quantity of grass bound round the waist.... It was, to me, very interesting to watch their regular motion, they seemed so exactly to keep time with one another; and with their dark shining skins, beautiful limbs, and lithe forms, they were by no means the least picturesque feature of the landscape." Later in the trip, breakfasting at an establishment called the Wild Yankee's, Shirley found herself "enraptured" by one young Indian woman she dubbed the "wildwood Cleopatra."

Shirley wanted to like the Indians she saw, but in the flesh they did not live up to her romantic predilections. "I always *did* 'take' to Indians," she reminded her sister, "though it must be said that those who bear that name here have little resemblance to the glorious forest heroes that live in the Leatherstocking tales." Those tales, including *The Last of the Mohicans,* had been written by James Fenimore Cooper, and they had fixed the image of the "noble savage" in the American imagination. Shirley wanted to appreciate the California landscape as if it were a scene in a novel or a painting, like those of Albert Bierstadt, who attempted to represent the grandeur of the American West. "I wish I could give you some faint idea of the majestic solitudes through which we passed,— where the pine-trees rise so grandly in their awful height, that they seem to look into heaven itself. Hardly a living thing disturbed this solemnly beautiful wilderness." It was almost better that way; she feared unknown Indians lurking in those woods, and she was aesthetically disgusted by some Indians she actually saw. She longed for "wildwood Cleopatras" that would complement and confirm her romanticized view of Indians and the wilderness.[4]

Goldsborough fantasized about killing and eating Ishi's people and their neighbors; Shirley dreamed of living out a romance novel with them. White communities establishing themselves in greater Yahi country in the 1850s alternated between these polar views: trying to expunge Indians or trying to find ways to live among them. In the town of Tehama in 1854 it was reported that Indians had stolen some cattle and that whites pursued them, cornered them in Dry Creek canyon, and killed twenty-three. "Such a course is to be deprecated," the local newspaper editor wrote. But he quickly took back his own moral condemnation, asking, "What are the settlers to do?...If there was a milder manner of teaching the Indians to regard the rights of property, the settlers would undoubtedly, willingly avail themselves of it." Rather than tracking down and murdering all of the Indians, the editor recommended gathering them up and confining them to a reservation. "If they are removed and taught to cultivate the earth," he proposed, "their present destitute and miserable condition would be greatly alleviated, and the settlers would be left in the enjoyment of their property." This would be the path of progress, he concluded.[5]

In the town of Indian Valley, along the Feather River not too far from Shirley's Rich Bar, George Rose walked into a shop and complained to the proprietor, "The Indians of this valley are '*no bueno.*'" Rose walked over to the fireplace, where two Indians, a father and son, sat peacefully. He casually lit his cigar, took a puff, and then pulled a pistol from his pocket and shot the son dead. The father fled. Rose assumed he could get away with murder, but the white community saw it another way. They arrested him, put him through a rough frontier trial, convicted him, and sentenced him to die by hanging. Though a nearby newspaper complained that a white man was executed for killing an Indian, residents defended the action as just and prudent: "Living amongst Indians in these wild mountains, some steps have to be taken for the protection of our families. We have hitherto lived at peace, and hope to continue. Indians must not be shot down as dogs."[6]

Rose was possibly not the first cold-blooded murderer to receive such justice in Indian Valley. Long before whites came, there lived a creature who hammered all day on a canoe hanging by the creek. It was a trick to lure people nearby. The creature had a collection of knives that he used for slicing up people before he ate them. One day Worldmaker, who crafted the whole landscape there, snuck up on the canoe hammerer. Can I see your cool knives, he asked. Proudly canoe-hammer brought them out. Worldmaker seized one of the creature's weapons and cut off the man-eater's head. That was a story the Konkow Maidu told.[7]

The story would have been a good warning for Goldsborough and Rose. After Rose was killed, the Maidu in Indian Valley would have been assured that some whites, like Worldmaker at the place they called Canoe-Hammering Point, delivered a form of justice they recognized. In Indian Valley in 1854 whites tried to create a middle ground on which they could live in peace with Indians. In Tehama in 1854 Americans sought to remove Indians from the land altogether, so they could pursue their ends unfettered by any human restraint.

In the town of Chico, just a few miles from Tehama and the cañons in which Ishi was growing up, one man spoke up for the Indians, or so he thought. John Bidwell was a wealthy farmer and rancher—indeed, "he was Chico," a visitor in the 1850s noted—and he saw himself as a friend of the Menchopa and other local Indians; in fact, he was their keeper. His white neighbors complained that Bidwell was merely opportunistic and hypocritical, that he loved Indians because he profited by having them work for him.

Bidwell preached peaceful relations between whites and Indians, and he took his opinion to the state capital, when he became a congressman. In Sacramento he helped draft a bill for the "government and protection of the Indian." Section 2 provided that Indians living on lands claimed by whites could continue to live there, and that they would not "be forced to abandon their homes or villages where they have resided for a number of years." Bidwell's language betrayed his biases. First, it assumed that Indian claims to land had been extinguished, which they had not. Furthermore, in practice this clause was meant to support the kind of feudal relationship Bidwell had with the Menchopa. They lived in a village on the land he claimed and provided him with the labor to transform what he saw as wilderness into an agricultural empire.

Tucked away into the law was a provision making it illegal to set fire to the prairie, extinguishing a key ecological practice with which Indians cultivated the plants they used for food and fiber. If an Indian stole cattle, the law said, he or she could be whipped up to twenty-five times or fined up to two hundred dollars. "Any Indian," the law's key provision read, "who shall be found loitering and strolling about, or frequenting public places where liquors are sold, begging, or leading an immoral or pro-fligate course of life, shall be liable to be arrested on the complaint of any reasonable citizen of the county." After hearing the complaint from the "reasonable citizen"—in other words, a white man—a justice of the peace could convict the accused Indian of vagrancy and "hire out such vagrant within twenty-four hours to the highest bidder."

Though Bidwell's original draft had some real protections of Indians built in, including the creation of a special court to mediate Indian-white conflicts, ultimately the state legislature removed them before it passed the bill into law. The Act to Protect Indians in fact became a means of uprooting Indians from the landscape and putting them to work replanting it for whites. The bill might well have been called an Act to Protect White Ranchers and Farmers. Their cattle and sheep, set loose by the thousands to eat up the grasses and forbs of California valleys and mountains, were being protected. Elk and deer, crucial game for Indians, suffered and dwindled at the onslaught of this livestock; if Indians hunted any of the new game, they would be whipped. And the Act protected ranchers' and farmers' ability to obtain Indians as quasi-slaves to work their ranches and farms. Indians who were not employed by whites were defined as "vagrants"—homeless people, refugees.

The *Sacramento Union* saw through the Act at the time, concluding, "If this does not fill the measure of the constitutional term, 'involuntary servitude,' we shall be thankful if some one will inform us what is lacking." The law allowed whites to claim Indian children, as long as a justice of the peace approved. As a result, many Indian children were abducted and sold into virtual slavery. One story illustrates the new reality. In 1857 whites attacked a group of Indians in Ishi's homeland at Inskip Hill. (They were Yana, and possibly even Yahi like Ishi.) After the battle a white man came across two Indian children, a boy and a girl. The boy fled up a hill, but the white man lassoed the girl, tied her to his pack mule, and took her to the livery stable at Red Bluff. He offered her as a servant to the owner, George Hoag, but he refused. "In that case," the packer responded, "I guess I'll just throw the little tot into the river." So Hoag relented and took in the girl.

The Hoag family thought "she was like a frightened wild animal and they had to keep her locked in a closet for a couple of weeks until she trusted them." The girl was renamed Mary and became the family's maid and nanny. She helped raise three generations of Hoag children. The Hoags came to think of her as family and were angered when anybody derisively referred to Mary as "squaw." George Hoag meanwhile was busy farming, hiring Indians and Chinese immigrants to transform the native landscape into a vast wheat field, and using a gargantuan mechanical thresher called the Monitor to get in what was then a record harvest (a feat memorialized in a famous painting).

Indian children were held captive between a rock and a hard place, and they often ended up in a hard place in white families, who loved them or not. Mary Hoag was one of the many Indian children whose families were destroyed and who found themselves working for whites who took over their land and virtually owned their bodies.[8]

Steadily American whites took the land and the law into their own hands. They ran cattle. They grew wheat and other crops. They hunted deer in the cañons and hill country for fun. H. H. Sauber was a young man of twenty-two when he came west to California to work on his uncle's ranch at the lower end of Deer Creek. The uncle grew crops on a hundred acres and ran cattle in the foothills, Yahi country. Working as a cowboy, Sauber was living out a fantasy of adventure in the West.

One day he went hunting. His "heart throbbed" when he caught his "first glimpse of a wild deer." But before he could muster the nerve to shoot the buck, another man took it down with a single shot. That man rode up and cut the deer's throat. Young Sauber stood transfixed. Before him stood a local legend, Hi Good, "the Boone of the Sierra," an Indian hunter. Sauber looked up to Good, who he saw as being "devoted to the destruction of the renegades and the protection of the helpless."

Sauber viewed Indians as "a black cloud" descending from the "dark, wild cañon of Mill creek" to rob, murder, and plunder white settlers. That cloud came down hours after Sauber first met

Good over the dead buck. A ranch hand turned up dead. Hi Good organized a posse to chase Indians into the hills. Sauber joined in, riding a mustang with the others into the night. To Sauber his "wild night ride" with Good was into another world: "In the midst of the darkness, the desolation, and the wild, cold storm, Hi Good spurred on, on, on, like a weird phantom, never stopping, never speaking...plunging into cañons, through dripping thickets, across wind-swept ridges, as though possessed of supernatural sight which revealed to him every inch of the scarred and ragged wilderness." Finally they made it to Lassen's trail on the ridge above "the black, wild, unfathomed cañon of sullen and dangerous Mill creek"—Ishi's home. Just "as the gloomy sky over the wilderness of the mountains to the east began to take on the cold gray hue of dawn," Good, "standing in the ghostly light," had the posse hide in a thicket to ambush the Indians.

A few minutes after the posse had taken their position, a voice whispered, "Injuns sure." Sauber saw a "dark form stalk out of the very head of the hollow." It was followed by another, and another. A shot rang out, followed by Good's "wild, fierce, exultant shout from the center of the pass. 'Now, boys, let him have it.'" Sauber "fired wildly into the hollow." The "fierce whites" pursued the Indians down a ravine. Sauber "ran nearly a mile, repeatedly firing a shot at some scudding form, and was in full chase of a tall half-naked savage" when he disappeared into a gorge. A moment later Sauber heard a "shriek, as of some wild beast...followed by a fierce execration from Good, and then with a swish and a thud a copper-colored body shot violently through vines and shrubs and fell at full length upon the rocks above the gorge. [Sauber] sprang hastily forward, but shrank back in horror a second later, upon beholding the quivering body of the Indian, his head nearly severed from his body." Good came into view, "coolly wiping his reeking knife on a bunch of grass." 'Guess that dog'll quit murdering,' he chuckled, with a fierce laugh, glancing at his fallen foe."

Good added the man's scalp to his collection, and Sauber took away the horror. Indian fighting was a way of releasing the wildness within, he learned, with thrilling and sickening results.[9]

Good kept at it. And he had help, and plenty of it. One of Good's partners was Robert Anderson. They first worked together in 1859. After a series of Indian raids, a subscription was put up, and a militia of Indian hunters went up into the hills. Good and Anderson worked together as scouts, and after failing to find any Indians in several forays into the hills, one day they discovered a camp near present-day Forest Ranch, about fifteen miles northeast of Chico. After surveying the scene, they turned back to their own camp. Along the way they saw an "Indian scout." Anderson and Good killed him. They scalped the man, and took the scalp back to camp: "[It was] the first trophy we had taken in the campaign."

Wanting more, the entire party of Indian fighters returned to the Indian encampment and set up an ambush. "As the gray dawn melted into daylight," the hunters slowly began to see that not all was as it seemed. Two lofty pine trees had been trimmed of branches; Anderson couldn't figure out why. But as "the heavens grew brighter," he saw to his surprise that large American flags flew from each tree. The men continued to wait. Finally someone stirred in the camp and began walking up the trail toward them. They could see that he was a Mexican, not an Indian at all. When he came closer, "Good's rifle spoke," and the "man, wounded, sprang back to camp." Anderson explained, "Birds flocking together on this occasion were to be considered birds of a feather." The party was intent on killing anyone in the camp, regardless of race or guilt, excepting only women and children.

The camp was aroused, and the ambushers poured in fire. Anderson wrote, "The bucks were armed and returning our fire. The squaws soon perceived that we were seeking to spare their lives, and so they clung to the bucks." Good made an offer to allow the women and children to leave the camp. They did so, but many of the men, disguised as women with blankets over their heads, also escaped, cross-dressing for survival. The Americans opened fire again. When the dust settled, they were satisfied, for "there was not a bad Indian around, but about forty good ones lay scattered about." The numbers were probably exaggerated for glory.

Anderson looked among the dead bodies for an Indian he thought he shot through the heart but couldn't find him. They did find two barrels of whiskey "as well as other evidences which pointed to the fact that whites joined with the redskins in the recent celebration." White Americans, Mexicans, and Indians had been partying together in a clearing beneath Ponderosa and lodgepole pines fashioned into American flag poles. Good and Anderson wanted clear racial lines, and this camp confounded them all. When Anderson returned to the scene of their massacre, he found that surviving Indians had cremated their dead.

The original militia was augmented by another company of fifteen men, who had been sent into the hills after a rumor spread that Good and Anderson's party had been killed. Still in pursuit of the Indians who had escaped and vexed by the Indians' ability to elude them and care for their dead, the Indian fighters descended on a mining town on Butte Creek. Good told them to shoot all Indians on sight. A white store owner named Wallace confronted the attackers, proclaiming that "if a single Indian were killed he would follow [the posse] up and kill six white men." Undeterred, Good's men held Wallace himself at gunpoint and lectured him on Indian culpability. Wallace was angry. He was married to an Indian woman, and she had been wounded during the Forest Ranch massacre. Wallace told the Indian hunters that if they had been there a day earlier they would have found him at the camp, too. The attackers coolly informed the man, whom they considered a traitor to his race, that "if that been the case he would surely have met with the same treatment as that accorded the Indians."

Anderson then pushed past Wallace into the back room of the store, where several Indians were being hidden. He found the Indian he was looking for seated on a keg. He grabbed the man's shirt and pulled it up over his head. There he saw the wounds, confirming that Anderson had in fact shot the man three days before; the bullet had entered his right breast and left his body under his left shoulder blade. Shot through the heart, and the man survived.[10]

"It is as impossible for the white man and the wild Indian to live together as it is to unite oil and water," the *Humboldt Times* editorialized in 1860. It was a common view among whites, though not universal, as the fact of Wallace and his Indian wife revealed. The Americans who unsettled the land with their crops and cattle continued to encroach on the lands and livelihood of the Yahi and their neighbors. Their own subsistence patterns left in shreds, the Indians took to hunting cattle, horses, and mules. They took flour and beans from cowboys' mountain cabins. The cañons of Mill Creek and Deer Creek became refugee camps for Indians of all tribes.

These were the ancient lands of the Yahi, a geological and social crossroads. Here the lava rock mountains of the Cascade Range left off; just to the south the granite Sierra Nevadas, with gold in their rocks and rivers, rose up. The northern boundary of the Yana-speaking groups, of which the Yahi were the southernmost, was the Pit River, the western boundary was the Sacramento River, and the southern boundary was the northern fork of the Feather River (though each of these boundaries was permeable and shifted over time). The Yana's neighbors were the Wintu to the west, the Maidu to the south, the Achumawi and Atsugewi to the north and east. Perhaps as many as two thousand people, divided into the three or four Yana groups, lived in the hills and cañons of Wahganupa (Mount Lassen) at the end of the eighteenth century.[11]

During the disruption and decimation following the Gold Rush, the Yana peoples were fractured and fissured. Other native groups had also been shattered, and some other Indians came into Yahi land as refugees; still others joined them in the 1850s and 1860s. The refugees fought terror with terror, killing or taking captive women and children. In the face of such violent resistance, the rhetoric of extermination grew louder. "It is becoming evident that extermination of the red devils will have to be resorted to," the *Red Bluff Independent* editorialized. Some whites believed that the Indians would vanish from the earth without the use of violence; others shared the view of the *Chico Courant:* "It is a mercy to the red devils to exterminate them.... Treaties are played out—there is only one kind of treaty that is effective—cold lead."[12]

There were many ways to extract treasure from the mountains of California after 1849, including, as it turned out, killing Indians. Bounties were paid to the likes of Good and Anderson for the scalps of Indians. In 1855 a white man could show up in Shasta City with the severed heads of Indians and receive five dollars for each one. A subscription was raised in Tehama County in 1861 to pay out bounties to Indian hunters. Indian-hunting militias submitted their expenses to the state government. Such men were paid over a million dollars in 1851 and 1852 alone. The State of California subsequently appealed to the federal government to cover these expenses, and for the most part it did. The blood money was paid out to further what Anderson called a "general clean-up" of all Indians who "infested" the land.[13]

There were voices, in and outside of government, that spoke up for alternatives to genocide. A letter to the *Alta Californian* signed "Shasta" expressed them this way: "You have but one choice—KILL, MURDER, EXTERMINATE OR DOMESTICATE AND IMPROVE THEM." Shasta preferred domestication and improvement, which was the very same view taken by three federal Indian commissioners who came to California in 1851 to settle once and for all the conflict between Indians and whites. Since the time of Jefferson, removal had been the national policy for Indians. Indians were perceived as an obstacle to national expansion, and whenever they got in the way they were sent packing west. But ultimately the policy of removal ran into an obstacle: the Pacific Ocean. As the commissioners noted, "As there is *no further west,* to which they *can* be removed, the General Government and the people of California appear to have left but one alternative in relation to these remnants of once numerous and powerful tribes, viz: *extermination or domestication.*"[14]

Wanting to avoid the immoral spectacle of extermination, the commissioners negotiated treaties up and down the state to promote domestication. Indians were to relinquish their claim to land and cease hostilities. In return they would be moved to designated reservations. There the government promised to furnish them with cattle and agricultural training. Eighteen treaties were negotiated and a system of reservations was laid out that would have encompassed about 7.5 percent of the state or some 7.5 million acres (somewhat less than the 11.5 million acres the Southern Pacific Railroad would be given as an incentive to build its railways in the state). But even this proved to be too much for California's politicians to stomach. A state commission argued that no land whatsoever should be given over to be "the home of the wild...Indians." So the treaties were ground into dust in Washington, like so many other promises.[15]

After the fiasco of failing to confirm the treaties it had negotiated, the federal government set up a system of smaller, military-run reservations in the 1850s. Under a "system of discipline and instruction," the Indians were to be taught agriculture, ranching, and religion, and thereby be domesticated. To advocates such as the *San Francisco Alta California* newspaper, the mission of these reservations was to eradicate the wildness they saw in Indians and replace it with its opposite: "The Indians will be transformed from a state of semibarbarism, indolence, mental imbecility and moral debasement to a condition of civilization."[16] This plan of cultural makeover reflected a widespread belief that Indians must be transformed from a "wild" to a "civilized" state.

One of these reservations was set up in 1854 on twenty-three thousand acres of land appropriated from the Nome Lackee Indians. Their homeland, situated on the foothills of the Coast Range on the edge Tehama County, some twenty-five miles west of Yahi country, was now to be the home of Indians displaced

Three white versions of California Indians. From Frank Soule, John Gihon, and James Nisbett, The Annals of San Francisco *(New York, 1855), which provided the following key to the image: "1. Wahla, chief of the Yuba tribe— civilized and employed by Mr. S. Brannan. 2. A Partly civilized Indian. 3. A Wild Indian."*

from all over the region. Conditions were so poor in the first year that many Indian internees died of starvation. Others fled. Those who remained started farming, as the government instructed. But in 1857 the harvest was so bountiful that neighboring whites took jealous exception to the reservation Indians. They soon demanded that they be "removed beyond the pale of [the whites'] thickly settled districts." To move them "beyond the pale" harkened back to the walled pale British colonists put up around settlements in Ireland, and later in the New World. Everything within was considered civilized and sanctified; everything beyond was a howling wilderness.[17]

Meanwhile William Kibbe, California's adjutant general, led a militia into the heart of Yahi country. Kibbe's Rangers intended to penetrate "the very haunts of the savages, with a view to conquer, and if possible, rid the country forever of their presence." Though the Indians had eluded previous raiders, Kibbe reported that he had outsmarted the Indians on their own ground. He had taught them once and for all how "utterly unable they are to cope with the great nation of people who are daily taking possession of the soil, and converting it from wilderness into vineyards and fields of waving grain."[18]

Kibbe captured twelve hundred Indians—guilty of being Indian—including many that were employed on Bidwell's ranch. Those prisoners probably included some of Ishi's people. Shipped by barge down the Sacramento River to San Francisco, these prisoners were paraded through the city's downtown. They were then shipped north to Mendocino and the Round Valley Reservation. According to Kibbe, whites were now free to fill up their vacated lands, which he estimated could support one hundred thousand head of stock and should now "be rapidly settled by our enterprising citizens."[19]

Contrary to Kibbe's picture of destiny settling irrevocably over Yahi country, the Indians hardly felt themselves vanquished. Even many of those shipped to Round Valley escaped back to their homeland. The early 1860s saw a reprise and intensification of raids and counterraids. Many whites still harbored fantasies of the country "cleaned out" completely of Indians. Wildcat militias killed more Indians, and Indians retaliated by stealing cattle, burning barns, and sometimes killing whites.

Walking home from school one afternoon in 1863, Thankful Lewis and her two brothers stopped to drink from Little Dry Creek. Suddenly a group of Indians appeared. They shot the younger brother and took the older brother and sister captive. The Indians may have been Yahi or refugees from other tribes; they most likely were a group that found refuge in the Yahi cañon of Mill Creek. Two of the raiders were mourning deaths in their family, for their hair was singed short and pitch covered their heads. This may have been an act of retaliation and an attempt at recovery of their own lost ones. Thankful asked to go home, but she was told, "No, we are going to take you to our home, your home no more." Her brother was later killed, but Thankful managed to escape.[20]

The abduction of Thankful and the murder of her brothers sent the white community into a furor. The vigilante group called the Oroville Guard set out on a rampage of revenge, killing any Indians they could find in Dogtown, in Yankee Hill, and on Bidwell's ranch. The *Butte County Appeal* announced its final solution for the Indian problem: "the last remaining son of the forest" should be gathered up, placed on the Round Valley reservation, put to work there, and warned, "[If he were ever] again seen meandering upon our valleys and mountains his life will pay for his audacity." More than thirteen hundred Indians were rounded up at Yankee Hill.[21]

The U.S. military was called in to "remove and protect" the Indians. The Army scoured the hills and took 461 more Indian prisoners. Most of them were Konkow Maidu who most likely had no role in the Lewis affair. In the eyes of authorities they were guilty by racial association. The Army drove the abducted Indians west toward Round Valley, 120 miles away. Only fifteen wagons were available; many of the Indians were sick with malaria but were required to walk nonetheless. Of the 461 Indians who left on what is called the Maidu Trail of Tears, 277 arrived in Round Valley. Thirty-two died on the trail, and 150 were left behind, too sick to travel further. James Short was sent back to rescue them, and he reported that the 150 "sick Indians were scattered along the trail for 50 miles...dying at the rate of 2 or 3 per day. They had nothing to eat...and the wild hogs were eating them up either before or after they were dead." In California as elsewhere, the official U.S. policy was domestication, not extermination, but it was easy to miss the difference amid such a scene. There were scarcely any safe trails left for Indians to walk in all of California.[22]

One day in 1865 in the Concow Valley, the homeland of many of the Indians who suffered on the Maidu Trail of Tears, a band of unknown Indians attacked the Workman residence, killing three people. White men of the valley vowed to take revenge. They set off toward Bidwell's ranch, where they assumed the band had come from. Along the way they met the now legendary Indian fighter Robert Anderson, who convinced the men that the attackers must not have been Bidwell's Indians but the Mill Creeks. The group then picked up Hi Good, and the two veterans took charge. Good and Anderson would lead the party into Ishi's home, "that everlasting haven of refuge,—the wilds of Mill Creek Canyon."[23]

Under the cover of night the Indian hunters silently waded up the creek to scout out a camp of Indians at a place known as Three Knolls. No one was on watch. Good, Anderson, and the other dozen rifle-armed Americans surrounded the camp. Good fired the first shot at daybreak, and the men with Anderson "poured a hot fire into the Indians from up-stream, while Good's men hammered them from below." Men, women, and children plunged into the stream. Some got away, but "many dead bodies floated down the rapid current." One Indian, dressed in a white shirt, tried to escape by scrambling up a ridge. Anderson recognized him as Billy Sill, an indentured servant of Dan Sill, who had run away to join the other Indians on Mill Creek. Anderson "cut him down" with a bullet just as he was jumping for a thicket. As Sill rolled down the slope toward the creek, he cursed Anderson "venomously with his last breath."[24]

The men from the Concow Valley did not stop with the last breaths; they now expressed their rage on dead bodies. Sim Moak saw that "one of them after an Indian was killed and scalped, cut his throat and twist his head half off and he said, 'You will not kill any more women and children.'" Good gathered up the scalps and meticulously prepared them for posterity; he took "a buckskin string and sack needle and tied a knot in the end and salted the scalp." He strung them together and tied them to his belt. "You can imagine a great tall man with a string of scalps from his belt to his ankle," Anderson wrote. Among the dead was probably one Indian man known to whites as Big-Foot Jack or Old Big Foot. His right foot was larger than his left, and the whites who continued to scour the hills on the lookout for Indian "sign" never saw his footprints again.[25]

But a child was discovered alive in the camp, a girl with six toes, presumed to be the daughter of Old Big Foot. Anderson wrote, "Good at once took a notion to the child and said he wished to take it home with him." Good "had odd tastes about such things." To carry the child out, one Indian woman, perhaps her mother, was also taken along. Perhaps fearing the worst, midway through the journey back she sat down and put a shawl over her head, refusing to take another step. Good took off with the child on his back; one man was sent back to execute the woman.[26]

Good kept the child on his ranch. When Moak visited that next spring, she was "out picking flowers." When she came back to the ranch house, Good patted her on the head, and then she took a nap. Good said, "When she wakes I will show you something." What would it be? When she awoke, Good had her greet Moak in three languages: "Hello," "Hola," and "Bonjour." The girl had picked up French and Spanish from one of Good's partners; it is not known if she retained any Yahi. Good lived in an enigmatic world: by night he could exterminate Indians in the mountains and by day he could smile over an Indian girl asleep in his cabin whom he had tutored in three languages. When Good needed work to be done on his ranch, he obtained a boy who was half-Indian from George Sill in Tehama, who seems to have run something of a business in

Indian servants. Indian Ned, he was called. Sill warned Good that he might be trouble, just like that runaway Billy Sill; Good laughed and said they'd get along just fine.[27]

The fates of Good, Indian Ned, and Ishi and his people became intertwined in a series of extraordinary events in the spring of 1870. They begin when W. J. Seagraves discovers some missing cattle in March. He suspects that Indians have stolen them, and enlists Good to chase them down. With dogs and two other men, the cowboy posse heads into the cañons of Deer and Mill Creeks. They discover a hidden Indian village, now deserted. They also find the bones of the missing cattle. Riding farther up Mill Creek the next day, the posse sees some fifteen Yahi returning to the village. The group of Indians splits in two, with six women and a one-handed man called the Old Doctor heading, unknowingly, right into the ambush. Good catches the eyes of the women and motions for them to crouch down, out of the line of fire. Some do—but one tries to run, though she is restrained by one of the other women. The Old Doctor has no choice but to run; Good fires—once, twice, three times, and brings him down with his fourth shot. He has twelve bullets remaining in his Henry repeater rifle. The men capture two women and a girl.

According to Seagraves, Ishi, walking behind an elderly Yahi man, comes onto the scene. The old man is caught, but Ishi is "too wild" and eludes them. The captives—the old man, the two women, and the girl—are taken back to the abandoned Indian village. The old man offers his captors a deal: in exchange for his freedom he will bring in the rest of his relatives. So he is allowed to return to the spot where the Old Doctor had been killed the day before. He calls out loudly to his people, presumably to draw them in. He asks Good to let him climb up on a boulder to look for them. And when he does so, he bounds away and escapes. The posse leaves Mill Creek with the three Yahis, whom Good takes charge of at his cabin.[28]

Two weeks later Ishi and the old man who escaped come to Seagraves's cabin, accompanied by three other men and seven women. Each of the men place before Seagraves a strung bow— an offering of peace, a token of exchange for the three Yahi taken hostage. But Seagraves is unable to make the exchange—to sign this treaty offer of sorts. The captured Yahis are not with him. And he is unable to unstring the bows. So he leads the treaty party to Good's cabin. As they approach, everyone can see the string of forty scalps hanging from a tree outside. Good and the Yahi women and child are away. So the Indians wait, along with Seagraves and George Spires. Spires decides to weigh himself (at least that's what Seagraves says after the fact). He takes a rope, and tosses it over a limb of a tree. To the Yahi, this doesn't look like a man curious about his weight— it looks like a man who's going to hang Indians. Negotiations are over and the offer rescinded. The Yahi vanish into the cañons.[29]

Good's Yahi captives speak to Indian Ned. Suspecting that they were plotting an escape, Good gives the two Yahi women and the girl to a white man named Carter who lives on Deer Creek. The next winter, Sandy Young will take the two women deeper into the cañons in search of their tribesmen. Rain and sleet pelt the band (according to a possibly exaggerated report). They come to a difficult creek crossing, and the women disappear. Young suspects treachery, but "suddenly there came floating out of the storm a thin young squeal." The younger woman has given birth. The older woman takes the infant to the creek and plunges him into the water. Young names the child Snowflake. According to the report, the "wild-eyed lad" came to live in Tehama. Seagraves believed that the child's mother must have been Ishi's sister, and so Snowflake would have been his nephew.[30]

Anderson thought that these resilient Yahi women had put ideas into the mind of Good's quasi-slave, Indian Ned, who certainly gets ideas that spring, wherever they came from. In April 1870 Good receives a large payment, around seven thousand dollars, for his herd of sheep that had been fattened on the grasses of Wahganupa's foothills. He uses half of it to pay a debt and buries the rest. In search of more money, Good, along with Sandy Young and Obe Fields, go prospecting in Mill Creek. They do not expect to find gold in the stream, however. Indeed the volcanic geology of Mount Lassen made it unlikely that any gold could be found in those hills. Gold was found in the Sierra Range, which started just south of Ishi's homeland. For that reason, his people were spared the direct onslaught of thousands of forty-niners who otherwise would have panned out every square foot of the streams of Mount Lassen. In 1870 Good, Young, and Fields have it in their heads that the Mill Creek Indians are hoarding some three thousand dollars of "booty"; that's the gold they seek. They head up the trail toward where Snowflake had defiantly been brought into this imperiled world.[31]

Back at the ranch, Indian Ned is at work trying to find Good's booty from the sheep. After all, it was the land of the Indians, and often it was the labor of Indians like him and Billy Sill that made such profitable sheep ranching possible. But before he can find it, Good, Young, and Fields come back, empty-handed. Ned and Good stare at each other, looking into eyes that were perfect mirrors. Each wants to plunder the other for riches. Each is wild and desperate, though they come to this condition from different directions. Each is consumed by the mercenary blackness at the heart of this wilderness.

Young leaves for Chico; Good rides off to gather vegetables from his garden at his other ranch, and Fields goes to sleep after Ned tells him he's going out to hunt squirrels. Ned goes out to the chaparral-covered ravine of Acorn Hollow and stands behind an old oak tree. We don't know what goes through his mind as he is waiting. Perhaps he's thinking about how he would later go to the cabin of Widow Lewis, who was fixing up Good's boots, and demand to see them. Was he thinking that earth clinging to their

(From left): Jay Salisbury, Sandy Young, Hi Good, and Indian Ned. Courtesy of the Pioneer Museum, Oroville.

soles might be a sign of where the gold was buried? Did he know deep down that the whites would force a confession from him, and that when they demanded to know why he did it, he would say, not *He was a killer of my people,* or *He was a cruel master,* or *I was after the gold,* but that he did it just to see how the legend *would act*? And that after saying that, Young would hang him from an oak tree, and then shoot him in the neck, just to see how Indian Ned would act? Did he have any inkling that his body would be left to rot beneath the oak, and that his bones would bleach out in the sun? That they would lie there for two years before two students from Colusa would come and take the bones away?[32]

Good comes into view, leading his horse, laden with the bounty of his garden, and singing. Ned takes aim and fires. One shot, and Good staggers but rises again and starts toward that damned Indian Ned (according to Anderson's telling of the legend). Ned fires two more shots, and Good is dead. Good and gone, good riddance, too. He was now a good white man in the wild eyes of Indian Ned.[33]

Renaissance: The Third World

The Yahi world had been turned upside down, and the people fell to the rocks and drowned in the streams running red. The things that happened in those cañons carrying the waters of Wahganupa down to the Great Central Valley were a reflection of Indian-white relations across the continent. Whites and Indians at first had found ways to live together, to trade and socialize with one another. They reached out to one another across the divide of culture. But these ways were torn apart and abandoned, and waves of terror and counterterror replaced them. Whites worried about being taken captive by Indians, and some were. But many more Indians were taken captive by whites. Whites worried about being killed and scalped by Indians, and some were. But many more Indians were scalped by whites. And whites saw Indians as wild and the land that they inhabited as wilderness. Whites wanted free land and freedom. They exiled the Indians or confined them to reservations, and said that this change would make Indians appreciate American freedom. Some whites were fond of Indians; they "took to them" in a romanticized kind of way. But most felt that the Indians, inevitably, must give up their wild ways and their wilderness so that whites could make that dark land into an Eden, a garden of new crops, towns, and commerce. In the reckless pursuit of that dream the whites themselves turned wild.

The Indians knew that it was they who were a civilized people; they had stories, a sense of place, and they listened to the land and cared for it. They tended it, and it was their home. The Indians saw the newcomers from the East as wanderers, homeless vagrants, and they pitied them and tried to help them at first. When whites transformed the Indians' home into a wilderness, Indians were left to struggle to survive in that new world, and somehow they did. But many had died.

The Yahi always knew there was death in their world. They were made that way; the story people, at the creation, talked about it. "Are there ones who kill people?" Yes: the rattlesnake bites, the grizzly bites, the scorpion stings. Healers could doctor them. But people would get sick, or fall from cliffs, or drown in rivers.

They would eat food poisoned by a disease arrow shot into it. The doctors might heal them. Or they would die.

The Yahi could not speak of individuals who had died. That would be disrespectful. It would interrupt the dead one's journey. But you did know the story of where they went, the journey of the dead:

> To tell about the dead, the dead,
> They see, the dead,
> They see a little at a time.
> See in the west, keep going, the dead.
> Seeing, they see.
> They don't hear, the dead, the dead.
> So many dead,
> Dead people, rolled up,
> Their bodies rolled up, flexed, stiff and cold.
> They go south,
> They jump through the hole (into the other world)
> One by one, they come this way and close the door.
> Make fire, make firelight....
> They stop and talk by the fire
> Then they go through,
> Go right through the door.
> The fire is put out....
>
> He takes one person through at a time,
> They shut the door and climb up the sky.
> They don't believe it.
> They go back down, go down and walk, the dead,
> Walk around on the ground.
> Then they whirl,
> A whirlwind, people say.
> They go up through the sky on a rope, the dead.[34]

Ishi's uncle was probably a healer, a *kuwi,* and Ishi may have become one as well. Many Yahi succumbed to disease. They fell on rocks. They drowned in streams. But the old stories did not tell of Smith and Wesson, of Henry repeaters, of cold lead. *So many dead; dead people, rolled up, their bodies rolled up, flexed, stiff and cold.* Those who remained had a responsibility to live on. After the killings of the 1860s, perhaps only a dozen Yahi—perhaps twice that number—remained alive in the cañons of Mill and Deer Creeks. Perhaps peace could be made with the *saltu.* The Yahi ambassadors went to them, offered to give them their bows in exchange for their women and children. The *saltu* took the bows and slung a rope over a tree, as if, by their own hands, they would pull them up into the sky. The Yahi knew this trick; they'd seen it before. And it was not unlike how Lizard tricked Grizzly Bear and hanged him. They didn't fall for it. They fled into the landscape and made a new life instead.

To survive, the Yahi appeared to perish from the earth. The *saltu* made their destiny so suffocatingly manifest that the Yahi had to hide their very existence to protect themselves. Humans have always impressed themselves into the landscapes they inhabit. They transform raw nature into a homeland. They make paths through it. They fashion tools from it. They cook it with fire. They create dwellings. They stack rocks on one another along paths at the top of ridges, telling others who would come that way how many ridges over they might meet and gather. All of this becomes evidence of their existence, for human beings are sign makers. But Indian hunters like Good and Anderson could read the signs, and they were ruthless in their pursuit. So the Yahi erased their existence in order to exist.

They covered their footprints and hid their trails through chaparral. They hid their fires. They watched from lava towers and hid when anyone came up the cañons. For a village, they took over a place beneath a cliff, covered with trees, hidden by chaparral, which was called Wowunupo'mu tetna, "Bear's Hiding Place." The Yahi had lived an exuberant life, in conversation with the rocks and plants and animals around them, with each other, telling stories, singing songs. Now they were being forced into a fugitive silence, careful to leave no tracks upon the earth. Almost like ghosts.

But the silence could not hold; the stories came back. To hide from the *saltu,* the Yahi found refuge in their deep knowledge of their landscape and in their culture. The streams and cañons of Wahganupa did not revert to wilderness, though it may have looked that way. It remained a storied place and a homeland. With their stories, the Yahi were reborn.

It is not known how old Ishi was when he became almost a ghost. When he was born he was put carefully into a basket, but it was coming apart. It was hard to make repairs. The grasses were changing because of all the cattle and sheep. The Yahi world was being torn asunder. When the Yahi went into hiding in the early 1870s, Ishi may have been six or seven, or he may have been fifteen or sixteen. It is certain that his early life was lived during the period of massacres, and then he, and the Yahi, became almost like ghosts.

But Ishi took breath from the stories. He heard the creation cycle. It told about Cottontail and the Sun, about Grizzly Bear going up on a rope into the sky searching for fire, about Coyote and how fire shaped the land, about how people were made, about how they would die, and what they would do to live. They would hunt deer, they would hunt birds, they would catch fish; they would gather sunflower seeds, which the story people made from sand; they would gather acorns, which the story people created from rain; they would eat grasshoppers, which the story people made from snow. And the people were taught all of this. Ishi heard it all.[35]

The story of Lizard is special; Lizard is a hero. He would "go to gather pine nuts west across the stream." He would climb a mountain, gather the pine cones, fill his sacks, but then the Ya'wi, pretending to be wind, would swoop down on him from the hills. Lizard wasn't fooled; he would fight them off; he would shoot arrows to the north, the south, the east, shoot them right in the face. The Ya'wi would scatter, and Lizard would return to the people with food. He would tell the children to eat. And he would make arrows, all day, patiently. Early in the morning Lizard rubs and smoothes the arrow shafts, working at it all day, and finally he is finished. He turns them on the ground, holding a brush to them to paint on the red bands. He soaks them in water. He wraps them with sinew. He trims the feathers. He chars the feathers, sealing them. He joins the fore shaft with the main shaft. He flakes the arrowheads from obsidian. He works all day. It takes several days.

But one day, his arrow breaks as he is working. So it's time for a party. Everyone dances and sings all night for three days. Then Lizard says, *All this sleeping around during the day is too much. Let's get back to work, back to normal.* Lizard goes out for pine nuts, with his quiver of arrows. Lizard was always there, working, crafting, providing, surviving.

One time his friend, Long Tail Lizard, was out gathering *báiwak'i* wood for the arrow fore shafts. But Grizzly Bear swallowed him up. So Lizard climbed into a tree to which he knew Bear would come, looking for grapes. Lizard climbed into the tree and draped himself in a wild grape vine. Grizzly came by and pulled on the vine to get the grapes. Lizard jumps down upon his back. He unstrung his bow, made a noose of the string, strangled Grizzly Bear, and opened her up. Long Tail was saved. Lizard could go back to making arrows.[36]

As the years passed, Ishi was one of the few able-bodied men of the survivors. There was his uncle, a medicine man, but his foot had been crippled in a steel bear trap. His mother lived on, growing old. Perhaps a sister was with him. Perhaps a wife. Perhaps others.

Ishi was a stalwart hero in the mode of Lizard.[37] He gathered food and braved encounters with potential enemies. He was the hunter and the fisher. He made arrows. He chipped arrowheads. But unlike Lizard, who lived in another time, the time of the story people, Ishi sometimes chipped his arrowheads out of the glass of whiskey bottles.

To keep their world together, they needed to use everything they could put their hands on. They snared rabbit. They speared salmon. They hunted deer. They gathered nuts and seeds, berries and acorns. But the land had changed since the time of Lizard, and so they began to take sheep and cattle, too. In the desperate springtime, after the summer stores of food had been consumed throughout the cold, spare months of winter, they looked for food in the mountain cabins of the cowboys. These were often stocked by the men who ran cattle in the cañons and hills, so that the cow-boys would have food to eat for the roundup. The Yahi broke into the cabins, careful not to break anything if they liked the owner of the cabin; they took beans and flour and the barley meant for horses. They left the canned goods, probably because they were a type of food—mushy, liquid, and opaque—the Yahi did not favor. Or perhaps because they once got sick from contaminated cans.

Ishi breathed the stories and was deeply traditional. But his environs had changed radically. Ineluctably in contact with the modern world, the Yahi picked from it to maintain their old way of life. Ishi and the remaining Yahi practiced something like what the French call *bricolage*. A bricoleur is someone who creates something from scratch, a creative and resourceful person who collects things from a variety of sources and puts them together in a new way, a way that was not intended when the individual pieces were made. A punk rocker may use a safety pin as jewelry. The Yahi took the cast-off goods of the white world—old clothes and tools, broken bottles, fabrics—to their own world, piecing together the chipped fragments into a whole.

In April 1885 four Yahi, two women and two men, entered the cabin of Mr. Norvell on Dry Creek. They began sifting through the contents of the cabin, assembling a pile of old clothes. One of the women put on three old jumpers. Norvell suddenly returned to the cabin, surprising them. They lined up, waiting to see what he would do. One woman motioned toward Mill Creek, say-ing in Spanish, "Dos chiquitos papooses"; she was taking the things because she had two small, hungry children back home. Norvell showed understanding, and let them leave. In October the Indians returned to the cabin and broke in once more. They took nothing; instead they left for Norvell two beautifully crafted baskets, two traditional baskets exchanged for the clothing they needed. And two children, the future, lived.[38]

In the 1880s a middle ground of accommodation and exchange was created in the cañons. Those who were friendly to the Yahi were given things in return. Without this middle ground, the Yahi would not have been able to survive. They cleaned out cabins in the spring, taking tithes to get them through the lean times. The ranchers were annoyed; some were incensed. One went so far as to leave his cabin conspicuously unattended. Inside he had poisoned flour—shot arrows of poison into it, as the Yahi might say—and left a note: "Poisoned flour for Indians." Presumably any whites who came to the cabin in search of food could read the sign and would not take it. The flour disappeared, and the rancher felt sure that some Yahi must have died. If they were poisoned, Ishi or his uncle surely tried to doctor the sick, but we do not know if they succeeded.[39]

Most ranchers came to a grudging acceptance. Some even left food out for the Indians purposely to assure goodwill. The Speegle family, who ran cattle in the area, had a cabin near Bear's Hiding Place along Deer Creek, and the Speegle children often swam in a pool that was also a good place to catch salmon. When the Yahi wanted to fish, they would hoot like an owl, and the Speegles would leave the water for them, sharing the streams of Wahganupa with the Indians they knew were still living there. But most of the outside world believed the Yahi had perished from the earth.[40]

One day Ishi was on his way down the cañon of Deer Creek to spear salmon. He came through a small opening in the brush to a clearing and was astonished to see two men sitting there, eating. He stood still, holding his rifle. He looked from one man to the other, in disbelief. One was a Noza, a Yana Indian, and one was a *saltu*. What was this? Should he run?

But the Noza said, "Come on in, come on in, have something to eat." Ishi didn't understand the language, but the tone seemed friendly. The Noza made a motion inviting Ishi to sit, and so he did, furtively. Then the man put some beans, bacon, and potatoes in front of him. Ishi kept his eyes on the men, and ate. The Noza started making signs with his hands—something about a woman, a pretty woman, did he have any back in camp? Ishi was worried. Then the Noza asked what he was doing. And Ishi told him, in sign; he made the motion of a salmon with his hands, and then that of spearing it, and that he would be going way down the mountain. Finally the Noza said, "That's all right, old-timer, you can go anytime you want," and motioned that he could go. Relieved, Ishi, grasping his old rifle, backed out through the opening and silently ran away, one meal richer from this strange and unexpected encounter.

The Yana man had come to Deer Creek in a roundabout way. For him, it was at once a homecoming and an attempt to find a new life away from the bizarre world of the modern city. He was born in 1884, probably not more than twenty miles from where he shared the meal with the strange Indian that day. His mother was Yana and his father was Irish Catholic, and they named him Benjamin Frost. He was orphaned when he was four, and so was sent by train to Sacramento to live with his Irish aunt. But when she married, she abandoned him. He lived on the street in the state's capital city. To survive he became a paperboy, selling copies of the Sacramento *Bee* to prostitutes, who paid him extra when they heard his story. Later he followed his aunt to San Francisco, worked for a lawyer, and then got a job on a riverboat that plied the Sacramento River. "The crew, it was a checkerboard," Ben explained. "They had half Indians, Kanakas [Hawaiians], colored and whites—so they couldn't consolidate together and strike." But Ben made friends across the divides.

The riverboat sailed all the way north to Red Bluff, and that's when he proposed to his white friend that they go looking for a homestead up on Deer Creek. They could get away from it all there, on a homestead that would be located in the ancestral lands of his people, though he didn't think of it that way. Like the salmon, Ben came through the San Francisco Bay up the Sacramento River into the streams of Wahganupa, to the place where the remnants of the most southern group of the Yana, the Yahi, remained. But everyone—everyone, that is, except for the few local ranchers who knew better—thought the cañon was empty of Indians, that the Yahi had disappeared. Ben Frost was very surprised by the visitor.

Even when he saw him, Ben had no idea he was a Yahi. But a decade later Ben realized just who he had met that day: "I see in the papers, everything like that, about Ishi." "[He] was dressed in, oh, white man's pickup clothes," Ben remembered. "He had an old coat wrapped around him and his pants was somebody's pants that he had picked up." Perhaps Ben, who was in search of his own homestead in his ancestral lands, saw a little bit of himself in the Indian. "I figured it was just some Indian who went berserk, or wanted to get away from civilization. And I didn't think it was a wild man."[41]

· *Two* ·

THE ANTHROPOLOGIST IN THREE
WORLDS

Origins: New York City and Environs

The German tutor—bespectacled, red-bearded, and plump—
led the four young boys out on the new suspension bridge connecting Manhattan Island to Brooklyn. When completed a year
before, the Brooklyn Bridge was celebrated as one of the wonders
of the modern world, longer than any other suspension bridge,
by far. It used all sorts of new materials, including cables of steel,
"the metal of the future," the bridge's engineer called it. It was
now the age of steel, and steel was, as an orator put it at the opening ceremonies on May 24, 1883, "the kingliest instrument of
peoples for subduing the earth." Another speaker remarked that
two hundred years earlier, when the first white men built a house
on the island of Manhattan, "Nature wore a hardy countenance,
as wild and as untamed as the savage landholders....Could there
be a more astounding exhibition of the power of man to change
the face of nature than the panoramic view which presents itself

to the spectator standing upon the crowning arch of the Bridge?" The Seventh Regiment military band, seventy-five pieces strong, filled the air with music as it escorted President Chester B. Arthur to this technological marvel, made in America. And a small band of Indians from the Carlisle Institute, a boarding school whose mission was to stamp out the students' Indianness and replace it with the culture of white America, was also on hand to celebrate the grand achievement with tunes trumpeted perfectly on instruments of brass. Luther Standing Bear, a Sioux student at Carlisle who led the band that day, proudly noted the irony: "The Carlisle Indian band...was the first *real American band* to cross the Brooklyn Bridge."

Two years later another Sioux man, Chief White Ghost, crossed the new bridge. He had been brought to New York City by missionaries. After giving speeches about the "encroachment of avaricious whites on his already diminished lands," the white missionaries gave White Ghost a tour of the city to behold what had been done with these lands. But his companions were disappointed to observe that "crossing the Brooklyn Bridge in mid-air and above the masts of large vessels, hardly evoked an expression of wonder."[1]

No song hung in the air the day young Alfred, along with his brother Eddie and the two Alsberg boys, Carl and Julius, made the mile-long trek following Dr. Bamberger to the apex of the bridge's crowning arch, but they all wore expressions of wonder. The boys, thrilled and scared, looked out over the rails to New York City and its harbor. The doctor called them to attention, then pulled two magic items out of his pocket, a compass and a map which he unfolded before them. The boys peered over the landscape and then its paper double. The doctor taught them how to read the map and how to use the power of the compass. He showed them how the needle was pulled to magnetic north, and how they could use it to plot the four directions. They could see north, south, east, and west on the map and also on the land and water. Their surroundings—houses and streets, ships and water—could be placed on a grid. It was a new way of seeing their home, a new way of seeing themselves and the world. The doctor was a huge man in their eyes, but as they looked over map, compass, and the world beyond, as they stood at the crown of the great bridge and surveyed the cityscape before them, the boys felt themselves grow a little as well.[2]

This was Alfred's first lesson in geography, but there would be many more to come. He would learn that the word *geography* was derived from the Greek words for *earth writing*. Dr. Bamberger also taught them the stories of Greek mythology, another kind of earth writing. To learn more about the earth and how to represent it scientifically in writing, the doctor took the young boys on field trips everywhere around the city, it seemed. Their most frequent excursions took them into Central Park. If the bridge was New York's monument to progress and development, Central Park was the city's grand celebration of nature. One of the park's designers said it was an "homage to the natural in contradistinction to the artificial." Frederick Law Olmsted, the other principal designer, wanted Central Park to provide "natural, verdant and sylvan scenery for the refreshment of town-strained men, women, and children." Cities had "grown so great that hours [were] consumed" in getting out into the country, but an oasis of simulated wilderness could be created in the heart of the city. Central Park was the place to escape the electric pace of modern life and the straight lines of the city's grid.[3]

For Alfred and his friends, who all lived just a few blocks east of the park, it was a second home. It was also a playground, a classroom, and a laboratory. They learned to read on park benches. The doctor pointed out the marks of glaciers on rock outcroppings in the park. The boys collected fossils and minerals, chased butterflies and insects, and put them all into bottles and collections, labeling them with their scientific names.

If we were to label young Alfred Kroeber, to give him a tag that might reveal his origins and milieu, it might begin with the line "Born, 11 June, 1876, Hoboken, New Jersey, to Johanna Muller Kroeber and Florence Martin Kroeber." The family grew up in New York City, first in a house on the corner of Madison and Seventy-eighth Street and then at 316 West Eighty-ninth Street. The houses were large: four stories high; the lots were twenty feet wide and a hundred feet deep. Our label might note that Alfred was the oldest of four children and that he was a quick learner, insatiably curious about the world, and small for his age. The first book he read, at age five, was *Robinson Crusoe,* the story of a castaway "who lived Eight and Twenty Years, all alone in an uninhabited Island on the coast of America." The Crusoe idea—a man left as the last of his tribe forced to reinvent civilization from scratch—was inscribed on the first layer of Alfred's literary consciousness.

We would need to know much more about the boy's place in the world to comprehend who he was and where he was going. We should certainly know that his parents were second-generation German immigrants. His grandfather had fought for the North in

Alfred Kroeber, age seven.
Courtesy of the Bancroft Library,
University of California,
Berkeley.

the Civil War. His father made his way up in the German American community of New York City. He imported furniture, art, and fine clocks, and he made a good living. The family blended into the progressive, free-spirited, financially successful community of German Americans, made up of Jews and non-Jews alike. They were appreciative of art and music and literature and of Kant and Goethe and American liberalism, and Alfred fit right in.

Alfred's household was quiet, orderly, and stern, but nurturing as well. With Carl and his other friends, the city was his playground and schoolhouse, an endlessly fascinating laboratory of education and entertainment.

Until he was eight Alfred studied at home and in the city under the guidance of his German tutor. He learned natural history and classical history. As his friend Carl remembered, "The Greeks and

Trojans were to us what Indians, trappers, cowboys, and Jesse James were to many other boys at that time." The boys pondered Bamberger's mechanical model of the solar system, which they could crank to revolve Mercury, Venus, and Earth around a pumpkin-size Sun. Bamberger told them about the new earth, about erosion and current theories of geological forces. They put soil in a pie pan to represent Earth, stirred it up with water, set it on a high shelf, and then looked at it the next week; ridges had formed, the earth had cracked and dried. Alfred did his own version of the experiment in the park, where he found a pair of stones carved into a bowl shape, like an acorn grinding stone, only these had been created for ornament. He put dirt into the bowls to start his experiment, excited to have a "chance to stir a pie-tin earth of [his] own."[4]

After his tutorials with Dr. Bamberger in his school without walls came to an end, Alfred entered a private school called Dr. Sachs Collegiate Institute, a college preparatory school, one of the best in the city. The education there was good, if by *good* we mean that it instilled knowledge into its pupils, but it didn't open up the world as a book. No matter—Alfred pursued his unbridled curiosity on the streets of New York City and in the parks and fields. With Carl he founded the Humboldt Scientific Society, a childhood fraternity of scientists in the making. Alfred was the smallest child in the class, though that was in part because he often sat in class with older students. His parents thought him frail. His size probably did not help as he and his friends probed the neighborhoods of New York and crossed the invisible social boundaries of the city. There was a geography maintained by gangs of kids, and Alfred learned it not through maps but through body-bruising lessons, being chased or pummeled in territorial skirmishes. The East Side gangs of New York had names like the Hell Benders, the Cave Men, and the Wild Indians. The Humboldts were no match for them.[5]

Alfred kept his head up, but his parents worried about his constitutional frailty. He had a reputation for being excitable and for tiring easily, for having an easily upset stomach, for being light-boned and small. They sought advice. The family physician, a German man, came to examine Alfred at his home. He asked him a series of questions, none medical in nature. Alfred proudly discoursed on a range of topics. Then the doctor turned to Alfred's parents and proclaimed, "Der Jonge weiss zu veil." *The youngster knows too much.* Hearing this, Alfred's "conceit was much fractured." Instead of praising him for his knowledge, the doctor was saying that Alfred was too wrapped up in books and learning. He saw a child who was suffering from too much cerebral city life.[6]

It was as if Alfred had the childhood equivalent of neurasthenia, a popular diagnosis for enervated men and women of urban America's professional class. One authority believed that the nerve energy of "brain workers" was being drained, like a battery being used up. Doctors were beginning to prescribe country living as an antidote to city life. G. Stanley Hall, the president of Clark University, would later present a psychological theory to support a "nature cure" for youths troubled by city life. Hall thought children as they grew up recapitulated the stages of civilization, growing from the most primitive conditions in infancy, gradually through higher levels of civilization, until at last they were ready for modern life. But impose modern life on a boy of six, Hall warned, and you would stunt his growth. Parents should allow their child "to visit field, forest, hill, shore, the water, flowers,

animals, the true homes of childhood in this wild, undomesti-
cated stage [in their life] from which modern conditions have
kidnapped and transported [them]." Children who had become
"flabby" and "anemic" from "easy-living" in the city could be
reinvigorated by going to the country. Let children run free and
express their "savage instincts," Hall advised.[7]

Hall's nature cure was rooted in the ideas of the European
Romantics, such as Rousseau and the Kroebers' beloved Goethe.
It's no surprise, then, that Alfred's parents readily accepted the
doctor's orders. On March 13, 1888, Alfred and his mother
boarded the West Shore Railroad to head out to the country in
Connecticut, where she had arranged for him to live on a "wild
farm" (as Alfred called the place). He thrived in the country, feeding the animals and doing chores as a working member of the family farm. His mother then took him to the Adirondack Mountains
in upstate New York, the favorite place for New Yorkers to get
back to nature. Finally it was arranged for him to spend a year at
the Gunnery, a boarding school in the Connecticut countryside.[8]

His experiences with nature in Connecticut were fantastic:
swimming naked in the water holes, climbing cliffs above the
river, sledding and skating in the winter. His experience with the
culture at the school was mixed. Alfred was one of two ethnically
German boys who came to the Gunnery; most of the boys were
Anglo-Saxon New Englanders. Everyone knew that Alfred came
from Dr. Sachs Academy, which had a reputation for being a
"Jewish New York private school." The other boy, Jim Rosenberg,
was in fact a Jew, but he hadn't come from Dr. Sachs.

Alfred became the target of hateful anti-Semitic taunts.
Classmates tried to ostracize him, using racial epithets to beat

down his morale. It stung, but Alfred took it as a joke. After all, Jim was the real Jew, and Alfred never let his tormenters know they had a case of mistaken identity. Rather than turn their fury away from him and onto Jim, he laughed inwardly at their folly.

The prejudice was embodied in Big John, the school bully. His target was not Jews, but the smaller kids; he would catch them, bend their wrists back, and make them beg for mercy. Alfred and Jim, along with three other boys, formed what they called the Scugee Society for Self Defense. The boys learned to quickly tie knots in a rope; Alfred studied Big John anthropologically, learning his movements and patterns. He discovered that Big John invariably went to a remote brook after football practice, so the boys hid in the bushes with their ropes. They waited for Big John to come by, and then they jumped him, tied him up, and took him down to the pond. With Big John half-submerged in the water, the boys held a kangaroo trial and found him guilty. They allowed him to plead for his life. After that Big John, taken down a notch, never bothered them again. Just so were the boys released from the clutches of the bully, something like the way Lizard rescued Long Tail from the Grizzly Bear.[9]

Alfred returned to the city healthier and stronger and more confident. It wasn't as if he was cut off from the natural world in Manhattan, though it was the most urban, the most constructed place in America. Central Park was a symbol and a touchstone of nature in the city. The Adirondacks and the family's summer house on Long Island were parts of his world, too, as were the farm and the school in Connecticut. The historian Richard Hofstadter once remarked that America was born in the country and grew up in the city. Alfred was born in the city, and though he learned a great deal there, he also grew up in the country.

The University: Columbia and Anthropology

At the age of sixteen Alfred entered Columbia College in New York City and coasted through his freshman year. Faced with courses that seemed remedial, he fed his intellectual curiosity in the library. He focused his surplus energy on pulling off principled pranks. Increasingly incensed by the sculptures in Central Park—"[They] offended our aesthetic senses," Carl remembers—Alfred and his friend tagged them as a "symbol of [their] scorn." Late at night they painted red walrus mustaches on the stately displays, stripes of blue and white (Columbia's colors) over leggings, red raccoon tails on the dogs. The pranksters also planned to release animals from the park's zoo: foxes, raccoons, and wild dogs. Alas authorities caught Alfred and Carl by tracing the paint back to the store where they bought it. Alfred's father was troubled by the behavior and by having to pay for restitution. But Carl's father thought it was a great joke, calling Alfred "Rembrandt" with a conspiratorial smile on his face.[10]

Under the influence of a great teacher of literature in their sophomore year, Alfred and his friends became enthralled with the world of letters. They founded a literary magazine that published short stories. It also featured critiques of the university, including Alfred's plea that Columbia hire a historian who studied not just politics but a deeper spectrum of humanity, something he called "cultural history." In the meantime he passionately pursued literature. He earned a master's degree and began teaching English courses. That year a new professor came to Columbia who would alter Alfred's life.[11]

Franz Boas, originally trained in physics and geography in his native Germany, had become one of the world's first professional anthropologists—not a "cultural historian," but in a sense just the kind of scholar Alfred had been seeking. Boas had been led into the field, and to America, in search of an answer to a question: Did different peoples perceive the physical world differently? He took his question with him to Greenland and was transformed by what he saw among the people Europeans knew as the Eskimos (but who refer to themselves as Inuit, or "the people").

With anti-Semitism on the rise in Germany, the Jewish Boas, scarred from duels with Jew-hating classmates, knew opportunities in his homeland would be few. He decided to make a life for himself in America. First hired by G. Stanley Hall at Clark University, he subsequently worked at the Field Museum in Chicago and helped organize the anthropological exhibits at the World's Columbian Exposition of 1893, which was held to celebrate half a millennium of progress since Columbus came to the New World. Boas brought Kwakwaka'wakw Indians from British Columbia and Eskimos from Greenland to the fair, hoping to open visitors' eyes to the beauty, complexity, and sophistication of the cultures Europeans had nearly wiped out in the wake of Columbus.

In the New World Boas couldn't escape Columbus, or at least efforts to honor him through names; he did field research in British Columbia, worked on the Columbian Exposition, and began teaching at Columbia University in 1896. Boas offered a course on Indian languages, teaching in his apartment in Greenwich Village.

Curious, Alfred went to see Boas. Boas looked the young man over and asked, "What makes you think you'd like these studies?" "I don't know," Alfred answered, "but I thought it wouldn't do any harm to 'shop around' until I found what I wanted. You see, whenever anything is published in the newspapers about Commander Peary's exploits...I find myself insatiably curious to know something of the early history of the Esquimaux."[12]

Under Boas's direction, the insatiably curious Alfred plunged into the linguistic universe of the Klamath, Eskimo, and Salish; he learned the Chinook trade jargon of the Northwest Coast. He was "enormously stimulated" by it all, especially Boas's way of allowing students to discover the grammatical structure, the skeleton of these languages, for themselves. "Boas' method was very similar to that of a zoologist who starts a student with an etherized frog or worm and a dissecting table," Alfred recalled. The analogy between zoology and anthropology was disturbingly apt, and that connection partly explains Alfred's fascination with anthropology—and later his repulsion.[13]

A star student, Alfred soon decided to take up anthropology as his life's work. Carl was shocked by his choice. If you're going to devote your life to research and scientific investigation, he demanded, why do it in anthropology, the study of man? It's inchoate, vague, intangible. Why not be a chemist, doing something that you can get your teeth into, a field where you know where you stand and get a result or not? Alfred replied that one may get a result in physics or chemistry, but it won't change people's minds. It won't set people free intellectually. Anthropology can make people see the world more clearly. It can dissipate superstition. It can free people from hoary tribal taboos.[14]

Alfred won the argument and went his way. But the superstitions he ultimately tried to clear up were not those of tribal peoples, but those of modern man. Modern men, or at least many of them, were deeply mistaken about their place in the world and in history. They thought they were at the pinnacle, the culmination of some evolutionary destiny, and that they were the carriers of the highest culture and makers of progress. Everyone else in the world, they thought, was behind and below them: behind them in time and below them in status and achievement.

Boas bucked the trend, seeing the world and its peoples in a completely different light. At the time, many scientists and philosophers believed that morality and culture were tied, ineluctably, to racial identity, which itself was considered immutable. Proponents of scientific racism had used biometrics, various techniques of measuring the body and especially the head, to undergird their belief in the distinctiveness of races, and that a natural hierarchy existed among them. But Boas used those same biometric techniques to undermine such racist assumptions. He directed a study measuring the bodies and heads of some eighteen thousand immigrants and their American-born children. The upshot was that the children's bodies and heads differed from those of their parents. Even bodily form was more plastic than the racist scientists believed; environment had a lot to do with bodily form, with "race." Race—understood as some unchangeable essence that defined life, morals, and intellectual capacity—was thus deflated, like a pigskin football punctured by a nail.

Boas's antiracism was deeply intertwined with how he looked at the native peoples of North America, and his views struck a chord with Alfred. For one, Boas wanted to close the intellectual gap most experts felt existed between modern Europeans and members of tribal societies. "The mind of the native enjoys the beauties of nature as well as we do," Boas insisted. "There is no fundamental difference in the ways of thinking of primitive and civilized man." "One man is as good as another mentally and physically," Boas told a reporter. "NO RACE IS INFERIOR, SAYS WORLD AUTHORITY," ran the headline. Intellectual capacity was the same, but cultures were different. At the time, culture was generally thought of as a synonym for civilization. The best and the brightest had culture, in the form of artistic works; others had no culture. But Boas democratized culture: everyone had a culture, he argued, for culture was the learned ideas and behavior of a people, their way of life. Culture wasn't a singular achievement; it was an endowment that every people enjoyed, and one should not put cultures into rank order.[15]

Boas championed what came to be called *cultural relativism,* an idea that carried enormous epistemological and political implications. It changed how people thought about knowledge and reinvigorated the democratic idea that all people are created equal. For an anthropologist and a director of museums, cultural relativism had practical implications as well. When Boas came to the United States, museums collected artifacts from all over the world. When putting them on display, they would often arrange them in a sequence from the most "primitive" to the most advanced or "civilized" form. Peoples and the things they made were thus ripped from their cultural and geographical contexts and placed on an evolutionary, hierarchical scale. Boas believed that objects of culture had to be understood in place, in context. A museum that lined them up was just creating a fiction using material objects instead of words. It was telling a just-so story ultimately designed to teach the moral that white Europeans had achieved the apex of evolutionary development. Anthropology, Boas preached, should demonstrate "that civilization is not something absolute, but that it is relative, and that our ideas and conceptions are true only so far as our civilization goes."[16]

Alfred learned these lessons well at Columbia. Early anthropologists, he later explained in a textbook he wrote on anthropology, may have been interested in distant peoples because they were strange, exotic, wild. But as they learned more about different peoples and their unique ways of life, they began to appreciate this diversity and to deepen their conception of culture: "[Anthropologists] became aware of culture as a 'universe,' or vast field in which we of today and our own civilization occupy only one place of many. The result was a widening of a fundamental point of view, a departure from unconscious ethnocentricity toward relativity." For Alfred that was anthropology's prime contribution. He insisted, "There is no room in anthropology for a shred of ethnocentricity...for prevaluations in favor of our civilization, our religion, our philosophy, our standards." Ethnocentricity, the belief in the superiority of one's own culture, was "one of the great perverters of truth" and the handmaiden of racism. The appreciation of culture "was the conceptual means of breaking hold of this shackle." It is next to impossible to prove that one race is superior to another, he wrote, but it is "easy to prove that we entertain a strong prejudice in favor of our own racial superiority." In that first debate with Carl, Alfred pointed to anthropology's potential to free people from "hoary taboos." What he ended up doing was freeing modern intellectuals from their hoary ethnocentrism, which amounted to a form of racism.[17]

Boas's relativity lit a fire under Alfred. If all of the world's peoples had created unique cultures that were complex and complete and beautiful in themselves, not just examples of earlier stages of civilization, the scrap heap of historical progress, there was much to be learned from each of them. But these cultures were threatened, vanishing. Whole languages were being swallowed into the void as the last native speakers died. Through imperial expansion, modernity was coming to every corner of the globe, intruding on all walks of life. Though Alfred and Boas did not dislike their own culture, they did recognize just how powerful and arrogant it could be. Modernity was "contaminating" the whole world, for good and bad. Before other cultural universes were erased or absorbed without a trace, anthropologists should mount a cultural rescue mission. Record the languages, the stories; see the material objects of the cultures in use; listen to the people. They should span the continent, span the globe, practicing what came to be known as "salvage anthropology."

People from different corners of the globe could also come to you, right at the bustling center of America. In 1895 Franz Boas told the arctic explorer Robert Peary, whose ultimate goal was to reach the North Pole and stand triumphant on top of the earth, about his desire to study an Eskimo from Greenland. Boas explained to Peary, "It would be of very greatest value if you should be able to bring a middle-aged Eskimo to stay...over winter. This would enable us to obtain leisurely certain information which will be of greatest scientific value." The anthropologist Lewis Henry Morgan had argued that Eskimos were trapped in an ice age stage of development and were among the most primitive versions of man, what he called "living fossils." Boas, who had himself observed Eskimos, thought otherwise, and he wanted to prove it. When Peary returned from his trip to the frozen North in September 1897, his ship carried six Eskimos as well as a huge meteor bound for the American Museum of Natural History. Boas got more than he had bargained for.[18]

The Eskimos, including a man named Qisuk and his six-year-old son, Minik, were housed at the American Museum of Natural History. At the Columbian Exposition in Chicago back in 1893, Boas had been troubled by feeling that he was being asked to act like a "circus impresario." This time his Eskimos would be sequestered for study, not exhibited for public amusement (though when they had still been on Peary's ship in New York Harbor, thousands of curious New Yorkers paid a quarter apiece to see the polar visitors). The man to study them, an oversubscribed Boas decided, was his bright twenty-one-year-old doctoral student, Alfred Kroeber. Alfred had already worked with Esther, a half-Eskimo woman from Labrador who was married to a mechanic at the museum. With her help as a translator, Alfred set about trying to learn as much as possible about the Smith Sound Eskimos' culture, their folklore and kinship relations, their ideas and behavior.[19]

But the Eskimos soon fell ill, afflicted with tuberculosis. Qisuk died in February. A funeral was held on the museum grounds, orchestrated by Boas and the museum's superintendent, William Wallace. It was a quiet ceremony, held at dusk. The body was laid to rest, stones placed over the grave. A bereaved, lonely, and tearful Minik took it all in. He made his mark on the north side of the grave, an Eskimo practice that keeps the ghost of the dead person from haunting you where you live. There were more things Minik had to do for the dead. Alfred reported that days after the funeral, Nuktaq, one of the surviving Eskimo elders, told Minik "to visit the (supposed) grave of his father, and instructed him how to act."[20]

Minik and the others were doing their best to perform the traditional mourning practices in what Alfred called their "strange surroundings." Strange, indeed. Minik, it turns out, was visiting not the grave of his father, but the "(supposed) grave site." Within those parentheses Alfred left a clue, a trace of something he knew that Minik and Nuktaq did not. What was the anthropologist's secret?

After the death of Qisuk, Boas hoped "to appease the boy" and spare the Eskimos "any shock or uneasiness. The burial accomplished that purpose." The surviving Eskimos would have been shocked and disturbed, Boas fully understood, if they knew the truth—that Qisuk's "body had been chopped up and his bones placed in the collection" of the museum. The museum wanted the bones and brain for science. To keep the remains for themselves, they performed a cultural sleight of hand, burying in traditional Eskimo manner not the actual body of Qisuk, but a substitute, a human-size piece of wood, a mask was attached to one end. The anthropologists had clearly gotten into the deceitful act, animating the piece of wood and then putting it to rest in a ritual worthy of study.[21]

Qisuk's preserved brain went to Aleš Hrdlička, who helped perform the dissection. Hrdlička was fascinated with skulls and brains and made them his life-long study. He was a physical anthropologist, devoted to understanding the biophysical shell of humanity. To get at his subject matter, he collected skulls and brains from all over the world and dug them up from many Indian burial grounds. Hrdlička stared at this new specimen and might have seen, as Alfred would later see in the cerebral folds of an Indian's brain in alcohol behind glass on his desk, a reflection of the cultural necrophilia with which anthropology was uncomfortably but inextricably intimate. Hrdlička published his first article, "An Eskimo Brain," based on what he did see; he reported facts and figures about the size and nature of Qisuk's brain, but nothing about the man or his culture.[22]

After the sham burial, the remaining Eskimos, some of whom were also showing signs of illness, left the museum for a private cottage on the outskirts of the city, "in the 'country,'" Alfred wrote, underscoring that the natural setting with its garden was thought by Boas to be better for the health of the remaining Eskimos. Later they were taken to Wallace's farm in upstate New York in the hope that the country life would restore them. Alfred followed them and got more stories. "The Eskimo experience," he wrote, "committed me to the exacting activity of eliciting the forms of a foreign culture by questioning members of its society." He found that it was "not difficult" to get them to "volunteer information," especially if one were "really interested," which he was.[23]

But death—more particularly, tuberculosis—followed them. Alfred witnessed the people as they succumbed, one by one, to consumption (as the disease was then called). Standing by, he felt it his duty to record the mortuary rituals of the Eskimos, which he did with great care, and some warmth, too. He was a scientist, yes; he treated the Eskimos as sources of information about their culture, for which he had great reverence. But compared to

Boas, who flippantly disregarded the feelings of Minik when they might get in the way of science, Alfred was more empathetic.[24]

Atangana died, and Alfred recorded everything her husband, Nuktaq, went through. Nuktaq adhered as best as he could to the observances of his people. He admonished his dead wife to come to him only at night, and he "ordered her to stay where she was buried, not to follow him when he was kayaking." Not long afterward, Nuktaq was dead as well; he would never again venture out on the water in a kayak. His remains went to the museum. His wife, despite his commands, did not stay in her grave, for she had no power over the living. The museum wanted her bones; they were cleaned in the bone room at Wallace's farm and then filed away in the museum's collection.[25]

Alfred was interested in the stories of the living, not the bones of the dead. For a twenty-one-year-old he did an amazing job with his ethnographic descriptions, though his "informants" were at times frustrated by his inability to transcribe fast enough to keep up with their "natural speech rate." He heard many stories, including tales of animals, and drew on them to put together his very first professional presentation at the American Association for the Advancement of Science meeting in Boston in August 1898. He was nervous, and no one from the audience asked a question. But during the intermission a black clergyman attending the scientific meeting approached him with a friendly inquiry. Alfred wrote, "I sensed that he felt as ill at ease as I, he on account of his color and I for my youth and inexperience. But also a certain assurance that he would not be rebuffed, and in my loneliness I was grateful."[26]

Alfred went on to publish three important papers on the Eskimos, his first publications, which amounted to his coming out as a professional anthropologist. In the process he struck a blow against the scientific racism that held that Eskimos were ice age fossils, frozen in time at the foot of the ladder of human progress. But he also discovered that salvage anthropology was not abstract scholarship in the Ivory Tower, not book learning removed from the vital world in which people live, struggle, and die. Anthropological salvage was like going into the dark basement of collapsed towers, looking there for survivors—and after hope of finding any was gone, looking for bodies and anything they could tell you about the identities of those who had been crushed in the rubble. Sometimes you crushed the bodies yourself as you were searching.

The New World: San Francisco and Rekwoi

A real anthropologist could not do all of his work by bringing his subjects to him, so Kroeber was called out to the field. His field was in the West, where he went to study the Arapaho and the Gros Ventre. While he was there, news of the death of his beloved brother Eddie came to him by pony messenger, as he was beyond the reach of any phone or telegraph.

Eventually Kroeber was called all the way to the edge of the West, to California, where his life's work would be. David Starr Jordan, president of Stanford University and director of the California Academy of Sciences, was looking for a curator for the Academy's museum. Boas told Starr to hire Kroeber, which he did. In August 1900 Kroeber took a train across the country to San Francisco. The Academy was downtown, and he took a room in a hotel on Eddy Street. He took in the sights and sounds and

tastes of his new city, indulging in Pacific crab, oyster, and abalone at Fisherman's Wharf. In the evenings he often attended the
local opera; a seat in the balcony could be had for twenty-five
cents, and he could relax with a beer and take in the spectacle.[27]

During the day Kroeber was very busy at the museum. He
organized its collection of artifacts in a mere six weeks, intensify-
ing his effort so that he could move on to what he considered the
real work of a curator: collecting in the field. Collect artifacts,
stories, information. See what was there. The salvage work was
urgent. He had to preserve and conserve objects, a great variety
of objects. By doing so he could preserve and conserve whole
worlds.

With one hundred dollars to pay for expenses, Kroeber headed
up the coast of California to the mouth of the Klamath River.
The place captured his imagination, as did the culture of the
Yurok Indians who lived there. He spoke to Captain Spott, asking
him for myths. Spott cautiously told him a few origin stories, in
English for the most part. For the benefit of the anthropologist,
Spott used the word "God" instead of "Wohpekumeu," and otherwise tailored his storytelling in a way that held something back.
As Kroeber himself recognized, Spott gave him a sample of "what
a Yurok at the time was likely to tell a strange white man." But
Kroeber persisted, and soon some Yuroks, sensing his genuine
interest, took pity on him and started to help, telling elders that
they thought Kroeber was "a friend interested in learning their
ancient manners...and [about] the effect the white man's coming
into their lives had made." With this help Kroeber was eventually
allowed to hear stories of the creation, of the First-time people
and the events that led to this present world. Spott told Kroeber

how Wohpekumeu, "'the widower from across the ocean,' the one who makes things as they are," asked the assembled creatures, "How shall we have human beings live? What shall we do for them?" Wertspit (Jerusalem cricket) answered, "We will make it bad for them, so that they will be constantly dying. Otherwise there will be too many and the world will be too full."[28]

Kroeber began to learn something of this place where the Klamath River now flowed into the Pacific Ocean. That hadn't always been the case. Once the river had flowed out to the sea a ways up north along the coast, at the village of Omen. But the people, standing on the banks of the river with their harpoons and fish gaffs, saw no salmon in the water. So the Wo-gey spirit changed the river's outlet, making it run out to the sea at Rekwoi. Sea lions would come barking up the river. They would catch salmon. The people would catch salmon. "People will be well off in this world on account of this river," the Wo-gey spirit said. The people saw the salmon coming up. And the Wo-gey spirit entered the rock at the mouth of the river, Oregos. "I shall watch this river where it enters the ocean, from this rock. I shall take care of it."

Crossing the river at Rekwoi was dangerous, Spott told Kroeber, but the Wo-gey had also created a song that people could sing to settle the waters when they crossed. By the time Kroeber first got to Rekwoi, a cable had been strung across the river, guiding a ferry boat for safety. The new people trusted steel more than songs. The salmon were being put in cans and shipped out to be eaten around the world. Kroeber came back time and again, learning about the old ways, about the first salmon rites, about respect and kinship, about the rocks and their history. Every part of the riverine landscape, Kroeber discovered, was named; it all had stories attached to it, and these stories animated the present, filled up the Yuroks' deep sense of place and identity. It was fascinating to him; the Yurok had built along the river a "remarkable civilization."[29]

This place was Rekwoi. To the Yurok this place was the center of the world, not some boondocks on the far western fringes of America. To impose the outsider's Anglo-Saxon toponymy and geography on this place was "incongruous," Kroeber insisted. Here was a different world, and he wanted to see it for himself, to understand it, to become part of it. And in his own mind, he eventually would. Many years later he traveled by canoe up the river with his wife. His old friends came out to greet him, hugging him. He hoped one day to write a "history of the Yurok at once more personal, psychological, and biographical than any" he had yet written. But then he wondered: "Perhaps I can not write of the Yurok this way. I feel myself too much a Yurok."[30]

But that was all far into the future. In 1900 Kroeber was a man fired with a mission, a man of boundless energy and passion, going out and gathering, trying to gain enough trust so that he could take away those things he wanted to take away. As his biographer described him, "He became part of the rural scene, going by stage, surrey, buckboard or on horseback or afoot up and down and inland over the dusty trails to the rancherias and villages of Indians who usually became his friends. Soon word of him preceded his arrival: he was the serious young man with a black beard, the pockets of whose khaki coat bulged with an assortment of pipes, a well-filled tobacco pouch, an all-purpose jackknife, notebooks and pencils, and a bag of hard candies for the grandmothers and children of the households he visited."[31]

Alfred Kroeber ready for fieldwork in California, 1911. BANC PIC 1978.128. Courtesy of the Bancroft Library, University of California, Berkeley.

Unfortunately the Academy of Sciences, strapped for funds at the time, was not entirely behind Kroeber's fieldwork, and he was let go. Yet Kroeber wanted to stay in the West; it represented freedom and a new field. It was a place where he could become his own man. He soon found himself sponsored by someone who was interested in this field work. Phoebe Apperson Hearst, the widow of the California senator and mining magnate George and the mother of the flamboyant media magnate William Randolph, had a passion for collecting artifacts from Egypt and around the world. She also had a vision for a museum. Hearst worked out an agreement with the president of the University of California: she would sponsor a museum and help the university establish a department of anthropology. Kroeber was hired as the executive secretary. He managed the museum's collections, which were brought to a building originally intended for the university's law school, on Parnassus Heights in San Francisco. With Hearst's support Kroeber planned to survey the languages and cultures of California Indian peoples. He would organize a mapping of the state, looking at the differences and similarities of cultures, tracing the complex and dense linguistic geography of the state, learning languages and talking with Indians, whom he referred to, and liked to think of, as friends (though anthropologists commonly referred to them antiseptically as "informants").[32]

Under the headline "Important Research," the *Los Angeles Times* in 1903 ran a story about the "systematic anthropological investigations throughout the State" that Kroeber was heading up. Newspapers covered his findings: California Indians had full and complex languages with intricate grammatical structures; they did not just "speak a random jargon as is popularly believed." This was news! The deep prejudice that had engulfed California's Indians for a century—a prejudice that held that they were "diggers" who lived off roots and insects and had no culture or even language—was swept away by Kroeber's relativistic research.[33]

Kroeber and his colleagues and students made remarkable progress on their survey, which amounted to a kind of *unmapping* exercise. As he was mapping languages, peoples, and landscapes, he was also unmapping California. He wanted to see a California that existed before the place-names brought by Anglo-Americans had been slapped onto the landscape. Whites called a river north of the Klamath the Smith River, after the American fur trapper Jedediah Smith. But to the Yurok the river was known by the settlement it passed through, Hinei, and by the stories and the actions of their forerunners along that river. Whites called the beautiful wine-growing county Sonoma and thought it was an Indian word meaning Valley of the Moon, a phrase so romantic Jack London used it as a title for one of his books. Kroeber pointed out that the name, which seemed to put the moon and no one else at the center of the landscape, in reality derives from the Yupian Wappo words for *earth* and *village; sonoma* means the village ground, a settlement that had been linguistically erased through fanciful translation. Whites were always doing this, emptying out the continent with their maps, mentally constructing it as an unoccupied wilderness ripe for the taking.[34]

Kroeber had to unmap what he saw before he could write *The Handbook of the Indians of California,* the great volume that was the culmination of the survey. In that book he attempted to "reconstruct...the scheme within which these people in ancient and more recent times lived their lives." The world of California Indians had been shaken, ploughed under. Kroeber wanted to find a way to see it once again as a whole. Salvage anthropology could retrieve the materials for reconstruction, for a narrative that would give modern Americans a sense of the "color and life in which...the characteristics of civilizations are manifest." The reel on which the movie of manifest destiny was spooled could be turned backward, Kroeber thought, so that everyone could see and appreciate the "remarkable civilizations" that had all but vanished from the land.[35]

But this unreeling of colonial history was possible only because California Indians and their cultures had somehow managed to survive. That they were threatened in fin de siècle California was not in doubt, and many whites became concerned with their precarious condition. In October 1909 the Commonwealth Club of California asked Kroeber, by then the leading white expert on the native peoples of the state, to speak at a meeting devoted to "the rights and wrongs of the California Indians." Kroeber outlined the history of the Indians, speaking of the Spanish *éntrada*, the coupled efforts to missionize and terrorize the Indian peoples; the effects of diseases; the population decline. "Far more Indians than fell in battle were massacred," he told his audience. Men, women, and children were killed by Americans—out of fear, suspicion, or simply because whites felt they were "in the way." The government's reservation policy was a failure, largely because it did not take into account the "localism" of Indians, and thus uprooted populations and put them in the land of other Indians they did not know, trust, or understand.[36]

What should be done about the current plight of the Indians? Did the scientist have an answer? Kroeber cut to the chase: it was all about land, and the autonomy that could come from controlling a piece of it. "To the ethnologist," he said, "the conviction is carried home very strongly that the solution of the California Indian problem lies above all in giving him land. Not money, not food, not advice, not even education, is what he primarily needs, but land—property which he can call his own, and by which he can at least subsist and thereby be independent." Restore land to Indians, and they would finally have a "foothold of independence." The Indian would cease to be "the football of circumstance or of the caprice of his white neighbor." He will be a "member of the community, instead of squalid half-outcast; and besides being self-supporting, will be self-respecting,—which under American institutions is equally important."[37]

Applause rang out for the anthropologist. He was followed by Miss Cornelia Taber, who told the audience that the author of *Treasure Island,* Robert Louis Stevenson, once said that "the redwoods and the redskins were the two noblest living indigenous things in the State and both were condemned." The noble trees had finally been preserved, but Indians were still having the land cut out from under them. She said that Indians were another kind of natural resource, that they were "natural logicians, natural artists, natural warriors." Taber insisted that they, too, should be protected: "We cannot spare out of our Anglo-Saxon population the qualities which the Indian could bring into our civilization.... Will you not help us save this race, these native Sons and Daughters of the Golden West?"[38]

Salvage anthropology was a form of conservation. But Kroeber would not be satisfied if the cultures of the Indians were confined to the hothouse of the museum and the university, with their artifact collections, their publications, photographs, and recorded songs, with their skeletons, too—just as a conservationist would not be satisfied if the last Giant Sequoia existed only as a specimen in an arboretum or the grizzly or bison lived on only in a zoo. Taber associated wilderness preservation with the protection of Indians. Kroeber would certainly agree that conservation of wilderness had gone further than efforts to help Indians. Ironically, sometimes one came at the expense of the other. He had seen it himself.

In 1906 Kroeber visited a group of Miwok Indians who lived on Big Creek near Groveland. They faced the "caprice of their white neighbor," as "at various times whites have endeavored to either dispossess them of their lands or at least trespass upon their rights." Now a white man had just squatted on their land and promptly proceeded to bar Indians from it. The Miwok were being squeezed between a rock and a hard place.

Both individual white property owners and the federal government through its management of the national park at Yosemite deprived the Miwok of their ability to subsist from the land and thus keep their culture alive. Kroeber witnessed this dire dynamic and felt compelled to petition C. E. Kelsey, the commissioner for Indian affairs in California: "[The Miwok] adhere to their old ways of living, particularly in the matter of foods, using the aboriginal foods to a large extent; and everywhere I heard them complaining that they had been dispossessed of their lands and were now obliged not only to live upon the land of the whites...but they were forbidden in many cases by the whites from gathering acorns, manzanita, berries, seeds, and other old time vegetable foods from the lands to which they had formerly had free access." Conservation was hemming them in as well: "Of this the Indians complain: that they are not allowed to hunt when the deer are in their vicinity, and that in certain parts, upon the forest reserve and national parks, they are not permitted to carry arms in the season when they might legally hunt, or else they are tied to their homes by the necessity to work for a living." He pushed Kelsey to come up with a plan to accommodate traditional hunting practices, telling him, "I am very much of the opinion that anything that might be done for them...would be in a very worthy cause."[39]

The subsistence patterns and ways of life of the Miwok conflicted not only with whites' ideas about the impermeability and sanctity of the landscapes they had turned into private property, but also with the management of the national parks and the conservation of wilderness. The Miwok found this out when their deer hunters were confronted by the U.S. Cavalry patroling the park lands in Yosemite in the 1890s; no hunting was allowed. Luther Standing Bear, who had made that inaugural march over the Brooklyn Bridge, the symbol of modern America on which young Alfred had his first geography lesson, got to the heart of the conflict between real Indians and the whites' idea of wilderness. "Only to the white man was nature a 'wilderness' and only to him was it 'infested' with 'wild' animals and 'savage' people," he explained. "To us it was tame."[40]

Kroeber traveled up and down the state for his survey, looking and listening and learning. He met a woman who was doing the same, Henriette Rothschild. They published their findings in the same journal, and they were joined in marriage as well.

In collecting stories the Kroebers followed in the footsteps of Stephen Powers, a journalist who in the 1870s had taken a keen interest in California's Indians and written the book *The Tribes of California*. Powers became an amateur anthropologist, but he was innocent of the exacting methodologies professional anthropologists like Boas would establish for the discipline. Powers was an untrained, untamed anthropologist, Alfred Kroeber's wild alter ego. Fingering through the pages of Powers's old *Tribes of California*, Kroeber, with his black beard and intense yet meditative eyes, would alternately "writhe and smile."[41]

Kroeber was particularly intrigued by Powers's account of a band of Yana Indians. In 1874 Powers wrote, "[They] seem likely to present a spectacle which is without a parallel in human

history—that of a barbaric race resisting civilization with arms
in their hands, to the last man, and the last squaw, and the last
papoose. They were once a numerous and thrifty people. Now
there are only five of them left—two men, two women, and a
child. No human eye ever beholds them, except now and then
some lonely hunter, perhaps, prowling and crouching for days
over the volcanic wastes and scraggy forests which they inhabit."
More than thirty more years had gone by, and to the outside
world the Yahi appeared to have vanished. Occasionally there were
reports of fleeting glimpses of red men in the wilderness, laughed
off like UFO or Bigfoot sightings in our own time. But Kroeber
was curious: Was this all just a story Powers made up? Could it
be that there were still Indians in hiding along the streams of
Mount Lassen? On November 10, 1908, the *Chico Record* broke
the silence: "CAMP OF WILD INDIANS REPORTED TO BE FOUND."
The *Oroville Daily Register* reported unequivocally "INDIANS IN
WILD STATE LIVE ON DEER CREEK." Reading these new reports in
black and white, Kroeber must have smiled, and writhed a bit,
and been intrigued.[42]

· Three ·

"WORLDS OF STUFF"

Wowunupo'mu tetna

Ishi was hard at work making things. He gathered materials from all around. You could make a whistle that would imitate the call of a buck, or fox, or coyote, and arouse the animal's curiosity. They would come close enough to shoot with a bow and arrow. You could make rope from grasses or barks. From the skins of wildcats and coyotes you could make a cape or a blanket; the cañons were among the hottest places in California in the summer, but in the winter and at night it was cold. There were salmon to harpoon. And river otters, too. Cure the hide, turn it inside out, sew the mouth shut with black flax thread, and you would have a quiver that could hold a bow and arrows, watertight.

Women made baskets. You dug up pine roots and split them for the weft; hazel switches or willow were good for the warp; slender twigs were used for coiled baskets. For designs, redbud bark for red, sedge for white designs. There were manzanita berries to gather, and acorns, and native tobacco. Grind the acorn with stone metates. Flat hearths of cedar wood, a wooden drill of buckeye: this was your fire kit. You needed fire to make it all work. With these things—bow and arrow, the calls of the wild animals you knew, the acorns and reeds, and salmon and deer—you could almost make a living. The few Yahi left did it this way. There were four or five, or eight or ten.

Ishi made good arrows. He knew the process. Arrow making was an involving art. Materials had to be gathered. For the bow, the *man'i*, you could notch out the heartwood from a living juniper, which would go on living. The bow was shaped with an obsidian scraper, then smoothed with sandstone. You curved the wood back by heating it with a hot stone. You boiled salmon hide for glue; deer sinew, the shredded fibers of its tendons, was soaked, chewed, and then glued to the back of the bow. Dried, the sinew made the bow strong and resilient, allowing the back to bend as Ishi pulled the twisted bowstring made from the fine sinews from the shank of a deer. It took days and weeks, drying in the sun and being reworked, sanded and filed, and finally strung. The finished bow, made of the materials of the earth, lived. It had to rest on the ground when not in use; to store it upright was to keep it working. It was a man's tool; if a woman touched the bow, it had to be scrubbed before it could be used again.

Hazel and buckeye, wild currant and cane were used for the arrows. A hardwood fore shaft, heavier than the wood for the main shaft, was often attached. Ishi made arrows five at a time. He would gather the shoots of hazel, remove the bark with his thumbnail, tie the bundle together to let it season. Then he would rub the shafts over a hot stone to make them straight. Sandstone smoothed the shaft. Paint pigment came from plants and from the eyes of salmon. Ishi rotated the shaft and held his paintbrush to it, making blue and red stripes. He would use eagle feathers when he could get them, or else feathers from the red-tailed hawk, the owl, or even heron, blue jay, or pigeon. Three feathers, carefully selected and prepared, were fitted to the shaft with sinew.[1]

Lizard was always busy making arrows:

Now he worked at it,
put on the red paint, put them away finished.

Early in the morning, as he turned them on the ground,
He flaked arrowheads

Now he chipped off flakes.

Early in the morning,
As he turned them on the ground,
He attached the points to the foreshafts—
Finished....

At sundown,
He trimmed the feather-vanes.

Now he was busy with it:
He charred the feathers,
Put them away finished.

"Eat, children!" he said.

Ishi's work was like that of Lizard. Making arrows. So that the people could eat. The storyteller would always say, after every step in the making of an arrow, "Finished." But it was never finished. You had to keep making to keep being.[2]

Ishi's arrow making was different from Lizard's. His arrow-heads were different. You could see it in their design. Most of Ishi's arrowheads were made of glass. And the way he chipped them was the way the Wintu did it, not his Yahi ancestors. Perhaps a Wintu man had joined the Yahi during, or before, Ishi's childhood and shown him the way. Ishi's technique was different in other ways. His flaking tool was not of bone or stone. He used an iron spike, latched by sinew to a wooden handle. Wahganupa had made the obsidian, a volcanic glass traditionally used for arrowheads. But the *saltu* left glass bottles all over the place, near their cabins and camps. Glass had become abundant; good material for his arrows. Ishi found that artificial glass worked well, and there was less chance of getting a chip in your eye.[3]

Ishi and the others gathered materials from all around. From *saltu* cabins and camps they took glass, nails, old saws, branding irons designed to burn *MF* and *MS* into cattle hides. Old Winchester rifles, disassembled; the triggers, cocks, and barrels were put to service as tools. All of these materials were taken back to their village, a village that had been created to be invisible to outsiders, a mini Shangri-la along the cañon. The lower camp, seemingly impenetrable on a flat area some four hundred feet above Deer Creek, was hidden by foliage from all vantage points above and below. The Yahi were careful to leave no tracks. Toeholds up the slope were often covered with leaves. Dense undergrowth and a laurel tree canopy above kept the site from being seen. The position of the houses was plotted so that they could not be discovered from the cliffs behind and above. They called the camouflaged village *Wowunupo'mu tetna*, Grizzly Bear's Hiding Place.[4]

It was a refuge in their eroding world, a place to live with three small houses, a place to work as well. The camp had a storehouse of parts, discarded or pilfered items from the whites around them. Square nails became harpoon points. An iron pot was used for cooking acorn soup; it was heated in the old way: a rock from a fire was dropped into the stew. A monogrammed razor became a flaking tool. Beer bottles became arrowheads, chipped at a place near the main lodge under cover of brush. A bushel of fragments lay on the ground where the arrowheads had been manufactured, tailings of Ishi's craft. In Wowunupo'mu tetna, the Yahi worked away in a factory out of sight, transforming the gifts of nature and the junk of the *saltu* into the objects they needed to survive.

They also wrapped a bar of soap up in fifty St. Croy flour sacks and placed it in a tree, as if it were a bundle of medicine. Shamans often placed their power stones in baskets and secreted them away in trees. More power for survival.[5]

Late one afternoon Ishi was looking for salmon, harpoon at the ready, from a rocky bank on the lower reaches of Deer Creek when he heard someone call out, "Hello there." He turned and saw two white men looking up at him. He did not recognize them. They were not cattlemen of the cañon, all of whom he knew by sight. The two were looking at him, puzzled and afraid. Ishi held their gaze, crouching slightly. They kept on looking, unsure of themselves and what they were seeing. When they looked away for a moment, Ishi vanished.

He did not know who these men were, but he probably climbed a lava tower to get a better look. There were nine men. Ishi was careful to go back to Wowunupo'mu tetna unseen. He climbed up the secret staircase of the cliff and put leaves over the toeholds and handholds. Back at the village the Yahi talked about what was to be done. Ishi's mother was old and sick. Her legs were wrapped in cotton cloth. She could not travel. Some of them would have to stay with her here. The white men would pass by and never see their village, they decided. No one had ever found it.

The next morning the Yahi started a very small fire, using their tricks to conceal the smoke. They were making acorn soup. But then they heard the men coming up their trail. The only way out was up and over the cliff, but this could not be done with Ishi's mother. They wrapped her up in a blanket and abandoned the village for hiding spots in the woods nearby. The white men came into the camp. They had guns in their hands. Ishi could see the cattleman now, Jack Apperson. Jack looked into one of their houses. He found the soup. The Yahi moved away from the camp but could not get far with Ishi's mother. They put her down, trying to hide the bundle in which she was wrapped. The white men came in pursuit. Ishi aimed carefully and let an arrow fly. He sent it flying, so that it would graze the man's hat. He shot it into Jack's face, like Lizard did to the Ya'wi. But the white men didn't scatter. The Yahi shouted, "Campoodee! Campoodee!" and motioned for the whites to go back. This is our village, the Yahi were saying. But the whites looked on, holding the ground they had taken. Ishi's uncle, the old shaman, crippled from long ago when his foot was crushed in a steel bear trap, had trouble getting up over the cliff. He was helped over by another Yahi, perhaps a woman. They all got away, but they had to leave Ishi's mother behind. Maybe the *saltu* wouldn't find her.

Ishi and the others watched and waited from a safe distance. The white men were there for a long time. When they left, Ishi came back to the camp. His mother was there, unharmed. She said she told the white men she was "muy malo." She said, "Muchacho vamoose." She said, "Agua," and the men gave her water. But the village had been ransacked. Their skin blankets were gone. Their fire-making kits. Their arrows, bows, and river otter quivers. Their food was gone, too—acorns and berries, salmon and white man's flour. All those things were gone. All that work was gone.

But the Yahi had taken a few precious bundles with them when they left. Their villages and caves had been raided before. The *saltu* always took the blankets, made of wildcat or coyote fur. These things were hard to make, but they could be made again, beginning by making arrows and calling the animals to you. They could get back some of the things they lost from the cattlemen's cabins: clothes and blankets and food. Ishi's mother was still alive. The white man had not taken the old saws. Some food was still to be had. They gathered these things together, seeds of civilization, and left Wowunupo'mu tetna. This village was no good anymore, at least for now. They would go to the upper village. Maybe they would have to go south to other streams of Wahganupa, over to the land of the Maidu, at least until this wave of *saltu* passed over them.

The two surveyors working for the Oro Water, Light and Power Company were stunned by what they saw. Stunned and trans-fixed. As soon as the Indian backed away, Ed and Al ran back to their camp as fast as they could, as if they'd seen a ghost. They had been searching unsuccessfully for a place to cross the roaring stream. Now they sped across the torrent, skedaddling back to the others. Breathless, the surveyors told their story to their foreman, Harvey Kluegal, and the local guides Jack Apperson and his two sons, together with Charlie Herrick, W. D. Polk, and Harry Keefer. "We both witnessed a 'wild man' down there," the surveyors said. "So, we had better leave this hell-hole of a cañon right now dam or no dam." Most of the others had a good laugh at the frightened young men, who they assumed were seeing things; maybe they saw a bear and thought it was a wild man, they teased. But Jack Apperson, the old-timer of the group, finally put in his two cents: "These men may not be as crazy as you think.... This region is extremely wild as you yourself know, and anything could happen here if you ask me." Well, they had asked him. Now the surveyors and the locals both were thinking about the man with the harpoon. They were thinking he must be "the survivor of a band of really wild and dangerous Indians who had inhabited the cañon in early days."

Survey work went on the next day, along with a nervous, half-believing, half-doubting search for the wild Indians. The local guides all had guns; the surveyors did not, except the rear rodman, the man who had to stay back to secure the beginning point of the survey line. He was given a Lugar automatic pistol, which he attached to his suspenders. Not being experienced with its use, and knowing that it would shoot seven bullets in succession if it was triggered, he was afraid of inadvertently setting off the gun, especially as "its muzzle prodded [his] abdomen and groin."

The locals took the lead when they finally got to the secluded, apparently deserted village. They searched the camp. They found a mirror, saws, food in barley sacks hung from trees. They found blankets, bows and quivers. Harry Keefer found a hand-laced pillow slip his wife had made that had been pilfered by the Indians. "Gee, I feel right at home," he called out.

Pistol in one hand, Jack threw open the canvas door of one of the dwellings and peered inside. "Come on boys," he shouted out to his partners. "Just in time for dinner!" He had found a pot of acorn soup, still hot. Maybe it was manna of the wilderness, they joked. They scanned the periphery of the camp but could find no footprints of any kind. They did stumble across ten steel bear traps, set. They were not meant for grizzlies, as any bears had abandoned this hiding place years before. The search party finally spied a trail out of camp, and Jack set off in pursuit. He felt something graze his hat brim. Maybe it was an acorn, Herrick suggested. Only acorns don't fall up, Jack said, and whatever it was grazed the bottom side of my hat brim. They searched the brush behind them and found the arrow that had narrowly missed his head.

Right then they spotted the two Yahi hiding, neither of whom had shot the arrow. The Indians yelled out, "Campoodie, campoodie," and then fled. Finally the men spotted the old woman, rolled up in a quilt. She touched her eyes and legs and said, "Muy malo." She said, "Agua," so Jack gave her water and shook her hand as a sign of friendship. They decided to leave her where she was, reasoning that the other Yahi would come back for her.

They went back to the camp and began gathering up all they wanted. The locals were especially intent on bringing back a good haul. After all, the Indians had cleaned out their cabins before; some of their own possessions had made their way to this village. If Jack were to march into the office of the *Chico Record* with his story of wild Indians in the hills, last of the treacherous Mill Creeks, he would need hard evidence to back up his claims or they'd say he was off his rocker.

On November 9, 1908, Jack Apperson did indeed take his story to the *Record*. To stave off disbelief, he laid out before the journalists the river otter quiver, holding inside the arrows of Ishi's manufacture. Convinced, the newspaper ran the story about the discovery of the camp of "wild Indians." The search for the Indians was quite an adventure, and a good news story. Cattlemen's stories of "wild savages" plundering their cabins, as the *Oroville Daily Register* put it, had long been dismissed as fabrications. The quiver and arrows and the eyewitness report were evidence of a different situation entirely. Wild men lived in the hills, and Jack Apperson had just written himself into the long saga of whites hunting the Mill Creeks. In this new era he was not looking for scalps, only artifacts that could prove his point. Bringing them back, Apperson and his party conquered and claimed the wild cañon. The legend of "the last of the Mill Creeks" had become fact. These things—otter quiver, painted arrows, fire kits, and coyote capes—were the facts. Now Jack and his sons could cloak themselves in the wild stories, and they would continue to do so for the rest of the century.

As for the surveyors, they each got part of the loot; the Lugar-toting rear rodman got three arrows, some flicker feathers, and an exquisite arrowhead. But they did not feel as entitled to the Indians' stuff as the locals who had lost things from their cabins. Besides, they were after something much larger: the cañon itself. They would turn it into a generator of electricity and feed the stream to the growing cities of the region, all of which wanted to be lit up at night incandescently. The new gold in the hills was power, and the Oro Company was preparing to supply it by damming the stream and submerging almost all of what was left of the Yahi's country. Oro dreamed of erecting its own sky wall at the edge of their world and thereby grasping the ball of the sun so that it could make it fly all around, from place to place.[6]

The stories in the Chico and Oroville papers brought the possibility that a few Yahi might still be living in a wild state to the attention of Alfred Kroeber. He was beyond intrigued. If the stories were true and these Yahi could be found, it would be a great coup for science. He sent an article to *Travel* magazine (for which he was paid a penny a word), laying out what was at stake in rediscovering the "elusive Mill Creeks": "These people must preserve, besides their language, many entirely aboriginal beliefs and innumerable native customs and practices....A record of their wanderings, their vigilance, their traits and habits, would appeal to the historian, while a knowledge of their ancient institutions and traditions, preserved from purely aboriginal times into the Twentieth Century, would be a rich mine to the...anthropologist of the future."[7]

Kroeber wrote letters to the locals, looking for information. He made plans for a university expedition into the cañons to open up communication with the wary band of survivors. But during this time Kroeber's duties at the university kept him out of the field. So he put his promising protégé, Thomas Talbot Waterman, on the trail. A Californian from the Central Valley, two hundred miles south of Yahi country, Waterman had attended the University of California as an undergraduate. Kroeber sent him to Columbia to study under Boas for his doctorate and afterward hired him back at Berkeley. Waterman was eager to see what he could see. He made a trip to Vina in 1909 and met with Jack Apperson. Under the secret sponsorship of the university, he returned to Vina in late October 1910 to embark on what he called "the wild Indian expedition." He told people only that he was going out somewhere on a "museum collecting trip."[8]

He was in fact trying to collect things. First and foremost, of course, he was trying to collect wild Indians. But Kroeber and Watermen knew that goal was far-fetched, for the Indians would most likely evade any effort to make direct contact. Secondarily, then, Waterman was to collect artifacts, or re-collect them from the people in the area who had already taken them from the Yahi. His camera was also a collecting tool; he would bring back images of the country and of the village or villages of the Indians. Finally, he was instructed to bring back the contents for two texts, one scholarly and one popular. As Kroeber wrote to Waterman just before he left Vina for the cañon, "Have a good time, take no unnecessary risks, and bring back a good paper for yourself and a magazine story for me."[9]

In Vina Waterman secured the services of Merle Apperson, one of Jack's sons who had been on the Oro survey trip. "[He swears] he knows the country like a book," Waterman assured Kroeber. Accompanied by an engineer, J. H. Hunt, Waterman planned to have Merle stay with them for a few days and then leave the two alone "to work out [their] own salvation for a week or more." Waterman thought they would have a better chance of making contact that way.[10]

Waterman was brimming with excitement. "Camp is full of venison, and life is certainly high," he wrote in his first dispatch from the cañon. "Young Apperson is a dead shot, of the old school. We have two deer in camp.... There are a number of caves, too. If the Indians are in there we will have them out. I hope to find a cave or two containing specimens, too. This country is the prettiest I have struck in California." The young anthropologist seemed to have fallen into Eden. But there is some foreshadowing of strife in that initial, hopeful letter: "Hunt has a bad case of poison oak, but while I have been scratched to a finish I seem so far to be proof."[11] Waterman thought he might be immune.

The next dispatch came from Wowunupo'mu tetna, reached on October 29. Waterman's disappointment was palpable. The Indians had been back to the site, he guessed, perhaps even in the past few days. He took photographs of "the region, and of the cabins." He also collected "some shredded maple bark for rope, some white man's netting, and a bad pestle." The artifacts were fragmentary, but he brought them back anyway, adding, "The climbing and beating through the brush was about as hard as any I've struck." Days earlier it was prettiest country he had seen; now it was the "roughest." The writing became rougher, too. "I lost my pen in the creek, so please excuse pencil," he noted. Kroeber wrote back, encouraging Waterman on: "Now that we have embarked on the venture we must leave no stone unturned." Waterman had to find the Indians, or at least decide "the probability of their existing and being wild."[12]

Waterman searched on but found little else. His correspondence ends dejectedly, poking fun at himself. From the Hotel Reading in Redding, Waterman wrote, "I enclose herewith the vouchers and statement of the wild Indian trip. I can give you a complete history of the Wild Indian expedition, but since we didn't bring home the bacon I won't inflict it on you unless you wish. I think the material, photographic and otherwise, has a picturesque value if nothing else."

The picturesque photographs were important mementoes. Waterman collected some artifacts, probably the most important of which was a flat basket with white acorn meal stuck to it, evidence that the Indians were living off of traditional foods. He also took photographs of other artifacts. Merle Apperson, who taught Waterman to read scat and find his way in the cañons (this was the book he knew, after all), modeled a few of them for Waterman. For one photograph he held up a deer decoy, used by Yahi to lure bucks near a thicket. For another he put on the cape made from the skins of wildcats and raccoons, standing for the photographer as a modern American, hair parted on the right but dressed up like a Boone of the Sierra or a wild Indian.[13]

Apperson wouldn't part with the cape itself, but Waterman was clearly interested in it. He wrote Kroeber about the "wildcat blanket which we ought to have." The cape was special, and there was not much else of true value for the anthropologists looking for pure artifacts, things that looked like they came from the time before contact with whites. "Culturally, and in the matter of specimens particularly, I don't think we will get much," he explained. The wildcat blanket was good; the "otter skin quiver however, is sewn with black flax thread. A mantle [a sleeveless coat] found was made of overalls, split up and patched together. The arrows...are pointed with glass." Culturally speaking, these artifacts were contaminated, for they were made of materials not purely aboriginal.[14]

Kroeber pondered the things Waterman brought back. To him a civilization or culture—which is an amalgamation, a patterning, a set of beliefs and practices—was made manifest in things. Purely aboriginal items were a manifestation of a purely aboriginal culture, alive and well. People didn't make objects so much as objects made people. Individuals were simply caught up in the stream of their culture, and that stream carried within it the resources to make the things they needed. Of course, the land directly held the resources, but it was culture that gave the individual craftsperson instructions about how to pattern it, how to shape it. It was not genetics or race, as the evolutionists and social Darwinists who wanted to put races in ranks thought. It wasn't nature, as environmental determinists thought. It was culture, and culture existed on a whole other plane. It wasn't organic; it was what Kroeber called "superorganic." "Civilization," he believed, could not be reduced to biology or race, nor did it amount simply to the sum total of the thoughts and beliefs of the individuals within any society. Civilization "is not mental action but...the stream of products of mental exercise."[15]

Now Kroeber could see signs of a purely aboriginal culture, from Stone Age America. But something was not quite right. Look closely at the quiver: manufactured black flax thread had been used. And the arrowheads were made of glass. Kroeber explained this away: the Yahi survivors turned to glass only as a last resort when "flint became scarce." They were really a Stone Age people, despite the change in the material of their culture.[16] Ishi's arrowheads were made of glass. You could see through them to the earth below. You could see yourself, reflected. You could see fractals of wild men.

The artifacts, tainted as they were, convinced Kroeber that there were still Indians living in "absolutely aboriginal conditions." He was prepared to put his hard-won reputation on the line and write that magazine article. For the August 1911 issue of the popular *Travel* magazine, Kroeber wrote "The Elusive Mill Creeks." He opened by asking, Could "a totally wild and independent tribe of Indians" be living along the streams of Mount Lassen? Indeed one could. The university expedition had established that, Kroeber maintained. After giving a thumbnail sketch of the history of the conflict between whites and the Mill Creeks, Kroeber brought the story up to the present, relating the Oro party's discovery of the village. He then divulged the details of the secret expedition, reporting, "The University party returned to civilization minus the sought-for Indians but with photographs and specimens which definitely established their existence." The scientist insisted that there was now "incontrovertible evidence of their existence in a wild state." It was a profound discovery, for they had found traces in the artifacts of "the smallest and most remarkable people, the last free survivors of the American red man, who by an unexampled fortitude and stubbornness of character have succeeded in holding out against the overwhelming tide of civilization twenty-five years longer even than Geronimo."

What should be done now? Kroeber worried that the Indians might be shot or poisoned by an irate rancher whose cabin had been plundered. He hoped that communication and negotiation could be opened up, that offerings and exchanges could be made. "Nothing would be more fitting than to secure them at least part of the ancestral territory which they have so long maintained and there allow them to work out their salvation in their own way." The government might offer advice, but Kroeber insisted that the Indians be secured in their land and that they remain free "to work out their own salvation in their own way."

During the expedition Waterman told Kroeber that Apperson would leave him and Hunt to "work out [their] own salvation." Now Kroeber echoed the phrase, in a way that would suggest to his predominantly Christian readers the righteousness of protecting

Yahi sovereignty, cultural and religious. They must maintain their autonomy in the land that was rightfully theirs. The land would now be their *property*, Kroeber hoped; nature would be turned into an object they could claim, a reservation on which to secure their right to life, liberty, and the preservation of their culture. Kroeber didn't know what would happen next to the elusive Yahi, but he predicted, "It is certain that before their record is finally closed at least one other chapter of entrancing interest will be added."[17]

Oroville

The phone rang at Sheriff John B. Webber's house. He picked up the receiver, and on the other end of the line was Ad Kessler, a young man who had worked for him back when he was in the meat business. "John, I got something out here at the slaughter-house but I don't know what it is. It is partly dressed and partly not. He ain't got no shoes, and he won't talk to me. I don't know if he's a Mexican or Indian or what." Ad was now seventeen years old, but the sheriff still referred to him in the same commanding way he did when Ad had worked for him. "Now listen, my boy," the sheriff said, "if this is your idea of a joke, and I come out there, I'll bring you back in irons."[18]

It was no joke. They had worked hard that day. They would slaughter four hundred beef that week, mostly to supply the crews of the Western Pacific Railroad. The slaughterhouse was a focal point of the new landscape; cattlemen brought their products in, the butchers transformed them into edible meat for sale, and the Western Pacific Railroad constructed its lines to link Oroville and its environs with the rest of booming America. Now, at the end of the day, something had come out of those environs and was hunkered down in front of an oak tree just inside the corral.

The butchers tried to talk to the man. They noticed he was different, dressed only in what the men called a sheepherder's jacket or Chinese shirt, a long shirt that came down around your knees. It was old, the denim faded. There was a knotted piece of buckskin in each of his earlobes, and a stick through the septum of his nose. They didn't know what he was. Ad gazed at his "big square feet." He even reached down to touch them, finding that they were "as hard as saddle leather." He'd never worn shoes. Ad rolled a Bull Durham cigarette. Ishi looked on. Ad thought he wanted one, so he gave him the pouch and a paper, but the man didn't know how to roll it. He did secret away some tobacco in his one shirt pocket. So Ad took out a paper and retrieved some of the tobacco from Ishi's pocket. Ishi grinned, caught, and then waited as Ad rolled a cigarette. Ad gave him a match and motioned for him to strike it; Ishi broke two matches, and then Ad held his hand with a third match. They struck it together and lighted up. Under lantern light the men shared a smoke as they waited for the law.

When the sheriff arrived the men stood Ishi up before him and made a thorough inspection. They found some dried meat in his pocket and some manzanita berries in his bag. The sheriff tried to speak to him in Spanish; no reply. The sheriff had brought along his irons, but they wouldn't go on Ad. "Well boy, you better put these on him," the sheriff ordered. So Ad put the handcuffs on Ishi. Ishi smiled, and they put him in the sheriff's buggy to take him into town, two and a half miles distant.

That call Ad had made to the sheriff was on a party line, so word passed along the grapevine that "a wild man had been captured at the slaughterhouse." Florence Boyle was one of the curious townsfolk who came out to her porch, hoping to "get a glimpse of the captured wild man." A crowd gathered at the jail, including the editors of the two Oroville newspapers.[19]

Ishi was taken inside, where the sheriff sat him down before Undersheriff White. White booked him. First he wrote the date, "August 28, 1911." Next, he needed a name. White made his entry—"Indian, wild. Alias Panama Kid Webber"—nicknaming him after Sheriff Webber and his constable, who called himself "the Panama Kid." The sheriff decided that he would keep the man in the padded cell upstairs, the one set aside for the insane. It was not that the sheriff thought he was crazy. It was just that there was no better place to put the wild man.[20]

Before he was taken upstairs, the crowd gathered around to witness Ishi's first meal in captivity. He was brought beans to eat and a spoon. He discarded the spoon and ate with his fingers. While eating the beans, he was handed a doughnut. He dropped it, then nibbled from it, and then ate it eagerly. After Ishi was finished, Webber took out his pistol, removed the cartridges, and made Ishi take it from him. As George Mansfield of the *Daily Register* reported, "The Indian showed no evidence that he knew anything regarding its use." In fact Ishi knew all about guns. His people had fought whites with guns. Ishi himself carried one around, for show. He had deconstructed guns. Sheriffs liked to give their captives guns to test them; that was part of Western lore. But in this moment, Ishi used his naïveté about the pistol's proper use to defuse the situation. The sheriff shrugged and decided it was time for everyone to go home and for Ishi to be taken up to the padded cell for the insane.[21]

Ishi's first days in Oroville were like that: people kept handing him objects to see how he'd react. More than three thousand people came to see him in his cell. All manner of things with which he was not familiar were pressed upon him. Matches and cigarettes. Doughnuts. Then a banana; he started eating it peel and all. They laughed. Then he tried to peel a tomato, and they laughed again. Then he was given something else to peel: a locally grown orange, an object being sold to Americans across the country as a little sun-kissed piece of the healthful California landscape. They took him out to see trolley cars, telephones, automobiles, electric lights, motion pictures, and railroad cars. All of these were tests, of a sort. Just how Stone Age was he? Was he a fraud? He passed the tests, showing naïveté about everything they all took for granted.[22]

But would civilization pass the test? Would the man be awed by modern technological achievements? Many pairs of shoes, all different sizes, were offered to him; they were all sent back. There was a trace of insecurity in this barrage of things directed his way. Like parents wondering if their children will like the presents they bought, they watched his reaction closely and found their sense of self-worth in each item. As they laughed when he tried to eat a banana with the skin on or broke a match trying to strike it, they were hiding their insecurity with haughtiness. Collectively the people of Oroville worried that maybe their things didn't all add up after all. Maybe all of these things didn't make them better than the man who had none of them. One man expressed this ambivalence in a poem published at the end of the week in the

Chico Record: What did "stone age man" think of "our speed and land train...of our houses and churches and clothes, cramped and unaired and confined?" The poet went on, "Collars and manners and fuss: / Let us 'improve' you and iron you out, / train you to flirt and to cuss, / Come let us aid you, but sonny, by 'Gee, / What if you've got it on us?"[23]

As these object lessons were taking place, the reporters looked into the wild man's possessions—and they were few. Newspapers reported his ragged dress, the manzanita berries and deer sinew in his bag, the "buckskin thongs" in his earlobes, his feet, "almost as wide as they were long, showing plainly that he had never worn either moccasins or shoes." This catalogue of possessions and attributes amounted to a list of lacks. There were all sorts of missing things about this man of few possessions; that was what made him different, wild.[24]

But as the week went on, scores of things of Ishi's own manufacture strangely began to pile up before him. Oroville seemed to be the place where all of the Yahi's missing works were hoarded. This allowed Ishi to reciprocate in the show-and-tell session the whites initiated. He was taken to the home of an attorney, William Duncan, an avid collector of Indian baskets and artifacts. Among these things, the newspaper reported, "the Indian was in his glory." Ishi took a special interest in the arrows and pantomimed how they were made. Later the brother of one of surveyors who had found Wowunupo'mu tetna brought some of the artifacts that had been pilfered: bows and arrows, paints, spears, and the wildcat and coyote capes. If he recognized them, this would be proof that he was one of the wild Indians rumored to live still in the cañons, the whites surmised. The *Register* reported, "The

Indian instantly seized them, and was transported with happiness." Ishi acted out the process through which all of these things had been created. He imitated the calls off the coyote, the fox, and the wildcat; he acted out how animals were snared or shot with bow and arrow. He showed how ropes, how bows, and again how arrows were made and decorated with paint. He demonstrated the flaking of arrowheads. A few arrows in the collection were not finished (as if Lizard had been interrupted before completing his story); Ishi asked for feathers to finish them. All of these objects held great meaning for Ishi, and he strove to share with the *saltu* just how they were constructed.[25]

This was not something the whites could do with their own guns, telephones, cameras, or cars. To whites, their things were magic; the *saltu* had no idea how they were actually manufactured, in factories far away.

The news of the "wild man of Oroville" went out on the wire. On August 30 the San Francisco *Examiner* carried a short piece titled "Last Lost Indian." Alfred Kroeber read the report. His article on the elusive Mill Creeks had just been published. Could this man be one of them? Or an imposter, some prankster who had read Kroeber's article and now was playing a trick on everyone? He composed a message to the sheriff, edited it to make it as concise as possible (it cost money to magically send words over wire), and then had it typed up for transmission:

> Newspapers report capture wild Indian speaking language other tribes totally unable understand. Please confirm...if story correct hold Indian till arrival professor State University who will take charge.... Matter important account aboriginal history.

Kroeber couldn't go himself. He had teaching duties; he was busy getting the museum ready to be opened to the public for the first time; he had "taken suddenly ill." These were the official reasons Waterman was coming in the professor's place. But something more personal was holding him back: worry about his wife's health. She had tuberculosis.[26]

Waterman was to be the official emissary of the university, the man to open up communication between the twentieth century and the Stone Age. Kroeber assembled all of the word lists of common nouns, *man, tongue, wood,* they had from of the tribes to which the wild man might belong. There were no lists for the southern subgroups of the Yana, but there were those gathered by Edward Sapir from Betty Brown and Sam Batwi, speakers of the Northern Yana dialect. The elderly Sam Batwi was still living, in Redding. Perhaps he could help translate if he could come down to Oroville on the train.

On Thursday, August 31, the *San Francisco Call* carried a story wired in from Oroville about the "least civilized man in the United States." A photograph of Ishi accompanied the story, taken in the padded cell. Requests for photographs of the Indian were coming in from all quarters, so Ishi had photo sessions with two photographers. Postcards were made, and images were secured for the newspaper stories. The man had little on his person that could be shared as tokens, but his picture could be taken. Through this means, the image of the man was captured, and everyone, far and wide, could consume a piece of the wild man.[27]

Waterman packed the *Call's* story in his suitcase; he intended to show it to the Indian. Of course, the Indian would not be able to read the story, but he could see the picture. What would he think of it? Would he even be able to recognize the image as himself? Waterman also packed an Indian fire-making kit. He said good-bye to his wife, Grace, and took the trolley to the ferry and the ferry to Oakland, where he boarded a Western Pacific train headed for Oroville. During his journey he anxiously looked through his word lists and planned his meeting with the man.[28]

Waterman was met at the station by Douglas Jacobs, the owner of the Union Hotel, and George Mansfield, editor of the *Daily Register*. It was 1:30 in the morning, but the two locals took the professor directly to the county jail. Waterman showed Mansfield the *Call* story; he was delighted to see it. He had sent it over the wire, his first big story. The officer on night duty took the men upstairs. Waterman was struck by what he saw: "The first impression received of the wild man was the sight of him, draped in a canvas apron they had hurriedly put on him at the slaughterhouse, sitting on the edge of a cot in his cell, still uncertain of his fate, and answering *ulisi (I don't understand)* to all questions that were being fired at him in English, Spanish and a half a dozen Indian languages, by visitors." Waterman wrote as if his brain had received another image of the man, a photograph stuck in his mind.[29]

Waterman proceeded slowly. He showed off his genuine Indian fire kit to Ishi. He began working through his word lists, but Ishi was still saying *ulisi, ulisi*. Nothing got across, until Waterman got to the word for *wood* on his list of Northern Yana. *I'wi*, Waterman said, and touched the yellow pine frame of Ishi's cot. The man's face "lit up" when he heard this, but he corrected Waterman; it wasn't made of *i'wi*, wood, but *si'win'i*, yellow pine. "It was a picnic to see him open his eyes when he heard Yana from me," Waterman told Kroeber. It was the first proof of the man's tribal identity.[30]

Ishi was especially fascinated by Waterman's word list. Waterman reported, "He looked over my shoulder at the paper in a most mystified way. He knew at once where I got my inspiration." Here was a technology that impressed Ishi. The words had been translated from their oral form into writing; a special orthography was used to represent the unique sounds of the language, including "cracked consonants." Edward Sapir had taken them down from Batwi and Brown, two of the last speakers of Northern Yana. Now Waterman, with no prior experience with the language, was able to transform the markings on paper into sounds intelligible to Ishi. Salvage anthropology proved its worth: it allowed Waterman to start communicating with Ishi. Ishi was clearly impressed by the power of the written word and the ability of Waterman to use it.[31]

Ishi was no longer alone, walled off within a private language no one else could speak. Were there others of his tribe still alive, Waterman wanted to know. "He has a yarn to tell about his woman, who had a baby on her back and seems to have drowned, except that he is so *cheerful* about it." Waterman couldn't quite follow him yet. Maybe he was happy to be able to tell his story. Maybe he was saying something else. Maybe he wasn't cheerful at all, just nervous. Despite the cultural chasm, Waterman believed he was making progress.[32]

Later in the day Waterman pulled out the *Call* article, showing it first to the newspaper editor to attract Ishi's attention. Then he gave it to Ishi. According to the *Marysville Appeal*, "The Indian gazed upon it, and a look of astonishment spread over his face. He still gazed upon it and with a half credulous look showed it to the callers and with wonder pointed at himself." Waterman nodded, and "an expansive smile broke over his features, and with great awe he carefully laid the paper aside." The *Appeal* concluded, "It is safe to say that the Indian is no greater wonder to the white men than the white men are to the Indian."[33]

Even if the *Appeal* exaggerated the drama of the moment, Ishi again passed their litmus test for aboriginality. Certainly, though, Ishi had seen his image reflected back to him before. After all, he had sat for the photographs in the studios the first day he was in Oroville. Before that, he could have looked at himself as often as he wanted to in the looking glass the Yahi survivors had in their possession. The white lawyer had Ishi's arrows and arrowheads in his collection in Oroville; Ishi had the lawyer's mirrors, triggers, and saw blades in Wowunupo'mu tetna.

Waterman and the *Appeal* were satisfied, but for different reasons. To the newspaper, the big news was that Ishi was as impressed with the modern white man as the modern man was fascinated with him. To Waterman, Ishi's reaction to his image was further proof that the man was truly wild. Waterman's own first impression, after all, was that Ishi was uncomfortable and out of place in the canvas shirt draped hastily over him. Waterman mentally removed it so that he could see the purely aboriginal man he wanted to see. But in fact nobody had put that shirt on him; it was the one he was wearing when he was discovered at the slaughterhouse.

Waterman wrote excitedly to Kroeber with the news, good news: "This man is undoubtedly wild." His conclusion was based on appearances and inferences. First, there were his objects and his body: "He has thongs in place of ornaments in the lobes of his ears and a plug in the septum of his nose." Next, there were his beliefs and practices. "If I'm not mistaken, he's full of religion—bathing at sunrise, putting out pinches of tobacco where the lightning strikes, etc." Finally, there was the proof of language, the solid sound of *i'wi* for wood. "He will be a splendid informant," he told Kroeber. Waterman knew that he had done well, but he admitted to his mentor that he hadn't understood much of what the man was trying to tell him. "I have not communicated with him successfully enough to get his story, but what can ~~you~~ I expect." Something of the relationship between Waterman and Kroeber was communicated in that strikethrough. He turned "What can *you* expect" into "What can *I* expect," as if acknowledging that he was trying to meet Kroeber's expectations but was trying not to put that onus on Kroeber himself.[34]

At the end of this first dispatch to Kroeber, Waterman expressed the sentiment shared by both anthropologists: "I'm getting wild to get information and phonetics from this old bird. I think there ought to be *worlds* of stuff in him."[35]

· *Four* ·

MAKING TRACKS

✳

DURING HIS SECOND DAY WITH ISHI, WATERMAN, HAVING already confronted the newcomer to modern America with a photographic likeness of himself, continued the game of technological show-and-tell with a telephone. He had Ishi stand next to the deputy sheriff. He then walked out and called the jail from an office across the street. The deputy picked up the telephone and handed it to Ishi. Waterman spoke a few words in Yahi. According to the *Oroville Daily Register,* "The Indian started back in astonishment and dropped the receiver."[1]

The *San Francisco Chronicle* reported, "Some of the modern inventions startle him more than would seem natural. The telephone he is afraid of. He imagines it something uncanny, yet he attempts to conceal the fear and wonder that is in him." *Uncanny*— that the *Chronicle* chose this word to describe the feeling of fear and wonder is revealing. Dictionaries of the day defined *uncanny* as "uncomfortable, uneasy, gloomy, dismal, ghastly; (of a house) haunted; (of a man) a repulsive fellow." Sigmund Freud, often considered the father of modern psychology just as Franz Boas and his students were the fathers of modern anthropology, took a special interest in the feeling of the uncanny, which in German is *unheimlich*. Kroeber was beginning to take a serious interest in Freud, himself a keen student of anthropology. Freud thought anthropology could be used to find out the origins of modern man's neuroses, which he believed were dramatized in the totems and taboos of "primitive" cultures.[2]

Freud pointed out that *unheimlich* is the opposite of *heimlich*, the homey and the familiar. A *heimlich* animal was tame, not wild. But not everything that was unfamiliar was truly frightening, just as many things about the modern world—matches and trolley bells, for instance—delighted rather than disturbed Ishi. Freud looked deeper into the word and the feeling it captured. Instead of a "haunted" house, the Germans speak of an "unheimlich" house. Feeling the uncanny is like being beside oneself; you experience something that was at one time familiar, but is now foreign. The feeling also came from seeing the dead, or seeing something that was supposed to be dead—a severed arm, for example—suddenly moving, reanimated, creepy.

For Ishi, Waterman's voice inhabiting the machine was uncanny; what was once connected to a living, breathing body was put into this metal container attached to a metal rope. Waterman's voice was displaced, and this unsettled Ishi, making him feel beside himself, not at all at home in this world of place shifting. The human and familiar had been rendered mechanical and unfamiliar—strange, weird, wild. *Unheimlich* was in a sense what modernity was: every place was home and not home, at the same time. You could go anywhere but never really be anywhere. All that is solid melts into air, Karl Marx said; place was one of those solid things liquefied and then turned to ether. You get used to this frightening reality, but you could never get away from its paradoxical and uncanny nature.[3]

Waterman's game of telephone backfired. He frightened Ishi instead of securing his confidence. But Sam Batwi was on his way from Redding, and Waterman hoped the old Yana man would be able to open up better lines of communication.

The advertising logo for Oroville's Gem Movie Theater depicted three people walking under the words "We're going to the Gem!" On September 3, 1911, the picture could have represented Ishi, Sheriff Webber, and his deputies, for they all marched off to the Gem on Ishi's last night in town. A mix of newsreels and one-reel comedies were screened that night. Ishi sat down with the crowd to watch. "With the greatest interest he looked upon the rapidly passing films," the *Register* reported. "Containing the pictures as they do, a tale which does not need an explanation in words, the aborigine was able to gain some kind of idea of the story told. The expression of astonishment first gave way to interest and amusement." The films shown that weekend included *The Diving Girl*, featuring one of the leading female stars of the silent film era, Mabel Normand; she would go on to work with Charlie Chaplin. She wasn't an Indian, but she played one for the silver screen in D. W. Griffith's *The Squaw's Love*.[4]

The Squaw's Love was a sympathetic portrait of Indians made out to be noble red men and women of the forest. Wild Flower, Normand's character, is in love with Gray Fox, and she follows him into the wilderness. But in a mix-up Silver Fawn thinks Wild Flower is after *her* fiancé. She attacks Wild Flower; they fall into a river, but Gray Fox rescues her. If Ishi had gone once again to the Gem in September, he might have seen that film. He might have viewed it with even greater astonishment. Here were white people playing Indians and somehow coming alive on the screen! But the story's happy ending contrasted with Ishi's own. Ishi had been trying to communicate his own story through pantomime for days; as Waterman and others understood him, his own wife and child had fallen into a river and drowned some time before he made his way to the corral in Oroville.

Griffith had earlier filmed a tragedy of native romance titled *The Call of the Wild: The Sad Plight of the Civilized Red Man*. George Redfeather has attended a white-run boarding school and assimilated into modern America. But he goes too far when he proposes marriage to a white woman. After she spurns him, he answers the "call of the wild." He takes off his white man's clothes, dons an Indian costume, and rides again with his tribe. However civilized Redfeather may have appeared on the surface, beneath lurked a wild beast that could suddenly call him back to nature. Wild Indians were all over the silver screen in these years.[5]

Ishi himself had already become something of a media star, meeting the growing demand for romantic images of Indians in the first decades of the twentieth century. The *Register* reported, "Demands come by mail for picture of Indian." Local photographers were "besieged" with orders from all over the country for "authentic likenesses of the savage." Two professional photographers, John H. Hogan and Morris E. Phares, were given access. Hogan photographed Ishi standing and wearing the tattered Chinese shirt Kessler had described; Phares photographed him sitting furtively on a chair. With his singed hair, his discarded white man's clothes, and his hunched pose, these images failed to meet the expectations of white fantasy. (Though Kessler, one of the men who had seen Ishi at the slaughterhouse, wrote on one of these photographs, "This is the true picture of Ishi as he appeared...at the Slaughter house.") The portrait failed to satisfy the public because there was too much contamination and too much resignation in it. The fugitive pose was pathetic and troubling, not tragic or noble. Images of Indians were meant to make modern white Americans feel sorry for them, but not uncomfortable in their sorrow.[6]

Hogan tried again. This time he pulled down Ishi's shirt over his shoulders to expose his bare chest. Hogan had him stand with his feet together and was able get him to look slightly upward. Placing the camera low and to the right, Hogan got an image of

Ishi. Photograph by John H. Hogan. Courtesy of the Phoebe A. Hearst Museum of Anthropology and the Regents of the University of California.

the "last of the Deer Creek Indians" that fit nicely into the genre of the stoic, vanishing Indian then being made famous by the photographer Edward Curtis. Whites were to be able to look into the eyes of these pictured men and see authentic Indians on the brink of vanishing. If the Indians had no traditional clothes or artifacts, Curtis, nicknamed "the Shadow Catcher," would supply them. In a sense, his photography turned living Indians into shadows of themselves. They could not smile or laugh, and they could wear no modern clothes. Hogan made the perfect Curtis-like image by highlighting Ishi's upturned chin and capturing a stoic expression; this time, without the distracting Chinese shirt, his body seemed more natural—pure, strong, and yet resigned. The image was made into postcards and sent far and wide. This Ishi was more easily digested into the visual culture of modern American, with its nostalgia for Indians it preferred to see as shadows.[7]

White Americans were used to seeing shadows of Indians flicker on the silver screen. But film tried to capture modernity as well; if there was one subject more popular than Indians it was the railroad. Many of the first films were essentially travel shows capturing the landscapes that could be filmed from a train heading west. These amounted to tourist photographs in motion, and every part of the country through which railroads ran might get a picture made of it, including Kroeber's University of California, which was captured in a film called *A Trip to Berkeley*. To regular patrons of the Gem, it would be no shock to see a railroad on the screen that evening. But to Ishi, it was a surprise. As the *Register* reported, it was only when the railroad appeared, billowing smoke, "that he gave any evidence of fright, and then his fear was most evident."[8]

*Ishi. Photograph by John H.
Hogan. Courtesy of Jed Riffe.*

Ishi would be making his own trip to Berkeley on an actual train the very next day, in the flesh, as it were. Ishi's departure was a big event; the local crowds wanted to see the spectacle of Oroville's Wild Man confronting the Iron Horse. Ad Kessler, one of the men who had first laid eyes on Ishi at the slaughterhouse, "wanted to see what kind of a circus he was going to put on when that big steam engine come out of the cut there by the depot."[9]

The next morning Waterman was at the jail early, looking to take the Indian out of the sheriff's custody. Back in San Francisco Kroeber had continued to work the telegraph and telephones to make the Indian's release possible. From the special agent for Indian affairs, Charles E. Kelsey, Kroeber secured permission to bring the unknown man to San Francisco. Kelsey sent a telegram to the sheriff, instructing him to release the Indian to the university's care. He sent another telegram to Waterman to let him know: "Will wire Sheriff there is no objection to taking wild Yana to San Francisco." Convinced that "the ethnologists would take good care of him," Kelsey later admitted to his superior, "I may have exceeded my powers a little, but I think it was the proper thing to do." Kroeber wanted more from the government: a treaty between the United States and the last survivor of the Yahi, or an executive order granting the man rights and land. But for now, Kelsey's permission to bring the "wild Yana" to San Francisco was much appreciated. The man who had been booked as "Indian, Wild. Alias Panama Kid Webber" was released that morning into Waterman's care and control.[10]

Local Indians had already tried, and failed, to talk with the mysterious stranger. Several Indian men came to the jail, some of whom claimed to be able to communicate with him. But some of their stories stretched credulity. After finishing harvesting the prunes and peaches on the Hazelbush Ranch, Billy Day, a Konkow Maidu elder, came back into town. The sheriff saw him and said, "We have an Indian over here that we'd like to find someone who could talk to him." "Well, I'll go and see," Billy replied, bringing along his nine-year-old son, Frank. "The sun was coming out," Frank remembers. Much to their surprise, they recognized the man in the cell.

Frank and his father had seen the wild Indian just a few weeks before, out in the country. They had been walking along the river at a place the Maidu called Lamin Mool, where the waters of the south and middle forks of the Feather River came together. Frank looked up and saw "this man and his buddy...resting under an oak tree." They were on "a mule trail where they haul supplies in to the railroad tracks for blasting powder." The buddy was suffering and could not get up. He had been shot and Ishi was ministering to him. "He was using a twisted grass rope, and tied to it were two rocks, two stones. Because they didn't have fire, he caught that morning sun and placed silica stone over here." The sun bounced off the silica and was directed into a lava rock bowl filled with water. The water heated stones, and Ishi placed them on his companion's wounds. Frank was not sure if the wounded Yahi was a man or a woman. It might have been Ishi's *mahala,* the word many thought he used for wife.

There were worlds of stuff in Ishi, indeed: tools and technologies of healing that almost nobody knew anything about. Yana healers often collected special stones they believed were imbued with power, but these were kept in a basket in a tree and touched before healing; there is no record of stones being used directly to treat patients. Ishi may have been a healer, using his tools as best he could to remove the pain and poison of the cold lead blasted into the Yahi's body. Frank never saw the wounded person again, though he walked the trail looking for bones or a grave. Lamin Mool is now submerged, covered by the water backed up by the dam put across the Feather River at Oroville. When he grew up Frank painted the scene from memory; it is a very different image of the man than recorded by the photographers at Oroville. In Frank's eyes, Ishi is strong, hopeful, and resourceful in confronting the shrinking circle of his world. Frank and his father couldn't communicate with Ishi in words that day in the jail, for the man did not understand Maidu. But Ishi did give young Frank a warm smile, and it stayed with him for the rest of his life.[11]

Ishi had another Indian visitor that last morning in Oroville. Sam Batwi, one of the two known native Yana speakers, had been considerably delayed, but finally he had been escorted by train from Redding to Oroville. Batwi wore a beard, spectacles, and a suit. The uncanny attire apparently made quite an impression on Ishi. The sheriff, Waterman, and reporters looked on in anticipation. The two men seemed to be able to communicate. Batwi immediately began pressing for answers. Where do you come from? Are there any others? Some responses came, but Ishi was evasive. He had a wife, and she died, Batwi reported. He had a camp not too far from the slaughterhouse and had been living on what he could hunt and pilfer. But he was afraid of being punished for killing sheep and taking things from cabins. He said that he

Ishi at Lamin Mool, *by Frank Day, 1973. Courtesy of Herb Puffer, Pacific Western Traders, Folsom, California.*

had been shot at, and he was the only one left living. He pointed to himself and raised one finger. He'd been doing this all week.[12]

But was this the truth? Or was it a story told to discourage the white men from looking for others? Feeling pressure from Batwi, Ishi began to counter with questions of his own, questions about Batwi's identity and allegiance. He pointed at Batwi's ears and nose. Batwi translated for the whites: "[He wants me] to put rings in my ears and a small stick in my nose and become an Indian." Ishi also began to laugh, uncomfortably but also sarcastically. The whites didn't know what to make of it. Why is he laughing? Batwi said, "It is because I have been asking so many questions." He explained that the Yahi said, "I know you are a man like myself. You have red skin and black hair. The white man want me to tell you about myself and my people." "The prisoner tells me, 'Sam, you are not my friend but the friend of the white man. I will not tell anything about myself.'"[13]

Waterman struggled to comprehend what was going on between them. "Poor old Batwee wished to impress his importance on the 'wild' man, while the 'wild' man looked upon the 'civilized' Indian as neither Indian nor white," he decided. Despite the impasse, Waterman hoped that they'd get over it, and with Kroeber's approval he invited Batwi to come along to San Francisco and work as a go-between. With communication you could learn everything there was to know about this man, which would open up the entire Stone Age world like a book. Waterman told a reporter, "The beauty of it is that he cannot lie if he wants to; he is untouched by civilization." Yet Ishi had just told Batwi that he would not reveal the truth about himself, that there would always be a gulf between what the scientists wanted to know and

Sam Batwi (left) and Ishi in Oroville. Courtesy of the California State Library.

what Ishi could, or would, tell them. Batwi accepted the invitation to serve as an interpreter, and the three men, with practically the entire town in tow, made their way to the railroad station.[14]

Everyone had to wait. The train didn't arrive until well after 2 p.m. Parked at the station was a beautiful example of America's new favorite mode of transportation: an Alexander Windsor Motor Company touring car, complete with a windshield. There were only a few automobiles in Oroville in 1911, so the idea of getting the most "primitive" man in America behind the wheel of the most modern technology in town proved irresistible. Seated in the car, Ishi was asked to remove the boater hat someone had given him, and he looked directly at the camera.[15]

Other Indians had been photographed in cars. Geronimo was photographed riding in a Cadillac. Kroeber had likened Ishi to Geronimo as two of the last holdouts against modern America. In some ways photographers meant to dramatize their capitulation to modern America by showing them riding in a car. As a white American you were supposed to laugh at Indians in cars, to confirm that you yourself were modern and the Indians belonged to another time and place.[16]

In this picture Ishi looks surprisingly dapper and at home in his vehicle, like a movie star driving to the set. Could the presumed gap be closed between the most primitive and natural person in

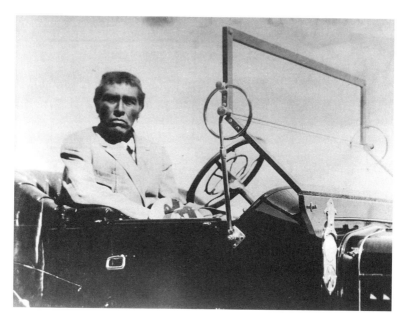

Ishi. Courtesy of Jed Riffe.

America and the most modern and mechanical means of transportation? Thousands of Indians were beginning to prove that they could close the gap by taking the wheel. Far-flung Indians, no longer having access to horse transportation, could still get together by driving an automobile. Jaime de Angulo, a self-trained anthropologist who knew Kroeber well (though the two were hardly friends), observed a group of Pit River Achumawi Indians caravanning through the landscape around Mount Lassen in seven Model Ts. When one of the cars broke down, the anthropologist was amazed at what he saw: "I was watching these Stone Age men unscrew and rescrew and take things apart." They deduced the source of the engine failure and made repairs. But had they adopted a machine age culture and logic as a whole? Not at all. One of the men surmised that the reason the car broke down in the first place was that the driver was "sleeping with his woman while she menstruating! That against the rules." That was taboo.[17]

Many white Americans looked at Indians and technology as essentially incompatible. But the truth was something different and more complex, as everyone could see when the train finally came around the cut and into the station in Oroville. Some people saw Ishi become terrified by the Iron Horse, galloping on its approach and then trotting metallically into the Oroville train station. The wild Indian, they reported, cowered, his primitive ignorance spurring him into a frantic search for refuge in the baggage room or behind a cottonwood tree. "The shriek of the locomotive," reported the *Oakland Tribune,* "caused the redskin to quake with fear." But if observers saw this, they conjured the scene in their imagination.[18]

What actually happened was that Ishi, dressed newly in gray overalls and a gray suit jacket—a kindly lady had even put a rose in his lapel—looked on with curiosity and caution as the train came in. He held his ground, if a bit nervously. Florence Danforth, who first saw him when he passed by her house in the sheriff's buggy, took issue with the sensationalist accounts, insisting that "he was among friends and he knew it." She had dressed up, too, and brought along her one-dollar Kodak Brownie to take her own picture of Ishi standing tall, surrounded by a curious and well-wishing crowd. It may be true that the Yahi regarded the train as an otherworldly presence, "a devil-driven, inhuman prodigy," as Waterman put it. In his travels with his band, Ishi had often seen the train ripping across the land. Always his people had hidden themselves in the grass or behind the boulders, taking care not to be seen. Now Ishi saw that the train ran on tracks, that white people rode inside, and that he, too, was to step inside. Anxiously, he stood by in plain view.[19]

Though whites thought Indians called the railroad "the Iron Horse," many Indians knew it simply as "the warpath." On the Great Plains they saw the laying of tracks as a threat to their very survival. Some Indians tore up the tracks, but still the tracks came, implacable. The first transcontinental road, built over the Sierras eighty miles south of Ishi's homeland, was completed in 1869 with the driving of a spike made of gold from those mountains. The railroad brought hunters in and hides out. Buffalo Bill and other white men shot bison by the hundreds to feed the track builders, and when the trains started running, tourists took potshots at the great beasts from their comfortable cars. Recreational shooters killed a few bison, but in the 1870s professional hunters selling hides to industrial processors and garment makers, who made belts to drive machinery from the bison leather and warm cloaks from the hides, downed these animals by the millions. The buffalo nation, com-posed of some 30 million members at the beginning of the century, was almost completely gone by the 1880s. Their bones were strewn over the territory. Sugar refineries and fertilizer plants demanded the bones, so they were gathered up and sent away, like the hides before them, to places such as the Michigan Carbon Works in Detroit. The industrial collectors turned the bleached bones into fertilizer to be used on the crops of white farmers.[20]

John Gast made a wildly popular painting in 1872 that depicted the Indians and buffalo retreating into the darkness as the railroad approached. Gast probably thought Indians would just disappear into the abyss as whites came through. But the Cheyenne and Kiowa and Crow, the Lakota and Pawnee and oth-ers knew they would have to find a new way of life now, and that it wouldn't be easy. Many would die. But they would be back, and a hundred years later they would bring the buffalo back as well. The demise of the buffalo and the coming of the railroad led to an ending, but not the end. The vanishing point was only an illu-sion, one conjured by the perspective of the observer.

For whites like Gast, this was all seen as a beginning, and an auspicious one. The West was being cleared and a new world was taking shape. The buffalo were gone, and good riddance, thought General Philip Sheridan. He told hunters, "Kill, skin, and sell until the buffalo are exterminated. Then your prairie can be covered with speckled cattle and the festive cowboy who follows the hunter as the second forerunner of an advanced civilization." Cattle would roam the country, and towns such as Dodge and Abilene would shoot up, and the railroad could come through to take the beef away to market in a distant city. The railroad and

American Progress. *George A. Crofutt chromolithograph, 1873, after an 1872 painting of the same title by John Gast. Library of Congress, Prints and Photographs Division [LC-DIG-ppmsca-09855 DLC].*

the market would make the emptied land grow and fill up with new plants and people and shops and houses. In Gast's painting it is as if the railroad brought pure light to the land. It seems to be guided by a luminescent angel, clothed in an ethereal white gown. The angel is overhead, stringing out the telegraph, and below a succession of miners, ranchers, and then businessmen arrive with the train. In the background you can see the starting place for it all: New York City's Brooklyn Bridge, where Kroeber had his first geography lesson and Luther Standing Bear marched across with the Carlisle Brass Band. Gast summed the scene as he saw it up with the title of his painting, *American Progress.* It was the American Dream made real. Destiny manifested.[21]

As a young boy Ishi may have learned from his mother that the train was a kind of demon following whites wherever they went. Whites knew the railroad did indeed follow them wherever they went, and that there was no escaping it, which even some whites found unsettling. It was a demon or an angel; whites weren't sure which. But they were sure it had the power to change utterly the course of human events, which is what angels and demons do, after all. In the gubernatorial race of 1910, just a year before Ishi's emergence at Oroville, Hiram Johnson got elected on an anti-railroad platform. He promised to shackle the power of the railroad, an entity that the novelist Frank Norris described as an octopus whose "tentacles reach into every community, however small," even into rural towns like Oroville. The railroad reached deeper still, into the forgotten village where Ishi lived, invisible from above and around—surely invisible to the railroad but not, it turns out, beyond its reach. By 1871 Stanford's Central Pacific Railroad had reached Vina, just fifteen miles from Ishi's homeland. By 1909 the Western Pacific Railroad had knocked through its line south of Ishi's homeland along the Feather River, and the slaughterhouse where he was found was supplying beef for the builders of more track.[22]

When the No. 5 engine came steaming into the Oroville Station at 2:50 p.m., everyone stood by, nervous and excited. Ad Kessler, the man who found Ishi crouched in the corral of his slaughterhouse, was watching Ishi, too. Now Ishi wore more clothes, and nice ones at that: a gray checkered suit and a straw hat. This wasn't the same unknown man, or beast, he'd gone after that first night armed with a hog gambrel. Looking down, he saw that Ishi wore no shoes; he was carrying them around in his hands. But Kessler knew there was more to the man than his clothes. "I always thought there was something there I should know, that I would like to know," he said. "I would have liked to have had some more time with him." But time was up: the train, just arrived, was anxious to leave.[23]

Shepherded by Batwi and Waterman, Ishi stepped onboard the Western Pacific no. 1 train, the only barefooted passenger that day. Not everyone on the train was a *saltu,* a ghost man, a white man. The porters in their blue uniforms were something else; they were not white, they were not Indian, and they were darker than both.

Waterman and Batwi showed Ishi where to sit down. The accommodations were much more plush than those of the crazy man's cell in Oroville. This was a Pullman car, the fanciest way to travel. Everything was new to Ishi, inside and out. The big machine steamed and strained into motion and soon was rolling down the tracks. Ishi could see Florence and Ad and the other people at the station fall back and grow smaller, into the size he'd preferred to see all *saltus*. He avoided the eyes of the *saltu* strangers inside, too close for comfort. The pine trees and the hills of yellowed grass of his country were outside, all around, and they began to swirl, as if in a dream.

For whites, the view from a railroad window had become commonplace, almost natural. But when trains first appeared, white Americans felt strange rushing through the landscape on them. They talked about the new machine, worried about it; it compressed time, it annihilated space, they said. It changed the way they knew nature, and the look of the land itself. Henry David Thoreau, camping out on Walden Pond, complained that the "devilish Iron

Horse…has browsed off all the woods on Walden shore." To ride the train skewed one's vision of the land and made everything seem unstable. A passenger in an 1851 Nathaniel Hawthorne story was jarred by the experience: "At one moment, they were rattling through solitude; —the next village had grown up around them;— a few breaths more and it had vanished, as if swallowed by an earthquake.… Everything was unfixed from its age-long rest, and moving at a whirlwind speed in a direction opposite to their own."[24]

Ishi and his people had already witnessed a whirlwind sweep over their land. In the old days the hills had never been so yellow, even in the driest days of summer. But along with their animals whites had brought new grasses, and the bunchgrasses that had kept their greenish tinge had retreated, leaving the hills golden, the color of the metal that had lured so many *saltus* to his country. Cows and sheep and horses ate up his country, and after they ate the country was changed. A living storm had blown through the land, much like the mechanical warpath that cut through Indians' way of life.

Traveling by train was utterly different from traveling by foot. Oroville had been the limit of the places Ishi knew, of places he had stories about. In his homeland places had names, and the names themselves were stories. Here might be the place where a grizzly had been killed, and over there, long ago, in the beforetime when animals could speak like people, the wood duck had told his many suitors that they were not good enough for him. You could tell the stories as you walked through these places. But moving through space at this speed would make the stories race. It would be like playing back a recording of yourself at double speed. It's your voice, but it's pitched high and strange. At twenty miles per hour and more, the land itself whines and buzzes. It's hard to hear where you are.

The train sped south down the Sacramento Valley, through Marysville, toward the capital of Sacramento. Waterman looked Ishi up and down. He was responsible for the Indian's "welfare and comfort." How was the Stone Age man holding up? He was nervous, Waterman could see. When he saw something new, he stiffened up, his hands clenched into fists. But his face sometimes lit up, and he also seemed to enjoy some of the sights. As the journey continued, Waterman could see orchards fly by, which meant that they were leaving the wilder country of ranches and livestock and coming into the settled realm of farms and orchards, coming closer to the city.[25]

The new landscape meant nothing to Ishi. This land had no stories. There were trees, but they weren't oaks or pines. Orange trees could be seen in Butte County early in the journey. Just a few days before, he had been given an orange in the jail, but didn't know to peel it. The *saltus* laughed when he tried to bite into a banana, and then again when he tried to peel a tomato. Before, he had tasted whiskey and wheat flour, but not these new fruits of the land. He would never drink whiskey again. It might be poisoned; it could kill you as it killed the others. But he liked the fruits. He'd eat more. Now he was bewildered by orchard after orchard of strange trees bearing strange fruit. They stood in perfect rows; you could look straight down the alleys in between. Train tracks could be laid right through these forests.

In Thoreau's Massachusetts the railroad consumed trees for power. In California it got farmers to grow fruit trees, neatly laid out on the land, not to burn up in its engines but to provide a payload for the trip back East. California, they said, was America's

Eden, but the Indians hadn't known what to do with it, and the
Spanish and Mexicans didn't either. It was once a wilderness, but
now we've made it into a garden, the growers announced. We've
even added to what God gave us, inventing new and improved
fruits. Everyone, especially the rattled denizens of Chicago and
New York, should, as they put it in their ads, eat California fruits!
These fruits had been kissed by the sun; put them to your lips
and you'd be lifted out of the dark city streets and placed in the
splendorous valleys of California.[26]

Waterman was anxious to get some more work done. He had
only begun to extract the "worlds of stuff" from Ishi. Kroeber was
waiting in the city. Waterman already had his man, but he wanted
to deliver more to his mentor. He needed Batwi's help, and Batwi
was happy to give it. Batwi wanted to show the anthropologist
that he could talk to this wild Indian, and he wanted to show the
Yahi wild man that he could deal with the whites. Batwi was blasé
about the sights. He wore his suit with casual aplomb. Ishi was
nervous about Batwi, this man who traveled with the *saltu*. He
could talk to him, but it was hard. (It was like being a Brazilian
trying to talk to a Spaniard.) And Ishi wasn't sure about this man
who could speak his language—in a distant, confusing way. What
did he want from him? And this man grew a beard. Strange. It was
something these *saltu* did. Did he forget how to pluck the hair
from his face? Did he think he was a *saltu*?

Maybe Batwi was like those boarding school Indians. It's
believed that one of Ishi's kin had once gone away to a school.
Children of other Indian tribes neighboring the Yahi or living in
other parts of northern California—Pit River Indians, Maidu and

Nisenan, Yana and Modoc and Yurok—had been run down these tracks Ishi was now traveling all the way to the Sherman Institute in southern California, a boarding school for Indians set amid the million-dollar orange groves of Riverside. Benny Lin and Stanley, from the Mountain Maidu and Hamawi Pit River tribes, were two of the boys sent to this school. They were born below Yo-Tim Yamne, or Medicine Mountain, not far from Ishi's homeland. When they arrived at the depot in Riverside, Benny Lin and Stanley, barefoot, were met by teachers and two Indian students from the school. They noticed that everyone in this new world wore "hard, stiff leather shoes." The school was a place of "sharp edges, shiny surfaces, and shouting bells." Its curriculum was designed to instill white knowledge and white values in the children.[27]

Since the 1870s reformers and self-styled "friends of the Indian" felt that Native peoples' only chance of survival was total assimilation. Like it or not, their culture, their old ways were doomed to extinction in modern America, with its electricity and steam power. Richard Henry Pratt was a ringleader of the reformers. Unlike the Indian fighter Sheridan, the one who had signed a death warrant for the buffalo, Pratt said he didn't believe that the only good Indian was a dead Indian. Pratt's motto was "Kill the Indian in him and save the man." He showed off before-and-after photographs: a Navajo man named Tom Torlino with long hair and traditional garb going into school, a modern suit-wearing American, hair shorn, coming out.[28]

Despite the uniforms and drills, Indianness was not so easy to kill. At the Sherman Institute at night Benny Lin dreamed of his grandmother telling him stories of Pa'nom, the grizzly bear who protects the people of Yo-Tim Yamne. He dreamed of his

The apparent transformation of Tom Torlino. Photographs by John Choate, 1886. Courtesy of Yale Collection of Western Americana, Beinecke Rare Book and Manuscript Library.

people's bear dance, and the *yo'koli* flag with tassels of maple bark, honoring the bear. At school the state flag of California flew, and it also honored the grizzly bear. The Americans found in the bear a noble symbol; when some of them rebelled against the Mexican regime in 1846, they put a bear on their flag. A year before the completion of the first transcontinental railroad, Bret Harte drew a bear for the cover of a new California magazine, the *Overland Monthly*. His friend Mark Twain complained that it was just standing there, so Harte added some railroad tracks beneath its paws. Twain now liked the picture of "the ancient symbol of California savagery snarling at the approaching type of high and progressive Civilization, the first Overland locomotive!" "Look at him well," Harte prophetically added, "for he is passing away." The bears were killed outright by hunters like Hi Good and much of their habitat was destroyed as valley lands went under the plow. One of the last was killed in 1922, though a few survived for years as fugitives hidden deep in the mountains. They found refuge in the Yahi's Mill Creek canyon and other out-of-the-way places; Ishi's hidden village, after all, was called Wowunupo'mu tetna, "Grizzly Bear's Hiding Place."[29]

Benny Lin's dreams of home made him want to go home, but the school did not help students return for the summer. As far as the administrators were concerned, the less contact the Indian children had with their family, the better. It would hinder their progress, allow them to revert "back to the blanket." Better to have them stay through the summer, get a job picking oranges, learn about money. The commissioner of Indian affairs even told the students that the school's insignia, with its *S* and *I*, looked a bit like a dollar sign, and "it is the dollar that makes the world go around." But Benny Lin and Stanley had other ideas about what made the world go round and about what to do with their summer. They took matters into their own hands, hopping a train and riding it through the night home to their families on Medicine Mountain.[30]

At the schools the first thing to go was language. To talk Indian was to be punished. But here, on the train, Waterman wanted to know the language. The anthropologist wants to know what you call *galaa-na*, Batwi would tell Ishi. *Galaa-na* is *galaa-hi,* he'd say. And then he'd hear Batwi repeat it to Waterman, but Waterman was already scribbling it down. Days before, in the jail at Oroville,

Waterman had looked at his paper and then said the word Ishi first understood, *i'wi,* wood. That *galaa-hi,* that "fish," was being put down on that paper now, Ishi knew. What magic. Maybe he had some exposure to writing already. Years before, while Ishi and the Yahi were in hiding, a Yahi girl named Red Wing was taken off to a boarding school, but like Benny and Stanley she returned to her people knowing how to read and write.[31]

The vocabulary session was a big success. Waterman completely filled the backside of a piece of paper that was handy, the release letter from the sheriff of Butte County. Then he turned it over and found some space for more words beside those that had been typed out:

> Received of Sheriff J. B. Webber of Butte county the person of an elderly Yana Indian, name and place of residence at present unknown, recently taken under the protection of the County of Butte, said person to be taken to the University of California for linguistic and phonetic study. The welfare and comfort of this said person to be duly looked after until the disposition of the case by proper authority.

The receipt was for the genuine article, a man like no other—purer, wilder. Now Waterman was already proving his value. Waterman wrote down *compani,* and its English equivalent, *cedar bark.* The word for *bark* was preserved on the page, which itself had come from some kind of tree somewhere else.[32]

After Stockton the train headed west, over the Altamont Pass and then through Niles Cañon. Sparsely populated, with an Old West look and feel, the cañon would soon become the home of Essanay Films. An actor named Gilbert Anderson was transformed into the cowboy star Broncho Billy. He made more than three hundred films, giving form to the early film western. Just a few months after Ishi passed through, trains coming through the cañon might be attacked by cowboy actors bursting out of the bushes and leaping from their horses onto the train. As one Niles resident recalled, passengers wouldn't always be informed that they had ridden their train into a work of fiction. One year after the Western Pacific no. 1 train carrying Ishi rolled through, Anderson was at work in the cañon filming *An Indian Sunbeam,* about a white girl raised by Indians and fought over by the cowboy and her Indian suitor, Big Wolf—who ultimately ties her to a wild stallion, of course.

Anderson loved the locale where he set up shop; with its hills and streams and fields, Niles Cañon could be made to appear to be any place in the West. "You walk out of the studio right into the scenery," he pointed out. This was a landscape that would have stories, many of them, but all telling the same western narrative. And the stories weren't really about this landscape; instead, nature had become a set for the peculiarly American origin story that was the western. The landscape was used to tell urban Americans stories about where they had come from and to entertain them with the drama of the Old West, a freer, more masculine, wilder place and time than the one they currently inhabited. It was a place modern Americans loved to go in their imagination. As for the cowboy star Anderson, he worked in rustic Niles Cañon but lived in San Francisco, commuting between the two by chauffeured automobile. Anderson recruited another performer who would gain even more fame than Broncho Billy: Charlie Chaplin, who would create the role of the little tramp in this very cañon just outside of the great metropolis of San Francisco.[33]

The train powered on to Oakland, arriving at the Transcontinental Gateway Entrance to San Francisco at 9:32 p.m. There was no bridge across the bay to the city; to reach their final destination, the three men boarded a ferry. Ishi grew nervous again, unsure of his footing as he walked onto this boat that was as big as an island. There were stories of the ocean, the place to which the waters flowed, but no one in his tribe had ever seen it. There was so much water. The ferry whistle blew; Ishi clenched his fists and bravely bore the ride over the water. At eleven o'clock, the ferry arrived at the terminal; it was time to disembark into a new world. As Kroeber described the scene, "There stepped off the ferry boat into the glare of electric lights, into the shouting of hotel runners, and the clanging of trolley cars on Market Street, San Francisco, Ishi, the last wild Indian in the United States."[34]

By then Ishi had already seen a good deal of modern America— its guns, telephones, photographs, fruits, and utensils had all been pressed on him. He'd seen the inside of a jail cell and a movie theater. He'd ridden in a horse-drawn buggy, seen a trolley car, sat in an automobile, ridden an oil-powered train, and crossed the bay on a steam-powered ferry. He'd struck matches, had a pistol blow up in his hand and a rose put in his lapel. And he'd already been photographed a hundred times and seen himself in the photograph. He'd seen a locomotive on a movie screen. But even before this last week of endless revelations, Ishi had been living in a landscape shaped by the railroad and all that it entailed. And he'd been living in a world shaped by the consequences of the image of Indians that whites held in their heads.

For Kroeber, Waterman with Batwi and Ishi coming into San Francisco was like a movie replay of Lieutenant Peary with Qisuk and Minik coming into New York Harbor. Kroeber's career had begun with these informants, who had been brought from far away right to him in the city. Now it was happening again, only this time the arrival seemed to hold even more anthropological value. Kroeber had already looked up and down the state, but all the Indians he saw knew too much and too little, he thought. They'd been around whites. They knew about church and school. They "live in houses and wear overalls." They had taken on new ways. They had forgotten old ways. Now he could work with a person he called the "last wild Indian," the last "uncontaminated man." Ishi knew it all, and knew nothing, which was just what Kroeber wanted. That night, Ishi, dressed in his suit jacket and overalls, was shown to his room in Kroeber's Museum of Anthropology, the place that he would learn to call *wowi*, home.[35]

Early the next morning the head of the museum was introduced to Ishi. Ishi tried to say something in English and then blushed in embarrassment when he was not quite sure if it was right. Kroeber, with his full beard and suit, tried to put his guest at ease. He felt that the man was shy in his presence and that he was fearful of the people around him and his new surroundings, a fear he was trying to mask.

Ishi decided that Kroeber deserved respect, and that he would call him "the Big Chief." But Ishi was not used to pronouncing *f*s, so he called Kroeber "Big Cheap." It amounted to a nickname, and not one that was entirely flattering. It was at once a sign of respect and deflating. It made plain to all around that Kroeber was the boss, the headman of the museum. But it was not a role Kroeber liked to assert through title, for he tried to relate to everyone around him with respect. When a graduate student presumed to use the museum secretary's typewriter for his own work at night, Kroeber pointed out to him that the secretary might not like that. She had typed through the earthquake and was entitled to respect, just as his informants were, the people he liked to think of as his friends. Back in June Kroeber had sent a letter to Sam Batwi. He enclosed a photograph Sapir had taken of him and let him know that the Indians in the hills Kroeber had been looking for had not been found. "I guess they are pretty shy," he wrote. "[I would] be glad to hear from you sometime, if you have anybody to write for you." He signed his letter, "Your friend, A L Kroeber."[36]

Now Batwi had come to him, bringing the shy Indian who had named him the Big Chief. It nominated the real distance between the two and underscored the power Kroeber had in their relationship. Kroeber had no choice but to accept the nickname and knew he would have to prove his goodwill before Ishi could see him as a friend.

But how could Kroeber welcome him as a friend? He didn't know his language, and he didn't know his name. It was taboo for a Yahi to speak his own name. A name was precious. Another Yahi might have told Kroeber his name, but there was no other Yahi, at least none at the museum.

Instead, there were reporters outside. They wanted the man's name and his age, neither of which Kroeber could provide. Kroeber explained the naming customs of the Yahi, but everyone wanted something to call him. "Wild man of Oroville" was not sufficient. Batwi suggested that they call him John. And of course he had already been nicknamed Panama Kid Webber. But these lacked individuality and dignity, Kroeber pointed out. He decided to call him Ishi. It was, he explained, an "anglicization of his word for man"; that word, which Waterman first wrote down as *i'citi*, was anglicized by dropping the suffix *ti*. Kroeber frankly admitted that the name was "not genuine," but he did feel that it was "singularly appropriate." With the name in place, Kroeber was ready to make his official announcement to the waiting tribe of reporters: "In 'Ishi,' as we have decided to call the Indian captured near Oroville, I can safely say that we have the most uncivilized and uncontaminated man in the world to-day."[37]

The reporters took to the name immediately, using it in their first stories about San Francisco's newest celebrity. It caught on, partly because it seemed so natural. What do we call the wild man, the reporters wanted to know. Call him *Man*, Kroeber responded. Call him *Ishi*. It helped convey one point Kroeber wanted to make: the "wild man" was a man, like them. But he was also a man unlike them, and the Yahi term underscored that as well. It seemed natural, but it was not genuine. It was a stage name, a name for the museum.[38]

"Ishi" was used right alongside Kroeber's name in the first newspaper stories after his arrival in San Francisco. Only days before, when the story of the wild Indian first broke, California's leading expert on Indians had been called "G. W. Kroeder" in one newspaper and "E. Krueder" in another. After Ishi appeared in San Francisco, Kroeber's name was fixed as well; the newspapers got the spelling right. Each man made tracks on the other; each man made a name for the other.[39]

There was one exception to the press getting Kroeber's name right after Ishi. The *Los Angeles Times* got not only his name wrong but also his picture: it labeled a photograph of Indian Sam Batwi "Prof Koerber." While Batwi momentarily took over Kroeber's public persona (that is, "the leading white expert on California Indians"), Ishi's nickname, Big Chief, began to subtly reshape Kroeber's private persona.[40]

· *Five* ·

CITY LIGHTS

✳

HEADLINE, *SAN FRANCISCO BULLETIN*, 5 SEPTEMBER 1911,
evening edition: "BIG CITY AMAZES CAVE MAN. PRIMORDIAL MAN
BLINKS AT CIVILIZATION'S GLARE." Ishi had just arrived late the
night before; when he woke up he saw San Francisco, and San
Francisco, through the eyes of several reporters, saw him. The
Bulletin's lede was typical: "The lusty civilization of the twentieth
century that is typified by San Francisco upon this shore of the
Pacific was viewed today by a primordial man, brought to town
from out of the furthermost savagery."[1]

Reporters had gathered that morning at the Affiliated Colleges of the University of California on Parnassus Heights to get
their first glimpse of the city's newcomer. They used as much
ink describing the man's perceptions of "civilization" as they did
describing the man himself. That made a certain kind of topsy-
turvy sense: their descriptions of *the other* were really descriptions
of *themselves*, using the man they beheld as a kind of measuring
stick for the "lusty civilization of the twentieth century." Five years
after the earthquake and four years before it was to host the grand
celebration of progress called the Panama-Pacific International

Exposition, San Francisco was at once proud of itself and anxious. That anxiety was reflected in the Ishi reporting that was, by turns, serious and silly.

The reporting recapitulated the exchanges of material items that had characterized Ishi's stay in Oroville. Reporters wanted to see, or stage, his initial encounters with civilization all over again. First, they wanted to get a picture of the man in his native attire. The anthropologists obliged by bringing a fur cape from their collection (though not one of Yahi manufacture, as these would be collected by the museum only later). When asked to undress for the photograph, Ishi, keenly observing his cultural surroundings, objected. He liked his overalls and his necktie, he said through Batwi. Besides, he didn't see anyone else wearing these kinds of clothes. He'd keep his on, thank you very much. He did agree, however, to put the fur cape on over his other clothes, and the photographers rolled up his pant legs to hide them. By nipping and tucking away the Western clothes, they finally succeeded in getting the staged shot they wanted. Six photographers began shooting away, while Waterman told Batwi to tell Ishi, "White man just play." But being shot by a camera is still being shot. As Mary Ashe Miller described the scene for the *Call*, Ishi "stood with his head back and a half smile on his face, but his compressed lips and dilated nostrils showed that he was far from happy."[2]

Ishi's refusal to return to a pure state of nativity became part of the story. Bemused and incredulous, reporters wrote that in his natural state he had gone about naked, "as God made him." Never mind that he had been wearing some amalgamation of whites' manufactured clothes and the traditional garb of the Yahi all his life. The *Los Angeles Times* headline read, "SHY, LAST YANA DONS PANTS, REFUSES TO POSE IN NATURE'S GARB." The reporting thus became self-reflexive, exposing the staged nature of this man's identity as it might be manifested (or not) in the clothes he wore (or not).[3]

Ishi had been set up in a publicity trap, but he found ways to wriggle free, ways to shape how he was seen and portrayed. After he was handed a bow and arrows from the museum's collection, the reporters wanted to see him shoot. A photographer put his new felt hat on a stick one hundred feet away. Thinking the Indian would not be able to hit the mark, he urged Ishi to make an attempt. His arrow flew true and hit the hat. Next up was a newspaper as a target; Ishi shot an arrow straight through the rag.[4]

The reporters were impressed, not just by what they saw but by what they heard from Kroeber. They readily picked up what the anthropologist said about the man's being "uncontaminated." The journalists called him a "human document" and a "treasure" and "the great anthropological find of the twentieth century"; they also likened him to a "specimen" put under the "microscope," and wondered what secrets of the aboriginal past the man might reveal. San Francisco newspapers were filled with the story of Ishi, and soon newspapers around the country were carrying stories about the wild man's arrival in the big city of the West.[5]

As in Oroville, a great variety of things were pressed into Ishi's hands. A government Indian inspector who happened to be there that day and who gave his approval for Ishi to remain with Kroeber, gave the man a knife as a keepsake. As Mary Ashe Miller reported, "His newly acquired pockets...are as keen a delight to him as are those of a small boy, and he has a great collection of odds and ends in them already." (She might have said the same of Kroeber's pockets, for his were always full of this and that as well.) Miller wanted to give the man something, too, but all she had was a cheap "white bone police whistle." But Ishi took delight in it, blowing into it, making the sound of authority. Reporters and anthropologists alike looked at him, listened, and noted the incongruity. The little whistle had captured his imagination, but the vast infrastructure of the modern city barely seemed to make an impression.[6]

From the grounds of the museum on Parnassus Heights the reporters and Ishi could take in a view of the city stretched out before them, and beyond they could see the waters of the Pacific. Ishi asked Batwi from which direction they had come the day before. Batwi gestured toward the San Francisco Bay. Miller asked what he thought about this place and his journey here. Batwi explained, "First, yesterday, he frightened very much, now today he think all very funny. He like it, it tickle him. He like this place here. Much to see, big water off there, plenty houses, many things to see."[7]

It is unclear exactly what Ishi's impression was of all those houses. Kroeber said that the whistle Miller gave "him roused more expression and spontaneity than the thousands of houses spread out before him as he stood on the high terrace of the Museum and looked over the city." The reporters, like the anthropologists, had a keen interest in seeing what Ishi would see. One newspaper reported, "Ishi is going on a real sightseeing trip about the city in a few days…the Primordial Man on a privately-conducted rubberneck wagon. And it will be worth more than the $1 for the alleged twenty-mile trip to know what Ishi thinks of San Francisco. There is a chance for the Fair publicity committee to get a brand new viewpoint of the city of the Panama-Pacific Exposition of 1915."[8]

The newspapers did not wait to see what he would see. They scooped not their competitors' coverage, but the sightseeing tour itself by depicting in cartoons Ishi's encounters with the modern city before he even left the museum. Under the headline "BIG CITY AMAZES CAVE MAN," the *Bulletin* printed a cartoon of Ishi startled and jumping back from the honk of a trolley car on Market Street. In another he is craning his neck to see the tops of the tall buildings, while a fashionable white woman is "what caught his eye." The *Examiner* drew him being arrested by a sheriff for hunting with his bow and arrow without a license. ("Nix the dummy act, yer Pinched!" the lawman says.) He also is seen carrying a woman off for a "stone age elopement" and sitting barefoot in a shoe shine booth "acquiring the polish of civilization." Tucked in and around these images of light ridicule were poems poking fun at modern life and warning the cave man to resist its lure; civilization wasn't all it was cracked up to be. After all, in his primitive state he never had to pay alimony or a mortgage, never had "to exercise for fear of getting fat":

> Happy old Ishi!
> Free from all anxiety!
> Bless your stars you weren't born
> In civilized society![9]

Five days after Ishi's arrival Kroeber took him out for a Sunday drive through the city. Their initial destination was the ocean, about which Ishi had heard. He had already crossed the Bay on a ferry, but now they were heading west toward the beach, where

"Big City Amazes Cave Man," San Francisco Bulletin, *5 September 1911.*

the waves of the Pacific touch the shore. Kroeber anticipated that the "surf,...as a phenomenon of nature, would interest him more than the works of civilization." The car stopped on the bluff above the beach, near the Cliff House, a famous San Francisco landmark. Ishi looked down but saw no nature. His eyes were filled by the sight of people. "*Hansi saltu,*" he intoned, over and again, *Many white people.* It was a warm day, and thousands of San Franciscans had come out to the beach. Ishi, living out most of his life with only a few companions, was overwhelmed by the sheer numbers.[10]

Ishi and Kroeber could look out and see the sea lions below; behind them rose the eight-story Cliff House, a complex of restaurants, bars, an art gallery, and a mineral museum built by the millionaire Adolpho Sutro. Sutro had made his fortune from mining the earth for silver, particularly at the big bonanza two hundred miles east of San Francisco, just across the Sierra Nevada at a place called the Comstock Lode. Other San Franciscans made their money by financing industrial hydraulic mining; huge pressure hoses trained water jets on mountains, reducing them to sludge from which gold was extracted. The machinery and technology for mining had been created in San Francisco, and money flowed back into the city, financing the growth of its towering buildings, its civic works, and its teeming population.[11]

When Sutro looked at the waves crashing in from the Pacific beneath his Cliff House, he saw its potential as a place where San Franciscans could bathe in ocean saltwater, warmed for their pleasure. With 600 tons of iron, 3.5 million linear feet of lumber, 270,000 cubic feet of concrete, and 100,000 square feet of glass, he built his marvelous public bath house. Sutro decorated by putting on display his collections of Egyptian mummies and Indian totem poles. There was room inside for seven thousand San Franciscans, and the various baths held 1.8 million gallons of sea water. When Ishi and Kroeber came by, the building's power plant was being connected to the lines of Pacific Gas and Electric. PG & E grew out of a group of hydraulic mining companies of the Gold Rush and now fed electricity to the city, supplied by plants called Rome and Electra in the Sierras and from a dam on the Pit River, one of the streams of Wahganupa. Its headquarters was on Market Street. The baths were outfitted with eighty-six 500-watt clear Mazda lamps, state of the art. San Franciscans from all walks of life had a chance to be edified by nature and the artifacts of various civilizations, brilliantly illuminated—and it had all been financed by the mineral wealth wrenched out of the Sierras.[12]

George Hearst also grew wealthy on silver. When he died his wife, Phoebe, an avid collector like Sutro, financed the University of California's initial growth and the Anthropology Department in particular, establishing the museum on Parnassus Heights that was Ishi's new home. George and Phoebe's son, William Randolph, ran the San Francisco *Examiner*. He was one of the inventors of "yellow journalism," a sensationalist brand of reporting that could turn any happening, such as the arrival into the city of a Stone Age man, into a media event. The *Examiner* had done just that with Ishi, when its reporter set up the action scene of Ishi shooting an arrow at the photographer's hat.

The museum and grounds were built by silver, Phoebe Hearst's and Sutro's, too, for he had given the land to the university in the first place. Sutro and Hearst were the great philanthropists among San Francisco's plutocracy, hoping to improve the lives of the masses by giving them access to artifacts and art as well as parks and natural ocean baths. They channeled silver and gold into the civilization of San Francisco, but that wealth had flowed to them only by turning vast sections of the Sierras into toxic wilderness. Everywhere Ishi went that day in San Francisco was connected in hidden ways to the mountain ranges south of his homeland. Even the streams and rivers of the Sierras and Mount Lassen had been dammed, their water converted to hydroelectric power that flowed into the cities on the Bay and lit them up at night.[13]

The tall buildings were also connected to the natural wealth of the mountains. When Kroeber pointed them out, Ishi looked on with no sign of wonder. Waterman reasoned that he "mentally compared a towering twelve story building, not with his hut in Deer Creek which was only four feet high, but with the cliffs and crags of his native mountains." To travel down Market Street was, topographically speaking, not unlike traveling through the cañons cut from the old lava flows of Wahganupa. What was arrestingly different was, as Kroeber put it, the "undreamed-of crowd of people." There were almost half a million people in San Francisco at that time. Ishi's whole nation numbered less than two dozen for most of his life. Yet many whites also found the crowds of the city disturbing. With its teeming numbers, a person was suddenly anonymous; you didn't know them, their family, their background, where they were coming from. And you were anonymous, too, adrift in the culture that defined you, caught up in a new world of possibilities and problems. It was exhilarating and disturbing to find yourself in the urban swirl wherever you came from.[14]

"Market Street, a world-known thoroughfare." From *promotional brochure titled* Panama-Pacific International Exposition–San Francisco–1915 *(ca. 1914).*

Kroeber tried to avoid more crowds of *saltus* on the rest of their tour that day. They drove the car through Golden Gate Park, a magnificent urban nature park, San Francisco's answer to New York's Central Park. The museum, situated just a few blocks above the eastern edge of park, could be seen from various points on their drive. Kroeber noted, "Each time a smile would break over his features as he pointed with a nod of his head and said *wowi* (home)." Ishi was already mapping this new landscape, and he pointed out landmarks that they had passed by before: street crossings, monuments, and statues. Kroeber was fascinated to see Ishi's "keen sense of locality" expressing itself in this terra incognita. A highlight of the trip was when the car "disturbed a flock of quail that roam the

Market Street in 1911. Detail from The "Chevalier" Commercial, Pictorial and Tourist Map of San Francisco from Latest U.S. Gov. and Official Surveys *(Aug. Chevalier, Lithographer Publisher, San Francisco, 1911). From the David Rumsey Map Collection. Copyright 2000 by Cartography Associates.*

park in a half-wild state." Ishi stood up, delighted, and watched them, calling softly, "Chikakatee, Chikakatee!" Kroeber, keenly aware of how shocking the crowds had been to Ishi, believed that seeing the quail in the city environs was a kind of antidote, giving Ishi a "feeling of home and kinship."[15]

Back at the museum the anthropologists later made a series of flash cards for Ishi, drawing a picture to the left and writing the word in Yahi in capital letters on the right. There was a picture of a tree beside I WI; a picture of a deer next to BA NA; a bow and

"Wowi" flash card. Alfred Kroeber, "Ishi Reading Lessons," A. L. Kroeber Papers, BANC FILM 2049. Courtesy of the Bancroft Library, University of California, Berkeley.

arrow next to MAN 'I and SA WA; a person dressed in Western-style clothes and a hat next to IH SI (looking like the Navajo man Tom Torlino transformed). For WO WI there was a picture, not of a dwelling resembling the houses of the Yahi, but a substantial two-story building, like a small-scale version of the Museum of Anthropology.[16]

At Kroeber's behest, Ishi soon went to work making a Yahi house on the museum grounds so that he could show visitors the traditional dwelling structure of his people. When a storm blew down the ersatz *wowi* Ishi was "chagrined by the havoc wrought

Ishi's model home, 1912. Photographed by Nels C. Nelson, 15-5424. Courtesy of the Phoebe A. Hearst Museum of Anthropology and the Regents of the University of California.

by the wind." He blamed Kroeber for selecting an exposed site, and Batwi translated Ishi's explanation, "At home he would have built in a brush thicket."[17]

When Ishi first arrived at the museum Kroeber was making final preparations for its public opening. Ishi suddenly brought more attention to Kroeber and the museum, some of it welcome, some not. The Indian agent Kelsey's one directive to Kroeber was to protect the man from circus impresarios and mountebanks, and Kroeber was dead-set against any such performances. He was a man of science and would have nothing to do with exploitation for commercial amusement. But the offers rolled in to put Ishi on display. *We'll pay two thousand dollars to show him in Sacramento. Let him join a traveling circus. Put him in a peep show dive on Market Street and charge sailors a nickel or dime to see the wild man. If that is too low brow, Professor, how about doing a two-person act at the Orpheum Theatre? It will be "edifying" and "educational,"* and lucrative, too. Kroeber refused them all. He didn't want Ishi to have anything to do with such cheap amusements; he believed they would demean both Kroeber and his profession and Ishi and his culture.[18]

There was a dark history of bringing people from other cultures into the cities of Europe and then America and putting them on display for the casual amusement of the audience. Often a self-styled anthropologist would present the strange aborigine and give a pseudo-scientific discourse on his or her culture and nature. San Francisco's ornate Orpheum Theater had hosted many of these performances over the years. Back in the 1890s one such showman brought a group of aborigines from Queensland.

Step right up, audience members were implored. See the "AUS-TRALIAN CANNIBALS!" See them perform "DEADLY BOOMERANG THROWING!" See King Bill, a man who "abducted the daughter of a chief, and ate her up!" But even the promoter of the aborigines found that his performers, whom he billed as "wild men," showed too many signs of contact with modernity to make his show work its primitivist magic. The *Chronicle* reported on September 25, 1892, that although they "were savage and barbarous in every attribute...they did not look like it as they stood watching [the showman] and waiting for the cue to give their performance." The public's thirst for the imagined primitive was seemingly unquenchable, but to Kroeber all of the Barnum and Bailey promoters trying to capitalize on Ishi's wildness represented nothing but a race to the bottom.[19]

The Orpheum burned down in the fires of 1906, but it was rebuilt and its management was still searching the city, and the globe, for acts when Kroeber rejected their offer. Then a reporter from the *Call* thought up an ingenious way to make Ishi and Kroeber play a role in an Orpheum show anyway. Grant Wallace, a reporter "in search of a story," as Kroeber later described him, cornered Ishi and invited him to go to the Orpheum. Batwi translated the invitation, and Ishi graciously accepted, so long as Waterman or Kroeber would go with him. Both Waterman and Kroeber good-naturedly decided to go, though Kroeber's taste in entertainment was for more high-brow fare than the Orpheum's vaudeville shows. Wallace described the evening one way, Kroeber quite another.

In Wallace's version Ishi, "the only really wild Indian in existence," walked down the aisle and "took his seat among the

Ishi, Alfred Kroeber, and others at the Orpheum Theater, October 1911. Courtesy of the Phoebe A. Hearst Museum of Anthropology and the Regents of the University of California, 15-25486.

crimson plush draperies and the glittering electric lights." The reporter set his titillating tone early: when "gentlewomen of the conquering race...gave the wild man a friendly nod and a smile, the wild man removed the cigar from his lips, dug the broad red toes of his bare feet deeper into the plush carpets and smiled back at these splendid women from another world." Wallace presented a colorful version of Ishi's history, and then quoted Kroeber: "We find that he has perceptive powers far keener than those of highly educated white men. He reasons well, grasps an idea quickly, has a keen sense of humor, is gentle, thoughtful, and courteous and has a higher type of mentality than most Indians." Wallace went on to press the anthropologists' buttons by saying that they called him the "uncontaminated man" as if they were circus barkers using that line: *Step right up, see the Uncontaminated Man!*

"Therefore," the reporter reasoned, "to permit the barbarian to mingle in our unsettled civilization is to expose him to contamination." Wallace then owned up to his own role in "the undoing of the last, lone spotless man." He had "inveigled him into the tinseled ambush of the temple of music and folly." Wallace described the various acts of the show and Ishi's supposed reaction: Brazilian dancers ("The dance illustrated the story of the Lying Coyote"), ax throwers from Australia ("Good work!"), various comedians (laughing on cue), a tragic soliloquy between an actor speaking on the telephone to his wife burning up in a hotel fire (Ishi accidentally laughed).

All of this led up to the performance of Lilly Lena, a singer from London. As Wallace had it, Ishi was transfixed at the sight of the "white goddess" and leaned over the box in desire. Kroeber "now leaned toward him, ready to grab the wild man before he could leap on stage." Everyone in the audience looked at Ishi; for the moment he had become "the headline attraction." According to Wallace, Batwi explained that Ishi thought the singer "must be the great medicine woman, the dancing goddess of the other world." Wallace then offered up his jaded reaction to Ishi's invented misperception: "Poor, simple-minded wild man! He could not know that the heaven of the white people is never likely to be so crowded as their vaudeville houses." After the performance Wallace brought Lena to their box. The *Call* illustrated the moment they met. Even though Ishi wore a suit and tie to the performance, the newspaper depicted him wearing a fur cape. It depicted a hulking and infatuated man-beast taking the dainty hand of the short-skirted and lily white Lena. She shook his hand, Ishi smiled back, and she gave him something, a "talisman" is what Wallace called it. He carefully put it in his pocket by his heart and explained to Batwi that he thought it was "the great medicine ball that would ward off all evil." But Wallace told his readers that "what the little singer from London had given the wild man of Tehama was only a stick of chewing gum."[20]

Bitter at the way the reporter had used Ishi, and him, to create a lurid fantasy scene of primitive man lusting after the decadent lures of the city and a white woman, Kroeber wrote, "The reporter got his story. But he got it out of his imagination." He noted that it was the great crowd that made the greatest impression on Ishi. He admitted that Ishi had laughed during the show, but explained that he was just doing what those around him were doing. Perhaps he was laughing out of embarrassment. The physical humor of the vaudeville show he did not grasp, and whenever anyone pointed something out to him, "he smiled politely... or watched the motions of the suggestor instead of the thing being pointed out. It was all absolutely meaningless to him." Wallace had woven his story around a set of misinterpretations, claiming that Ishi understood the acts according to his own supposed culture: the myth of Coyote and stories of medicine women goddesses. Kroeber asserted an absolute cultural gap. "Yet," the anthropologist insisted, "there is nothing undeveloped about him; he has the mind of a man and is a man in every sense."[21]

Kroeber explained that, after his first month in San Francisco, Ishi was "no longer bewildered." But he did not yet understand much about modern American culture. It was as if we had gone to the moon, Kroeber suggested. Soon the novelty would wear off, though we still wouldn't understand 90 percent of what was going on in the alien world. At the end of his article, which was printed next to the account of the evening by Wallace, Kroeber revealed more about his relationship to Ishi. Kroeber had taught him English words, but Ishi "refuse[d] to use them": "He does not consider himself a part of the civilization around him, and makes no effort to become part of it." Kroeber seems to have tried to prepare Ishi for acculturation, but the Yahi was steadfastly remaining apart. Furthermore Kroeber thought Ishi was vulnerable: "If he were turned out to shift for himself he would attach himself to the first person who came along." Kroeber seemed frustrated with what he perceived as a lack of initiative and paternalistically mused, "[Ishi's attitude] is just like that of a puppy. He comes running when you call him, and if you were to tell him to stand in the corner or stand on his head, if he were able he would do it without hesitation."

Protective of his charge, frustrated by Ishi's seeming unwillingness to meet him halfway, Kroeber also worried that Ishi was "unhappy." But when Batwi "asked him if he would rather live with the white men or the Indians he said he preferred to stay where he was."[22]

The Museum of Anthropology was the place where Ishi would live and work. Others lived there, too. There was a live-in caretaker and a hired hand who slept in an apartment upstairs and looked after the specimens after hours. But the museum caretakers weren't also museum attractions, as Ishi was. When Ishi moved into the museum, the crowds came to see him there, a living exhibit amid the artifacts of antiquity.

But before the crowds came to see Ishi at the museum, San Francisco's high society got a chance to see him there at the opening reception, an invitation-only affair. Kroeber had been busy getting everything ready, almost too busy to spend much time at all with Ishi. The day the story of the Wild Man of Oroville broke in the newspapers, Kroeber was busy writing out bills, asking about a coal shipment that never came, paying the Spring Valley Water Company, and writing letters to various people about the opening of the new museum, the precise date of which had not yet been set. Finishing touches were being put on exhibits of artifacts from the world over. The objects were placed on stands or on shelves and lit up with electric lights. Now the glare of San Francisco's gaze was on the museum because of Ishi, and Kroeber didn't blink. University President Benjamin Ide Wheeler and Phoebe Hearst would greet the invited guests, almost a thousand of San Francisco's elite. Many wanted to see Ishi; indeed, as a newspaper reported, "the wild man" was one of the "chief attractions." Kroeber situated Ishi as comfortably as he could in an exhibition room where he could meet with the curious; the newspaper reported that "Ishi was shoeless and sockless, but otherwise he was garbed in true American fashion, with stock collar, shirt and tie and with a coat and vest." Kroeber brought small groups to see Ishi, who good-naturedly shook their hands—though he did not like to touch strangers. Kroeber said the names of the people to Ishi, and Ishi repeated them, smiling at the guests. One woman, who had been stationed at an army post twenty-five years earlier and had picked up some of the language of nearby tribes, "talked in the guttural lingo of the redman to the stolid figure who sat in the chair." All Ishi could do in reply to the well-meaning gibberish was laugh.[23]

When Waterman first saw Ishi in Oroville he thought he would be a great draw for the museum. "If this fellow don't die before we get him to the museum, or some other unheard-of thing occur," he wrote to Kroeber, "why can't we put him in a case, and have him make arrows....Good exhibit for the public." Kroeber agreed, though he wanted to avoid the implication that he would somehow be "putting him in a case." Ishi would not be put in a case or labeled, though of course "Ishi" was a label, as was "uncontaminated man," for that matter. His position at the museum would not, Kroeber hoped, bear any resemblance to the horrific treatment of the African pygmy Ota Benga, who was once displayed in the Monkey House at the Bronx Zoo. Visitors were supposed to come away with the idea that Ota Benga was a lower form of human being, a "missing link" between *Homo sapiens* and apes and orangutans.[24]

Ishi would always be respectfully introduced to an audience. Kroeber would receive visitors, explain something of Ishi's background and culture, and insist that he was a man in every sense, though his culture was far removed from that of modern Americans. Visitors would be allowed to see him at work crafting artifacts. In the second week of October Kroeber sent announcements to all of the city's newspapers, not just its major dailies like the *Examiner* but also those published for various immigrant communities, such as the *Chinese Free Press,* the *Japanese-American, La France Californien,* and the German weekly *New San Francisco.* In a cover memo he wrote, "Enclosed notice regarding the wild

Indian Ishi being on exhibition at the Museum of Anthropology at the Affiliated Colleges this Sunday afternoon may be of interest to your readers, and I shall be glad to have you mention the fact in your columns." Kroeber and Ishi would be at the museum from 2:00 to 4:30 on Sunday afternoons for the next several weeks.[25]

Kroeber's emphasis on education and edification didn't keep the press from describing Ishi as "a novelty act," "about to enter upon professional life as a one act specialist under the management of the University of California." As many as a thousand people came to Parnassus Heights on any given Sunday. Ishi would sit down to work, drilling fire or making arrowheads. Sometimes he played a guessing game with visitors, inviting boys onto the platform and concealing a small bird bone in one of his hands. They would have to guess which hand it was in. Often school groups would come to visit, and Ishi would greet all of the children. One eleven-year-old schoolgirl was told that Ishi was the last of his tribe: "He shook hands with each and every one of us with a kind sweet smile." At the end of the museum sessions, Ishi would hold up the arrowhead, finished; then he would bequeath it to some lucky visitor. It was as educational and edifying as it could be, and as authentic as possible. "It was obsidian that Ishi used by preference in his wild state," Kroeber wrote, "and it was in obsidian that he demonstrated his skill one Sunday afternoon to more than 1,000 marveling visitors to the museum of anthropology."[26]

The anthropologist went to great lengths to keep Ishi supplied with his native materials for his crafts, even though he knew that Ishi had come to prefer glass for his arrowheads. Whenever any of the university anthropologists went into the field, they were instructed to bring back wood or acorns for Ishi. Kroeber also made connections with whites in various locales who might send what Ishi wanted. He corresponded with a Mr. Green of Santa Cruz: "You will remember me as the man who left Goldman's on the 4 of July and for whom you brought down the bundle of sticks the next day. My Indian was much pleased with the buckeye which makes him fine fire sticks, but he says the black oak is no good to him for any purpose. He says also just what you thought, that hazel makes good arrows and I therefore take the liberty of reminding you of your promise to cut a few straight shoots of hazel for me on your next trip and leaving them at the railroad station to go per Wells Fargo, collect." Despite Kroeber's effort to bring the native landscape of California to Ishi, Ishi was busy collecting materials from San Francisco for his craft. For feathers he made an arrangement with the keeper of the aviary at the Golden Gate Park; he also obtained feathers from wild pheasants and from discarded women's hats and boas. He liked to use metal files. For arrowheads he liked glass. Sometimes, led by his new friend, Dr. Saxton Pope (who took a keen interest in Ishi's archery), he would go down to the city dump, scavenging for empty bottles of beer and Bromo-Seltzer.[27]

Ishi did not drink beer. He did not consume Bromo-Seltzer either, an effervescent elixir invented in the 1880s and sold as a cure for headache. Sales of the fizzy stuff bottled in distinctive blue glass skyrocketed as America urbanized and more and more people sought a quick cure for their headaches brought on by their fast-paced lives. Ishi took these discarded products of industrial America and turned them into arrowheads, at once beautiful and functional. But Kroeber did not much like Ishi's cutting-edge use of Bromo-Seltzer, which in his view lacked authenticity.

Ishi ended up becoming something of a street sweeper, turning the trash of San Franciscans into things he valued. He also literally swept up, serving officially as a janitor at the museum. He would sweep the museum floors, and even tidy things up after a visit from a group of schoolchildren. He gave them arrowheads and then cleaned up the trash they left behind.

Ishi was a craftsman, and that is the role he played at the museum. He was a maker of things, a producer. Americans went to the museum on Sundays in their leisure time and acted as consumers. More and more, American identity would be shaped by consumption, acquiring more and more things and then discarding them just as quickly. It is somehow fitting that someone from the American Society for Thrift, newly formed in 1914 to celebrate producer values and warn against the danger of becoming a consumer republic, gave Ishi a Society pin. Ishi kept it, not because he agreed with their program, but because he liked the button itself, its smooth metal face featuring in red, white, and blue the American flag. Ishi was a consumer, too, though he was also very thrifty with the money he made from janitorial work. And despite Kroeber's intent on making his performances free and open to the public, in January Ishi reportedly began to ask for contributions. The *Oakland Tribune* reported, "The 'uncontaminated' one has become civilized to the extent of knowing that it takes money to buy good things." Eventually Ishi refused to perform until a collection was taken up.[28]

Being a janitor meant cleaning up the dirt and discarded debris of others, and modern Americans tended to stigmatize this activity; waste contaminated those who touched it. Certainly middle-class Americans who could get out to museums saw the work as beneath them. But Kroeber did not think the work was demeaning, and he was certain that Ishi took pride in it. By giving him the job, Kroeber was hoping to do several things. First, he wanted to make Ishi self-sufficient. The budget for the museum was tight, and there was no budgetary code to pay a live-in exhibit. But even if he could manage to cut through bureaucratic red tape and get money allotted for Ishi's support, Kroeber was reluctant to do so. He did not want to pay Ishi for his Sunday demonstrations, for that would turn him into a professional performer. It would smack too much of the traveling circus Kroeber detested. Kroeber would have found such an arrangement demeaning, though Ishi himself seems to have seen no problem being paid to show others how he chipped arrowheads and made fire.

In addition, teaching Ishi this practical skill of sweeping was considered a sign of his acculturation and could be held up as a sign that the museum was taking good care of him. It was preparing him for survival in the city. The Bureau of Indian Affairs was asking about Ishi. Kelsey, the California Indian agent who had granted Kroeber permission to take Ishi from Oroville in the first place, forwarded Kroeber a missive he had received asking after the status and "capacity for civilization" of "Wild Indians":

> Make inquiry with special reference, first, to the possibility of training him to conform, at least to a reasonable degree, to the customs of civilized life; and, second, as to the possibility of training him for the performance of simple manual labor.

The note amounted to bureaucratic dehumanization underlying an official interest in the welfare of the Indian, who was ultimately considered a ward of the government.

Kroeber fired back in kind:

I beg to state that from the outset Ishi has conformed very willingly
and to the full extent of his understanding, to the customs of civilized life. Further that he is now being trained in the performance of
simple manual labor, such as sweeping, dusting, washing windows,
and other janitorial work about the Museum. He is entirely unfit
to take care of himself on account of his understanding practically
no English and not speaking any whatever. He also has shown no
inclination towards the initiative, but appears to look upon himself
as in every sense a dependent who is ready to take orders.

Kroeber thus dehumanized Ishi in return, motivated by a desire
to keep him at the museum and a belief that Ishi was better off
there than in the hands of a government bureaucrat. He also
genuinely believed that Ishi wanted to stay. Kelsey went to see
Ishi in San Francisco and asked him if he would like to go back
to his homeland or live with other Indians under the care of
the U.S. government. According to Kroeber, Ishi said, in Yahi,
"I will live like the white people from now on. I want to stay
where I am. I will grow old here, and die in this house." Kelsey,
noting the "fair amount of work [he does] for his keep," reported
to his superiors, "[Ishi] shows no apparent desire to get away or
return to the wilds."[29]

Giving Ishi the janitorial job was a compromise between ideals and pragmatics, but it seemed to work out all right for Ishi. He
made twenty-five dollars a month, paid to him by a check from
the University of California. Kroeber taught him to write his name
so that he could cash his paychecks. Ishi had found a way to turn
sweeping into silver, a trickle of the stream of wealth the Hearsts
and Sutros had extracted from the mountains. He took the silver

half-dollars he was given, stacked them neatly into discarded film canisters, and deposited them in the safe in Kroeber's office, next to gold artifacts and other museum treasures that visitors might be tempted to walk away with.[30]

The Sunday performances were for the public; the janitorial work was for spending money and for show as well. But behind these tasks there was real work for Kroeber and Ishi to do. It would be the most arduous kind: the work of recording and understanding Ishi's language and culture. There were documents to collect and no time to lose: Ishi was the last Yahi and his culture needed to be extracted form him and put in the university vaults, or it might perish from the earth.

Following his teacher Boas, Kroeber was a pioneer in the use of phonographic technology for salvage anthropology. The heart of his work was to listen to his informants, writing down the narratives they told him and recording their language. The oral performances of stories were flattened into text, and then the text could be taken back to the university. The phonograph, literally, "sound writer," had certain advantages, including preserving the voice of the storyteller or singer. When phonographs first became available they captured the impression of the speaker's or singer's voice on a cylinder of wax, not a plastic disc. Anthropologists soon put Edison's cutting-edge technology to work recording ancient traditions. Each cylinder could record about three minutes of precious sound. Kroeber, Waterman, and other university anthropologists had made some sixteen hundred wax cylinder recordings of songs and stories from across the state by the time Ishi arrived at the museum.[31]

On September 7 Ishi was introduced to the phonograph. The anthropologists, recalling Ishi's wariness of the telephone, thought that he might be frightened by the machine. But after its purpose was explained he readily agreed to speak a story into the phonograph. He chose to tell the story of Wood Duck. Wood Duck decides that he wants a wife, and so he sings his sweet song of seduction, *Wino-tay, wino-tay*. Suitors flock to him. But Wood Duck is very particular: he turns each away, starting with Skunk Woman, who is rejected for her strong smell, of course. Flint Woman, Crane Woman, Beaver Woman, Abalone Woman: all are sent back. Even Turtle Woman, who Ishi said was dressed in elk hide and came from the very place he was speaking, the Affiliated Colleges, was turned away. Ishi, like many California Indian storytellers, was situating the narrative in the local setting, making it relevant and pleasing to his audience, in this case adapting it to the cultural life of the city.

The story went on and on, with each suitor presenting herself and then being turned away. It proceeded in fits and starts, as Waterman had to change the cylinder every three minutes, parsing out the sounds and words of Ishi into a mounting stack of cylinders. The longest recording of a piece of music at the time, Beethoven's Fifth Symphony, considered to be Western civilization's pinnacle of cultural achievement, was just thirty minutes long. The Berkeley anthropologists recorded over two hours of Ishi's command performance, and in the end Wood Duck does find someone to love. Alas the beautiful young woman falls for Lizard instead. Lizard cuts Wood Duck in two, though with the help of his sisters Wood Duck is put back together again.[32]

The sound of Ishi's voice, and parts of his cultural repertoire, were split off and stored away in the fifty-one wax cylinders. Ishi clearly enjoyed telling the story of Wood Duck, with Batwi there and Waterman and the Big Cheap. But it was rude to leave in the middle of the story to take a telephone call, as Waterman had done. Once a story has begun you should stay and listen to it all, he told him through Batwi. Listen to it all the way through, and hear how Lizard, the reliable arrow maker, gets the girl in the end. Waterman put the phone away in a drawer to muffle the incessant ringing. The anthropologists had been dealing with all sorts of inquiries coming in, phone calls about putting Ishi on display or making a movie about him. The anthropologists, too, wanted to make a movie about Ishi, but they did not want to exploit his image for commercial purposes.[33]

An arrangement was finally made with the California Motion Picture Corporation, which was instructed to make an ethnographic, not a sensational, film. It was to record his culture. Ishi was filmed making fire. He was filmed entering and leaving the Yahi dwelling he had constructed on the grounds of the museum. It showed him making an arrowhead of obsidian and stringing a bow and shooting. It showed his hands. And it showed him singeing his hair, performing the way a Yahi cuts his hair, then mourning for the camera. All of this went into the canisters.[34]

Pieces of Yahi culture had been flaked off and put into storage. With the help of electricity, metals, plasters, chemicals, and manmade light, Ishi had been photographed, recorded, measured, and now filmed. As the fifteen hundred feet of film on the reels rolled along—Ishi called film the *lopa pikta* (rope picture)—anyone could see Yahi culture preserved in the shadows and light. But in the recording and presentation there was also an invention. The silver screen, just like the field notebook page, the photographic paper, and the wax cylinder, reflected one's own projections. Ishi was full of treasures and surprises, but so were the people who were looking at him for something. Those treasures and surprises—compassion for one's fellow man, repulsion for modern civilization, a desire to be wild themselves—came to the surface when they presumed to be only looking at Ishi.[35]

After hours and in between recording sessions, Ishi went on making arrowheads, went on making arrows, went on making fire, and started making friends as he made his way into his new world.

The reporters were the first to ask all of the basic questions about Ishi: What is his name? His age? Is he mentally a child? Is he a lower form of human? What is he? The social evolutionists had their answers: Indians like Ishi represented a lower stage of human development, and their elevation on the ladder of humanity was determined by their heredity, what scientists were just beginning to call genetics. But Kroeber didn't believe in that; he saw clearly Ishi's intelligence. He rehearsed his answer to such questions Sunday afternoons at the museum, and then he wrote it all up for a popular magazine, the *World's Work*. He began the article with his vignette of Ishi stepping off the ferry boat into the "glare of electric lights" on Market Street. He ended it with an assessment of Ishi's place in modern culture: "The strange history of this survivor of the past seems to show that intelligence is not the monopoly of civilization. . . . Ishi has as good a head as the average American." Here was Kroeber's attempt at descalping:

Indians were as smart as whites were, not inferior in intellect. But, Kroeber added, he is also "unspeakably ignorant. He knows nothing, or knew nothing, six months ago, of hours and years, of money and labor and pay, of government and authority, of newspapers and business, of nine hundred and ninety of the other thousand things that go to make up our life."

Though Ishi had "lived in the stone age," Kroeber explained, this did not "involve a semi-animal, brutal, merely instinctive, and inferior mental capacity." But his culture had not given him the same opportunity that modern Western culture had given its sons and daughters. "Ishi himself is no nearer the 'missing link' or any antecedent form of human life than we are." Kroeber attributed difference not to race but to culture, but he did arrange those on a scale: "[In what Ishi's] environment, his associates, and his puny native civilization have made him, he represents a stage through which our ancestors passed thousands of years ago, and which is therefore as significant when understood as it is remarkable to have preserved until today." But in the published article, the magazine chopped off Kroeber's concluding clause, altering the impact. The magazine left the reader with an image of Ishi living in a "stage which our ancestors passed thousands of years ago." A chasm between "us" and Ishi is opened up: difference, hierarchy, and historical distance is what the reader is left with. In Kroeber's original version, Ishi's culture has remarkably survived, and it is imperative for us to try to understand it, to treat with care what Ishi carried with him.[36]

But what did Kroeber mean by "puny native civilization"? It is not a neutral evaluation. Did "puny" pop into his mind because the scale of San Francisco was ever expanding—outward and

upward, like modern civilization—while the Yahi world had contracted to a few small dwellings concealed by laurel trees? In 1911
San Francisco was on the march, midway between its leveling in
the earthquake of 1906 and the 1915 Panama Pacific International
Exposition, its party celebrating its coming out on the world
stage. Reporters had even suggested that Ishi might be able to give
the exposition planners some ideas from his fresh perspective on
the city. They certainly expected him to be impressed. But to Ishi,
used to the mountain Wahganupa and the deep cañons of Deer
and Mill creeks, the city might indeed appear to be "puny, scarce
worthy of comment."[37]

San Franciscans were busy rebuilding the city and giving it
a face-lift, hoping to create buildings that were so artistic, substantial, and timeless that the city would live up to its imperial
ambitions and put to rest any notion that it was but an over-
grown mining camp. To cap their efforts, artworks were being
installed all over the city, statues honoring Greek gods and white
pioneers. Each time a new statue went up, there was a big celebration. Theodore Roosevelt even came to one.

It was just this kind of imperial civic pride manifested in statuary that Charlie Chaplin, who got his start in movies in Niles
Cañon just months after Ishi had sped by on that fateful train
ride into the city, poked fun at years later in his masterpiece, *City
Lights* (1931). In Niles Cañon, Chaplin had first created the figure of the little tramp, a hobo who dressed in a refined suit with
tails but that was ragged and fit badly, the archetypal outsider in
the city. *City Lights* opens with the unveiling of a new statue, but
the celebration is spoiled: the cover is raised to reveal the homeless tramp sleeping and snoring on it, a deprecating gesture akin

to young Kroeber's painting raccoon stripes on the statuary of Central Park.[38]

In *City Lights* a blind flower girl mistakes the little tramp for a wealthy businessman, and he doesn't have the heart to correct her. Instead he plays the role and even decides to get together the money she needs for an operation to restore her sight. He tries earning money as a street sweeper. He even tries boxing for money, but is clobbered. Finally, through a friendship with a drunkard millionaire whom the tramp saves from suicide, he obtains the money the flower seller needs for the operation. He gives it to her, even though he knows that when she lays her restored eyes on her pathetic patron, she will likely send him away, as Wood Duck did to so many.

Chaplin, the tramp trickster, together with the blind flower girl are outsiders in the city, but they are the ones who ultimately reveal and redeem its heart. She cannot see, but is more perceptive than the civic leaders, recognizing the nobility in the man that others fail to see because of his appearance. He has no place of his own and no money, but is actually more generous than the wealthy elite. When the girl's sight is restored and she sees him, she asks, "You?" He responds with a complex smile—hopefulness, embarrassment, astonishment, appreciation for her and the wonders of life, all mixed together on his face.

It is precisely the way Ishi often smiled, as when he gave an arrowhead to someone who had come to see him work or when he looked up at an airplane and queried, "Saltu??" The newspapers may have tried to make a joke of Ishi, but his strong presence and his ability to laugh at the city's leading lights—his pantomime communication, often done without words—made him a trickster in the imperial city. The effect of Ishi was precisely the effect of Chaplin.

Herb Samuels and Fred Burton, dental students at the Affiliated Colleges, ate their lunch together on the lawn, and while they were eating "quite often Ishi would stroll over to [them]." They would exchange greetings and give him a sandwich or a piece of coconut layer cake, which was a favorite. They admired Ishi's "perfect denture" and paid him fifty cents to make plaster casts of his extraordinary teeth, kept perfect, they thought, from his native diet of acorn gruel—at least until he got to San Francisco, with its cakes and ice cream. Herb and Fred enjoyed hanging out with Ishi. After lunch Ishi would "take pebbles, gravel from this path and let them filter through his hands and pick the right size and put it on the finger nail of his thumb and aim it at a light pole across the street. And he hit it every time."[39]

· *Six* ·

NATURE WALKS IN THE CITY
AND THE SIERRAS

❋

IN FEBRUARY 1912 KROEBER AND ISHI RECEIVED AN INTRIGUING invitation. This was not to see a vaudeville show or attend a ceremony. Instead they were invited to explore on foot nature in the city:

> A party of fifty or more of the Sierra Club will start from the Baker St. entrance of the park at 9.30 on the morning of Washington's Birthday on a seven mile walk by way of Buena Vista Park and Twin Peaks through the Sutro Forest to the Anthropological Museum.

"We shall be most happy to receive the parties from the Sierra club," Kroeber replied. "As to Ishi we shall be very glad to have him a member of the company for the day provided I or some one from the Museum can accompany him."[1]

Harold French headed the local walks committee of the Sierra Club, and he had been doing a splendid job organizing these rambles through the woods. They were very popular that year, better attended than ever, and brought more and more San Franciscans into the ranks of the Sierra Club. The Sierrans preferred to walk on the wild side of the state, in the mountain range from which they took their name. But they certainly enjoyed their walks through the San Francisco parks and over the forested Sutro Peak that stood above the museum. The Sierrans could forget that these lands had once been a potato patch supplying the Gold Rush city with sustenance. They were now well forested, for when Adolpho Sutro owned the mountain he had schoolchildren plant it with eucalyptus trees, a nonnative species imported from Australia. French called it "a mountain wilderness in the city's heart." He would have pointed out to Ishi the geology of the mountain and its eucalyptus, pine, and cypress trees; the mining shaft sunk by some old miner and the "poppies, floral nuggets of great beauty"; the hundred-yard wall of stone presumed to have been made by a "pre-historic people"; the caves half hidden by vines "in which a man might live in comfort"; and how you could look out from the high forest for a panoramic look at the vast civilization below and hear the whistle of the train.[2]

Twenty years before this ramble through the woods, 180 men and women—naturalists, University of California professors, lawyers, businessmen—gathered in a San Francisco law office and formed the Sierra Club, which would become America's signature environmental organization. The club elected the bearded, charismatic naturalist John Muir to be its first president. He would become America's most famous environmentalist, a wild man who captured America's imagination.

Born in Scotland, Muir moved to a farm in Wisconsin when he was eleven. He worked hard for his father growing crops, but his great love was technology. By the age of sixteen he was inventing

barometers, hydrometers, and clocks. Many of his gadgets had to do with time and work. An ingenious alarm clock tilted the bed of the slumberer when it was time to get up; a mechanical reader opened up a new book at a desk at set intervals. His skills soon came in handy in the business world, and Muir got a job in a carriage factory in Indianapolis, where he made improvements to the machinery. While he was fixing a belt one day a file slipped and struck him in the eye. Muir went blind.[3]

In the darkness he contemplated his future. Mercifully his vision came back, and a grateful Muir gave up mechanical inventions and dedicated himself "to the study of the inventions of God." Through walking he would find his salvation. He set out

---

Ishi and Kroeber's San Francisco, looking west from the Affiliated Colleges. Legend: 1—The Museum of Anthropology, the westernmost of the three main buildings of the Affiliated Colleges of the University of California; 2—Hugo Street, where Ishi did his shopping, passing by the home of Marcella Healy along the way; 3—Golden Gate Park, at the buffalo paddock; 4—The home of Fred Zumwalt Jr., who with Ishi would walk around Mountain Lake and visit patients at the Marine Hospital; 5—The Cliff House and the Sutro Baths, just south of the terminus of the Lincoln Highway; 6—Ocean Beach, where Ishi first beheld a crowd of San Franciscans and exclaimed "Hansi saltu" and where Kroeber walked after the funeral of his first wife, Henriette; 7—Beginning point and general route of the Sierra Club walk with Ishi, February 1912. Ishi and Kroeber also traveled to downtown and other parts of the city and across the San Francisco Bay by ferry to the main campus of the University of California. Base map is detail from The "Chevalier" Commercial, Pictorial and Tourist Map of San Francisco from Latest U.S. Gov. and Official Surveys *(Aug. Chevalier, Lithographer Publisher, San Francisco, 1911). From the David Rumsey Map Collection. Copyright 2000 by Cartography Associates.*

in search of wilderness, walking south a thousand miles to the Gulf of Mexico. Eventually he made his way to Panama, where he boarded a steamer bound for San Francisco in 1868. He spent one day in the bustling city and then desperately asked a man what was the best way to get out of town. "But where do you want to go?" the man asked. "To any place that is wild," Muir replied. Muir suspected that the man thought he might be crazy. He quickly directed Muir to take the ferry across the Bay to Oakland, which he did; from there, he walked east across California's Great Central Valley toward the Sierras, toward Yosemite.[4]

Muir fell in love with Yosemite, seeing it as a pristine wilderness where he could find meaning and inspiration. He became the great spokesperson for the wilderness idea, eloquently sanctifying these landscapes and fighting for their protection. He saw himself as a champion of nature imperiled by encroaching civilization. "Let a Christian hunter go to the Lord's woods and kill his well-kept beasts, or wild Indians, and it is well," he wrote. But there was no toleration for Indians or animals fighting back. "I have precious little sympathy for the selfish propriety of civilized man," Muir said. In a fit of species treason, he proclaimed his allegiance to the wild: "If a war of races should occur between the wild beasts and Lord Man, I would be tempted to sympathize with the bears."[5]

Muir revered bears, but just how much he sympathized with Indians is an open question. He admired their ability to gather food from the land but did not recognize how much they had done to shape the landscape he regarded as untouched wilderness. The fact that the valley floor of Yosemite featured acorn-bearing oaks and open prairies was a result of land management by Indians using fire.

For Muir, Indians were picturesque parts of the landscape, not shapers of it; they were little different from birds or bears. Such dehumanization, coming from the sometime misanthropic Muir, was not intended as an insult. Yet Muir's identification of Indians with the natural landscape was sometimes knowingly insulting. During his first summer in Yosemite he encountered a group of Paiute Indians on their way to the valley. They asked for tobacco and whiskey, but Muir insisted that he had none and looked at the Indians as fallen beings: "[These] specimens [were] mostly ugly, and some of them altogether hideous. The dirt on their faces was fairly stratified, and seemed so ancient and so undisturbed it might almost possess a geological significance." Muir made no effort to understand culturally why the dirt was there: Was it used in part to mask human scent and aid in hunting? Wilderness represented cleanliness to Muir; it was pristine. Indians, especially those he found ugly and dirty, polluted his ideal vision. "Nothing truly wild is unclean," he maintained. To Muir these Indians were "dirt-specks" mucking up his wilderness, desecrating his temple. "Somehow they seemed to have no right place in the landscape," he wrote, "and I was glad to see them fading out of sight down the pass."[6]

That same perspective was adopted by the managers of the national parks: they would prefer to see Indians, if at all, as "fading out of sight." Yellowstone and Glacier saw violent expulsions of Indians, whom park managers came to see as a threat to wildlife. With the active involvement of the army, park administrators made sure that Indians "had no right place in the landscape"—or rather, that their rights to hunt and gather in the landscape, many of which had been secured by treaty, were violated and nullified.

But a particular place was reserved for Indians by park officials and promoters, who wanted them to add a romantic element to the wilderness scenery; they were to act as "specimens of a Great Race soon to disappear."[7]

After Glacier National Park was created in 1910, the Blackfeet were told that their traditional hunting grounds were now off-limits. The park superintendent vigorously enforced these rules, hoping to increase the population of deer and elk and other wild-life. He even tried to prevent the Blackfeet from hunting elk on their own reservation, arguing that those animals had "originated in the Park" (which bordered the Blackfeet reservation because the park's lands had been carved out of their reservation). Many Blackfeet resisted these proscriptions, but in the government's drive to promote uninhabited wilderness, the Blackfeet were driven off the backcountry of the park. In return some were given jobs as performers for tourists. When they appealed, citing treaty rights, they were told that the treaties no longer applied because Glacier had become a national park. Before, progress and development had been cited as a reason that the Blackfeet must cede land; now the U.S. government was saying that the need to protect pristine nature—a nature that the government outsiders depicted as unaltered by man—took precedence. Any footprints of the tribe must be removed from the landscape in order to support the story that no one had ever really lived there.[8]

In a novel the Blackfeet writer James Welch describes a young man's first encounter with the *napikwan,* the Americans, at a fort where a treaty council was to be held. The young man "looked up the pole beside him and saw the red and white flag with the patch of blue in the corner. The white sharp-pointed designs on the blue represented the many territories conquered by the Napikwans." One star represented Montana, but another star might have been added to represent Glacier National Park, a place the whites called the Crown Jewel of the Continent, now secured for wilderness preservation and white tourism in the American empire.[9]

Some Indians tried to make their living by working for the tourist industry. Blackfeet performed dances at the hotels and greeted visitors at the railroad station. The Great Northern Railroad was the main private promoter of the park and sent Blackfeet Indians—it dubbed them the "Glacier Park Indians"—on a traveling junket, complete with tepees that were set up on skyscraper rooftops in New York, Chicago, and San Francisco. Arriving in San Francisco in time for the Panama Pacific Exposition, these traveling Blackfeet would meet Ishi in person.[10]

The Central Miwok Indians were at first forced out of the spectacular Yosemite Valley, then they made a reappearance. Their caches of acorns were burned by militia, and some of the Indians of the area turned to making a living off of the thousands of white tourists. They sold fish and strawberries, made baskets for tourists, and did a brisk trade. Many of the tourists, seeking a true wilderness experience, enjoyed the chance to meet real Indians. The Miwok found a way to make a living from this interest, charging a dime or a half-dollar to allow the Kodak-carrying visitors to snap their picture. The baskets and images were collected as tokens of a wilderness experience, one far removed in geography and time from modern America. The Indians of the park no longer lived off the land but off of images.

The Park Superintendent barred hunting in the backcountry of Yosemite. Park officials were like the sheriff depicted in the

Examiner cartoon arresting Ishi for hunting with a bow and arrow. It was these very proscriptions on hunting and gathering, so central to the Miwok way of life, that roused Alfred Kroeber to complain to Agent Kelsey back in 1906, pointing out that the park regulations were preventing the Indians from maintaining "their old ways of living." Instead they were to become part of the wilderness pleasure ground, bit players on the set. They were expected to become ghost-like images of themselves, two-dimensional actors who would complete the picture of a romantic wilderness landscape for two bits a shot, or less.[11]

Ishi may have walked the city's wilderness with the Sierra Club, but he also walked it on his own. During his first few weeks Kroeber put limits on how far from the museum he could wander. But as he learned a few words in English, Ishi ventured farther and farther away. He learned how to ride the trolley on his own, and he would take the Number 6 down to the Ferry Building, and then take a ferry over to the East Bay to visit Thomas and Grace Waterman at their home in Berkeley. Waterman showed Ishi the expansive campus of the University of California, and the two walked along Strawberry Creek, past the Faculty Glade to the anthropology building. Waterman brought him to his classes, and Ishi demonstrated making fire to rapt students.

A year after Ishi came to San Francisco, Kroeber hired Edward Gifford as a curator at the museum. Kroeber sent him to do fieldwork among the Central Miwok of the Yosemite area. Gifford and his wife, Delila, lived in the East Bay near the university campus, and Ishi befriended them as well. Ishi often went on walks with Delila, in the hills, looking for birds. The two sat on the ground,

waiting for the birds to come to them. Ishi made bird calls, and
Delila looked on with fascination. But Ishi was also impressed by
Delila's whistling. At home she whistled popular songs, recorded
them, and played them back for her canaries to learn. As these
songbirds were then in vogue with "Hollywood people," Delila
was able to add to the Giffords' income. Many plants in the hills
above Berkeley were different from the ones Ishi grew up among,
but he could identify several wild varieties, much to Delila's
delight. She transplanted a few of them to her own garden, giving them Yahi names. Delila's garden reflected a growing interest white Californians were developing in the native plants of the
state, and in this she was aided by a native guide to that native
landscape.[12]

Back in San Francisco the Museum of Anthropology had its
gardens, too, and Ishi even did some work weeding them as part
of his janitorial duties. But he spent much more time wandering
through the gardens of the nearby Golden Gate Park. He sometimes walked alone through this expansive park that stretched
from the foot of Parnassus Heights westward all the way to the
Pacific. There he found the quail he had seen from the automobile ride, and many other small animals.

Near the park's aviary was a special paddock that held several
large animals Ishi had never seen before: buffalo. Where had they
come from? In 1890 the population of buffalo had dropped to
just over a thousand. Whites suddenly were shocked at the near
obliteration of the once numerous animals; Indians were devastated. Their sorrow was reflected in the spread of a new religion
in the 1880s, the Ghost Dance. The Ghost Dance was inspired by
the visions of an Indian prophet named Wovoka, a Paiute, one

"In Golden Gate Park, Showing Affiliated Colleges, University of California."
Postcard, 1899. Courtesy of the San Francisco Public Library.

of the tribe that Muir had described as "mostly ugly, and some of them altogether hideous." Wovoka taught the Indians to do a special dance, which would bring back their world. He prophesied that a cataclysm would shake the continent, whites would disappear, and the buffalo would all return. The Lakotas sang hopefully, "Over the whole earth they are coming. The buffalo are coming, the buffalo are coming." But the U.S. government was apprehensive about this millenarian religion and decided to stamp it out. In their efforts to repress the Ghost Dance, U.S. Army soldiers opened fire on a group of Lakota believers at

Wounded Knee in South Dakota in 1890, killing more than two hundred men, women, and children. The Lakota would never forget Wounded Knee, nor would they give up hope that the buffalo would one day return.[13]

In response to the demise of the buffalo, some whites drew on conservation rather than religion, and started captive breeding programs. San Franciscans brought a small group of buffalo to the Golden Gate Park for safekeeping in 1891. One of the bulls was swapped for one from Buffalo Bill's Wild West Show when he came to town in 1902. But the bull given to Buffalo Bill escaped and ran into Sutro Forest above the Affiliated Colleges; fifty cowboys were dispatched to bring him back. The park's herd was augmented by birth. (A crowd gathered when a cow named Sarah Burnhardt give birth; the calf was to be named Buffalo Bill until it was discovered that the new buffalo was a female.) A few more were transported to Golden Gate Park from Yellowstone National Park in 1905. There were almost thirty buffalo in the park when Ishi first saw them. To the white civilization that had nearly exterminated them, these buffalo preserved in the park's paddock represented a hope of redemption. Some saw the great animals as pets, others as emblems of wild America.[14]

The park staff befriended Ishi. The aviary keeper gave him feathers for his arrows. A gardener gave him slips of roses and fuchsia, which Ishi brought to others as gifts. For Ishi the park was a rich landscape composed of people, plants, and animals he came to know. Often he had friends along for his walks in the park. One was a new doctor at the university hospital, Saxton Pope. Pope had seen Ishi a few times at the hospital, but one day he saw him working on arrows on the lawn of the museum. Pope was fascinated; he had made bows as a child in Texas and wanted to recapture the magic of a child's desire to play at being Indian.

Pope approached Ishi and, using sign language, asked if they might shoot arrows together. Pope became Ishi's student; he watched every step of the process of making bows and arrows, recording it faithfully. He watched Ishi shoot arrows and studied his methods. Ishi liked "Popey," and the two soon were walking into the park together, perhaps even shooting arrows at quail or squirrels. Ishi called out to the birds and small animals, imitating their sounds. He could wait for them to come to him. Pope had much to learn, especially about being quiet and patient. "My love for archery blossomed again," Pope wrote. Through Ishi's eyes, Pope lived out a fantasy, playing Indian in Golden Gate Park and searching for a sense of authenticity through archery. Pope took Ishi to see Buffalo Bill's Wild West extravaganza when it came back to San Francisco. At the show Ishi met one of the Sioux performers, and Pope was pleased to report that Ishi made a very favorable impression on him. "He is a very high grade of Indian," the Sioux said. That's what Pope and Kroeber thought, too. In turn, Ishi thought the Sioux showman was a Big Cheap, like Pope and Kroeber.[15]

"[Ishi] was my teacher in the old, old art of the chase," Pope acknowledged. Soon Pope was hoping to make trips with Ishi out of the city, perhaps even back to the Yahi homeland, where Ishi might show him how to shoot a deer. In the meantime Pope set up targets and practiced. Using a longer and more powerful English long bow, Pope found that he could send arrows sailing farther, and with more accuracy, than could Ishi with his Yahi bow. Ishi could shoot a squirrel at forty yards, but was unaccustomed to shooting at flat targets with their rings of color. He complained that the colors were distracting and that they sent his arrows in the wrong direction. Ishi changed the paint on his arrows in response, but he did not take up the long bow. "Too much *man-nee*," he said; *too much bow*.[16]

Prompted by the editor of the outdoor magazine *Forest and Stream*, Pope set up competitions with Ishi, shooting formal rounds and keeping track of scores. Pope was quite pleased to have been Ishi's student, and then to prove that, with a superior bow and a complete understanding of the "optics and ballistics of archery" (something that Ishi, "in common with all savages," could not grasp), he could surpass the master, at least in the abstract form of archery that is target shooting. But even as Pope bested Ishi in the archery competition, he saw him as someone who could teach him, and the culture he was part of, valuable lessons about nature, truth, and wisdom. Pope believed, "[Ishi] looked upon us as sophisticated children—smart, but not wise. We knew many things and much that is false. He knew nature, which is always true."[17]

Ishi enjoyed his time with the sophisticated child Pope, but he especially lit up around actual children. Dorothy Stevens was ten years old when she met Ishi at the museum. They played jacks, and he later visited her home. "I thought him one of the nicest men I had ever met," she remembered. "He did not treat me as a child—but, as an adult." On his way to do his shopping for food and sundries on Hugo Street, he passed by the homes of Marcella Healy and her friend Bess on the hill on Third Avenue. On his way down Ishi would carry one of them "papoose style." The next day the other would get to ride. The girls weren't allowed to cross the street, so they would wait at the bottom of the hill for Ishi to come back from shopping. The three would walk up the block together on the sidewalk. They would sometimes rest on Marcella's front steps. Ishi carved each of them a wooden doll. Marcella cherished hers, and she passed the doll on to her own children, along with stories of Ishi.[18]

Ishi formed a special friendship with a young boy named Fred Zumwalt Jr. Fred lived next to Mountain Lake, located on the uncultivated and undeveloped grounds of the Presidio (an army base that would eventually become a national park). Their walks began with a visit to the Zumwalts' kitchen, where Fred's mother supplied them with cookies, chocolate, and jerky. The jerky could have been some that Ishi himself made, for Fred's father once brought home a freshly killed steer and asked Ishi to show him how to make it into the tasty dried meat. The two hikers would then visit the Zumwalts' garden, where Ishi was particularly interested in the growth of fuchsia and rose plants that he had brought to Fred's mother from Golden Gate Park.

With Fred's pet chipmunk in Ishi's pocket the two would walk around the lake. They would climb the pine tree and look at birds' nests. They gathered watercress and nasturtium leaves, and Ishi taught Fred to "suck the sweetness from the blossoms." They gathered berries and called quail. Fred learned to walk silently and learned respect for the animals. Their walks also brought them by the Marine Hospital, and the two paid visits to patients who were out convalescing in the hospital's sunny garden. Ishi and Fred shared their chocolate and cookies with them.

Fred himself was often ill as a child, and sometimes he couldn't go for walks. But he could see Ishi from his window when he was out by the lake. Ishi would wave to him and smile. He brought Fred samples of soil from different points around the lake. He taught Fred to smell the soil, really smell it, so that he could tell one from another just with his nose. He then drew a map of the lake and showed Fred where each sample had come from. Another time, Ishi brought him leaves of grass on which two butterfly cocoons were attached. They put them in a glass jar in Fred's room and watched the butterfly emerge from the chrysalis. Under Ishi's guidance Fred was learning the science of the land, having a childhood that paralleled young Alfred Kroeber's, who also gathered butterflies. When the butterflies emerged Ishi and Fred set them free. Indeed Ishi did not approve of keeping animals in cages, and eventually even the chipmunk was set free. Only once did Ishi become angry with Fred, when he smashed some frogs for no reason. "Then he really thundered," Fred recalled in shame.

For young boys of the time playing Indian was a popular pastime. All across the country Boy Scouts were trying on Indian identities and learning to shoot arrows. Fred's walks with Ishi around the lake, learning the songs of the birds and the uses of plants, as wonderful as they were, did not match his dreams. He wanted there to be a tepee, and his father obliged by making one and putting it up near the lake. As Fred remembered, "[Ishi and I] played at being Indians to which he good naturedly gave in. It must have amused him to 'play' at being an Indian; particularly when he would submit to being scalped, burned at the stake etc." But Ishi also got his turn to scalp young Fred. For Ishi the friendship transcended this postmodern playacting. Everybody seemed to want to be an Indian, whether they were an adult like Pope or a child like Fred.

Ishi had a chance to play, too, and learn about other cultures. On Chinese New Year in 1915 the Chinese man who did the Zumwalt family's laundry brought Fred a present: a dragon kite. The man, whom Ishi nicknamed "Kite," taught him how to fly it. As Fred recalled, "We must have been a sight to watch, the Chinese with black baggy pants, wearing a queue, a black skull cap and felt slippers, Ishi in a scotch plaid wool shirt, but barefoot, and I in a sailor suit."[19]

Ishi's beloved Scottish plaid shirt was a gift from John McLaren, the superintendent of Golden Gate Park. The plaid was most likely in the McLaren clan colors and pattern, and thus it made Ishi an honorary Scot. McLaren had been born in Scotland and early on developed a love of trees and plants. "Work and life in a good garden were the nicest things I could think of as a boy, and I've not changed my mind," he recalled. He was a good friend of fellow Scot John Muir, and the two often hiked together in the Sierras. From these trips McLaren brought back ideas for the city park. On one occasion Muir brought McLaren to a waterfall in a gorge in Yosemite. Looking up at the falls, Muir teased McLaren, "You've nothing like that in your park John." McLaren responded, "No but we will have." In 1894, using money donated by the railroad magnate Collis P. Huntington, McLaren created a 110-foot waterfall cascading down the east side of Strawberry Hill into Stow Lake. Water was then pumped back up the hill to keep this one-twentieth scale model of the Yosemite Falls going year round.[20]

Unlike in Yosemite, the water for Huntington Falls did not fall from the sky; it was provided by a private corporation, the

Spring Valley Water Company. Spring Valley monopolized the water supply for the city. Situated on a peninsula surrounded on three sides by salt water, the city was parched from its beginnings. During the 1850s San Franciscans often bought their water by the barrel from sailing ships. In 1851 a company was formed to supply the city with water from Mountain Lake, the lake that Ishi and Fred walked around. By the 1860s Spring Valley, whose stock was owned by railroad magnates Huntington and Leland Stanford and other wealthy men, had swallowed several water companies to become the city's primary supplier. It had its fist around the city's water hose and could squeeze it dry if it was crossed. The company erected dams, flumes, and conduits throughout the region south of San Francisco, building up a supply for the city. It made astronomical profits. Like the railroad, Spring Valley eventually would be seen as an octopus; rather than supplying the country with transportation and water, the monopolistic companies were portrayed as sucking the life blood out of the land and its people. Henry George, a fierce critic of monopoly, complained, "Water in San Francisco costs more than bread, more than light."[21]

In return for providing water, the private company was granted enormous power, including that of eminent domain: it could take over land and water rights from private individuals. In return the company was supposed to provide water at reasonable rates to city customers and throw in free water for Golden Gate Park. A vast amount of water was a necessary ingredient for the park, for San Francisco's answer to New York's Central Park was built on an arid landscape once called the Sand Dunes. City developers envisioned a grand park in the 1860s, bigger than New York's, and grander as well. They even hired the designer of

Central Park for the project, Frederick Law Olmsted, who was in California managing the newly created state park at Yosemite.[22]

In a report he wrote in 1865, Olmsted celebrated the wonders of Yosemite, which he insisted were beyond the power of words or photographs to adequately represent. He wrote about all of the valley's features, but his description, he admitted, fell flat in comparison to the grandeur of the place itself. He was one of America's most fervent promoters of nature. If Americans, pressed by business in the city, could not get out into places like the Sierras, they should have a park in their city where they could contemplate "natural scenes of an impressive character." Science, Olmsted insisted, had proven that if men and women were shut off from nature, they would not only lose the capacity to be happy, but they would experience a "softening of the brain." In Olmsted's view, Americans deprived of green scenery would be driven mad, succumbing to a kind of nature-deficit disorder. Olmsted saw urban parks as the antidote to the ills of modernity; he wanted to provide to urban-bound Americans a transplanted experience of Yosemite, "the greatest glory of nature," he called it, right in the midst of their city's high-rises.[23]

But when he looked at the sand dune site San Franciscans had in mind for a park and heard their dream of creating a lush and even larger Central Park of the West there, Olmsted balked. The city should not to try to deny the arid reality, but instead create a park that would work with the climatic conditions of the region and be accessible to more of its population. A greenbelt should be built crossing the city, and the landscape should use drought-resistant trees and shrubs, he thought. But the city leaders wanted a big park that would make a big statement, and they would accept no compromise with nature—or Olmsted, for that matter. So they hired an engineer, William Hammond Hall, to give them a thousand acres of lawns, trees, and gardens where the sand dunes currently stood.

After much experimentation, Hall found a way to anchor the blowing sands of the site, first planting barley and then lupine to keep the landscape from blowing away. All of the manure from the streets of San Francisco went to the park as fertilizer, and soon an amazing transformation was taking place. As if out of thin air a verdant landscape of hills, streams, lakes, forests, and meadows appeared. Hundreds of thousands of trees were planted. But this reinvented landscape depended on having more water. Hall himself recognized the costly implications of his creation. "Water is required for some large city," he wrote, "and forthwith an area many times as great is robbed of its rivulets and brooks—and its fertility—to supply the demand, and the consequences are not seriously considered." In this way Golden Gate Park symbolized the relationship between the metropolis and its hinterland, a region that had to pay tribute, in the form of natural resources, to the big city.[24]

Suddenly Spring Valley reneged on its promise to supply a free flow of water to the park, and the city was left scrambling. When large bills came due for the water, the city began looking for an alternative source, one that would be publicly owned and that would fuel unlimited urban growth. When the earthquake hit in 1906 and there wasn't enough water to put out fires, the drive for more water became an obsession. Mayor James Phelan and others had their eyes on a site within the boundaries of Yosemite National Park, a glacier-formed valley, rimmed with granite walls and waterfalls called Hetch Hetchy, second in grandeur only to Yosemite itself. Dam the mouth of the valley, build a 150-mile aqueduct, and the city would have all the water it could ever want.[25]

John Muir, outraged, campaigned to stop San Francisco. He preached about the beauty and sanctity of the valley. But rhetoric alone could not win the point; after all, he was fighting a plan backed by money and power. He needed recruits, and luckily he had been creating a following ever since the Sierra Club formed in 1892. He was wildly successful in promoting his vision of the mountains as a restorative and renewable Eden for urban Americans. In 1901 he noted, "Thousands of tired, nerve-shaken, over-civilized people are beginning to find out that going to the mountains is going home; that wildness is a necessity." In effect they were following in Muir's own footsteps, for his own nervous anxiety had been cured by wilderness. Sometimes they were literally following in his footsteps, hiking—or, as he preferred to call it, "sauntering"—through the mountains on trips organized by the Sierra Club.[26]

"Lured by the call of the wild," the Sierrans headed to Hetch Hetchy for the High Trip of 1911. First, beginning at the Oakland Mole, the terminal through which Ishi would come for the first time in a few months, they boarded a train to cross the Central Valley to the edge of Yosemite, where they would set off on foot. After more than a week of hiking and climbing, the trip culminated with "two days...spent in luxurious idleness" in Hetch Hetchy. It was a time for solemn and purposeful reflection. "As we left the valley early in the morning," wrote the author of the official narrative of the trip, "each breathed a silent prayer that this temple of the gods, with its stupendous walls and magnificent falls, its picturesque oaks sheltering innumerable birds ... should not be transformed into an unsightly storage reservoir to satisfy the as yet unjustified demand of a municipality at the irreparable expense of the nation."[27]

When the Sierrans wrote about the "expense of the nation," they did not mean the Miwok, who would be taxed completely out of their Hetch Hetchy homeland so that it could become a wilderness retreat or a reservoir to slake the city's thirst for growth. Alfred Kroeber had researched the Indian origins of California place-names, and reported that Hetch Hetchy got its name from the Miwok term for a kind of grass that grew in its lower meadow, a grass that bore edible seeds, gathered by Indians for food. Women often used woven fans to harvest the tiny grass grains. But by 1911 many of the native grasses had already retreated from the valley, pushed out by the disturbing presence of sheep, which at once decimated the native grasses and helped spread invasive species. Harvesting the seeds of grasses for food was something any native California was accustomed to, and it led to one of the early scenes of cross-cultural confusion when Ishi came to the museum in San Francisco. Smiling at Ishi's misconception, newspapers reported that when he saw the gardener picking flowers and cutting the grass, he made signs asking if he were collecting something to eat.[28]

To whites in the city, nature had become an ornament, a piece of scenery, something to be consumed mentally, not physically. Gardens themselves were grown not for food, but to demonstrate the wealth and power of the gardener. As the Berkeley economist Thorstein Veblen pointed out at the time, there was a kind of conspicuous cultivation that went along with conspicuous consumption. The lawns of the university, growing outside the windows of Veblen, Kroeber, and Ishi, were at once a sign of modern Americans' desire to be close to nature and a sign of their alienation from it, as were the parks of the city and the national parks in the mountains; they were places where they could again see for themselves the natural world they had shut out of so much of their lives. Their alienation from nature fueled their desire to preserve pieces of the landscape as protected wilderness.[29]

Muir recognized this and welcomed the urbanites into the mountains, even as he also gently mocked them. "Even the scenery habit in its most artificial forms," he said, "mixed with spectacles, silliness, and kodaks; its devotees arrayed more gorgeously than scarlet tanagers, frightening the wild game with red umbrellas,— even this is encouraging, and may well be regarded as a hopeful sign of the times." Yosemite and Hetch Hetchy became the wilderness counterparts of Golden Gate Park. (Such places were only "half wild.") They were places where San Franciscans could go to get away from it all. When proponents of the scheme to dam Hetch Hetchy said that the dam would enhance the valley's beauty by creating a picturesque alpine lake, Muir shot back angrily, "As well say damming New York's Central Park would enhance its beauty!" They would be outraged if someone tried to convert Central Park or Golden Gate Park into a reservoir; they should be doubly outraged if they tried to drown Hetch Hetchy.[30]

Muir certainly was. The mountain parks were all the more worth fighting for, more sacred, because they had been shaped by God, not man. He called the proponents of the dam "Satan and Co." and fought for the wilderness with lyrical paeans to the sanctity of wilderness. "These temple destroyers, devotees of ravaging commercialism, seem to have a perfect contempt for Nature, and, instead of lifting their eyes to the mountains, lift them to dams and town skyscrapers," he scolded in one of his fire-and-granite sermons. Muir worshipped at the altar of Nature; his opponents, he claimed, worshipped civilization and its works.

Though Muir's words may have persuaded many about the sanctity of wilderness, ultimately he lost out to his pro–urban growth opponents. In 1913 Congress authorized Hetch Hetchy to be submerged to supply San Francisco with water and power. Before the valley was inundated, its trees were razed to create a desolate plain, not unlike the Outer Lands of San Francisco before they were artificially built up into the landscape that mirrored features of Yosemite and Hetch Hetchy.

Hetch Hetchy was the most famously dammed valley, but all over California the drive for water and electrical power to fuel economic growth was turning valleys and rivers into dams and lakes. The Oro Light and Power surveyors who blundered into Ishi's village in 1908 were part and parcel of the larger transformation of the state's landscapes. Muir might have gladly swapped the damming of Deer Creek for the damming of Hetch Hetchy, if that had been possible. He was willing to accept alternative sites to Hetch Hetchy for a dam, because Hetch Hetchy was especially beautiful and because it was in a national park. And even if Muir had won the battle over Hetch Hetchy, Indians would have been left out of the picture—or rather, left in but only as ghosts of themselves pictured in a primordial wilderness of the white man's imagination.

Back in 1877 Muir had spent five weeks with John and Annie Bidwell in Chico, just fifteen miles from where Ishi and his band of survivors were in hiding. When he left Chico he sailed down the Sacramento River on a makeshift raft, all the way to the San Francisco Bay. "It is seldom that I experience much difficulty in leaving civilization for God's wilds," he wrote to the Bidwells, but he had enjoyed his time in and around Ishi's homeland so much that it had been hard to leave. He wrote of how drifting down the great river, "[My] thoughts wandered upstream back to those grand spring fountains on the head of the McCloud and Pitt. Then I tried to picture those hidden tributaries that flow beneath the lava tablelands, and recognized in them a capital illustration of the fact that in their farthest fountains all rivers are lost to mortal eye, that the sources of all are hidden as those of the Nile, and so, also, that in this respect every river of knowledge is a Nile." As far as we know, Muir encountered no Yahi during his "ramble in the mountain wood." He described Ishi's Indian neighbors as "scattered, few in numbers and miserably demoralized, though still offering some rare specimens of savage manhood." Muir walked Mount Shasta and Mount Lassen, the peak Ishi called Wahganupa. But there was a limit to what he could see of the source of the waters as well as the lives into which they flowed, as he well knew and yet did not fully comprehend.[31]

At the museum Ishi was in charge of the Egyptian room, into which many artifacts of the Nile had washed up. He carefully swept the floor and kept the room tidy. In his free time he walked Sutro Forest, he walked Golden Gate Park, he walked the Presidio, and he walked the streets of San Francisco. Next to the museum was the hospital, and Ishi walked there, too. He was interested in Pope's methods of healing, in his surgical operations. Sometimes he told Pope what the Yahi did for certain ailments, curing tonsillitis with honey rubbed on the throat instead of surgical removal, for example. And he offered medicines to some of the people he met outside of the hospital. In September 1913 Ishi met with U.S. Secretary of the Interior Franklin K. Lane, honoring him with a gift of two arrowheads, and bay leaves for his cold. After first following Pope around, Ishi started to do his own rounds, visiting recovering patients. He would fold his hands together and walk from bed to bed, bestowing on each patient a warm smile.

Ishi did not practice medicine at the hospital, though his bedside manner was excellent. He was a favorite among doctors, nurses, and patients, raising spirits with his songs and stories told in pantomime and broken English. Ishi himself went to the hospital as a patient several times, suffering from respiratory infections. He recovered from each of these; every test Pope made for tuberculosis came back negative. Pope encouraged Ishi to stay outdoors as much as possible, and everyone tried to keep him away from infectious diseases. Like Kroeber, Pope asked him if he would rather go back to his homeland, if he wouldn't be happier, and healthier, there. "No," Pope understood Ishi to reply. "Everyone was dead, only evil spirits inhabited the places of his former pursuits."[32]

Ishi was often a houseguest of Waterman and Kroeber, and he saw the suffering of Kroeber's wife, Henriette. She had met Kroeber when he spoke at a Folklore Society meeting, and she was a collector of Indian folklore herself. Like Kroeber, her parents were immigrants from Germany, and like him, she was smart as a whip. Two months after the earthquake shook everyone in San Francisco, the two got married. They worked hand in hand, traveling to Indian country and gathering stories; they published the stories they heard in their own articles in the *Journal of American Folk-Lore*. But Henriette came down with something in 1908, a few months after her own father died of tuberculosis. At first doctors thought she was afflicted with nervous exhaustion; they prescribed rest and retreat to the country. Henriette and Alfred went together to a health resort, but she did not recover. She lost more weight, her cough grew worse, and the doctors knew then that she had contracted tuberculosis. She was sent to Arizona, in the hope that the dry air would help. It may have helped some, but she came back to San Francisco because she wanted to be at home. In the spring of 1913, one and a half years after Ishi arrived in San Francisco, Henriette died.[33]

After the funeral Kroeber took a streetcar west all along the south side of Golden Gate Park to land's end, to the ocean. He walked down "the wet sand where the surf breaking over the rocks and against the shore drowned out other sounds; within the rhythm of the reiterated ebb and return of the breaking waves the solitary man pondered the multiple patterns of the universe. As for the pattern he believed each life must have, he saw his own as torn, disordered, without design or meaning. He turned inland away from the wet shore sand, back over the dunes, on into Golden Gate Park, walking, walking."[34]

Kroeber could not bring himself to go home, to his empty house, so he went to the museum, Ishi's *wowi*. After his long and desolate walk, he entered the museum, reliving the journey he had made to the building after the earthquake in 1906. Back then his apartment had burned down, but the museum and its contents remained safe, and he had camped in Golden Gate Park to guard the building. This night he was not anxious about the contents of the museum, but his own insides were ashes. He went to his office. He heard the sound of work, not the tapping of a typewriter but the chipping of glass being shaped into an arrowhead. He went into Ishi's room and sat with him. Ishi knew Kroeber's wife had died, but he could not speak of it. He smiled at Kroeber and went on with his work. Ishi had gone on with his work, making arrows, after he had come to the museum with singed hair and a world reduced to ashes behind him. Kroeber went back to his office, opened up the safe where he kept his Yurok field notes next to Ishi's silver coins, and went to work deciphering the grammar of this most remarkable civilization's resilient language.[35]

· *Seven* ·

THE CALL OF THE WILD

✴

Nature Men

In the summer of 1914 two different white Americans, each dubbed "the Nature Man" in the media, entered briefly into Ishi and Kroeber's circle.

Nature Man No. 1, a.k.a. Ernest Darling, had been introduced to the reading public in a magazine article by Jack London. "I first met him on Market Street in San Francisco," London wrote. "It was a wet and drizzly afternoon, and he was striding along, clad solely in a pair of abbreviated knee trousers and an abbreviated shirt, his bare feet going slick-slick through the pavement slush." The second time London met the Nature Man was when he sailed his boat to Tahiti, where Darling had taken up residence. Darling told the famous writer that he was a writer of sorts himself. "'This is the book I write,' he explained, smashing himself a resounding blow on the chest with his clenched fist. 'The gorilla in the African jungle pounds his chest till the noise of it can be heard half a mile away.'"

Darling's natural body was his life's work, his oeuvre. A dozen years earlier he had been lying on his deathbed, "a bag of

The Nature Man's Plantation.

bones...a perambulating corpse with just the dimmest flutter of life in it to make it perambulate." In desperation he "turned his back upon men and the habitations of men and dragged himself for five miles through the brush, away from the city of Portland, Oregon." Secluded from the city, he sat naked in the sun—and made a miraculous recovery. He saw the birds and animals around him and took note of their perfect health; it dawned on him that "they lived naturally, while he lived most unnaturally; therefore, if he intended to live, he must return to Nature." At that moment Darling became a full-fledged nature man: he began to run around on all fours, flap his arms like a rooster, and imitate animals in a thousand ways, such as pounding his chest like a gorilla.

His health recovered, Darling migrated south to California to study medicine at Stanford. But he soon came to believe that modern medicine failed to acknowledge the power of "solar therapeutics." He moved to famously sunny southern California but was arrested for indecent exposure and charged with insanity. He fled to Hawaii in search of a Garden of Eden in which to live his simple, stripped-down life, but was promptly deported. Missionaries had been telling Native Hawaiians to cover up for decades, and they weren't about to let some foolish white man play out his fantasies of going native. Darling sailed on to Tahiti and found a secluded place on the island where he could live out his dream. His story was an extraordinary feat of bodily recovery, the ninety-pound weakling transformed into a healthy, strong man. He was like Edgar Rice Burroughs's fictional Tarzan, an Englishman who finds strength in a primitive environment. For that matter, he was like Buck the St. Bernard mix in London's own *Call of the Wild,* the pampered dog languishing on the estate of a San Francisco millionaire who recovers his strength and fighting spirit in the wilderness of Alaska.

Darling returned to California in 1914, making a pilgrimage to San Francisco to meet Ishi. Ishi taught him some quail calls, and the Nature Man invited the Wild Man to spend the night with him in the forest above the museum. Ishi declined the invitation, preferring to sleep in the museum. So the rebuffed Nature Man set off on a long walk all the way down to Los Angeles, where he lectured on the benefits of natural living. The Nature Man was a very natural speaker indeed, for he lectured in the buff, entirely "unembarrassed by clothes."[1]

Nature Man No. 2, a.k.a. Joseph Knowles, was a newspaper illustrator living in Boston. "In the city," he explained, "I always heard the call of the wild." But after growing quite pudgy from his life of urban indulgence, Knowles got to wondering "if the man of the present day could leave all his luxury behind him and go back into the wilderness and live on what nature intended him to have." Backed by the Boston *Post,* Knowles stripped off his clothes and headed into the woods of Maine to live for two months as a "cave man." He scrawled reports on birch bark with charcoal, which were carried in the *Post,* and soon tens of thousands of readers were following his struggle to "defy nature." One sensational dispatch described how he killed a bear. Two months later Knowles emerged from the wilderness. He was leaner, stronger, and in far better health, as a Harvard physician certified. One hundred thousand fans turned out to see him in Boston, and he toured the country getting top billing in a vaudeville show. Even though a rival newspaper run by William Randolph Hearst claimed that Knowles was a fraud who had spent his two months in a comfortable cabin in the woods, the public wanted to believe in this Nature Man.

Even Hearst decided to cash in on the public's interest in city men getting themselves lost on purpose in the wilderness. Hearst's *San Francisco Examiner* sponsored a second stunt, in

which Knowles would have to prove that he wasn't a fake. The paper decided to hire an anthropologist who knew a thing or two about real wild men to lend intellectual gravitas to the stunt. The editors must have known Kroeber would turn them down, so they asked Waterman to be their "special commissioner." Waterman first asked Kroeber's permission, noting, "[I hesitate] to involve the University and the department in such a deal. My connection will certainly be emphasized." But Kroeber overcame what must have been his initial distaste and gave his blessing. Waterman went off in July 1914 to spend three weeks in the Siskiyou Mountains, two hundred miles north of Ishi's country, with the man the *Examiner* would variously label the New Adam, the Modern Crusoe, the Nature Man, and the Wild Man.

Just as he had done from Oroville, Waterman excitedly wrote back to Kroeber, saying, "Our wild man wants me to write a book with him." He assured Kroeber, "[Knowles] has the goods, is a regular fellow and a blamed good scout. I like him ever so much.... Am having the time of my life." In the *Examiner*'s stories Waterman was labeled "the anthropological expert" and his connection to the University of California was emphasized. He slightly deflated Knowles's wild gambit by placing it in cultural context: "There's no use arguing whether it can be done or not. The whole human race has done it." But Waterman also played up Knowles's adventure as cultural time travel: "When he walks into the woods unarmed... he places himself where the first naked man walked the earth." Would he, like Ishi and other California Indians, be able to use some 250 species of plants to live? Could he fashion snares or traps like Ishi? With a bush providing strategic covering, the *Examiner* photographed Knowles in his "nature garb" about to disappear into the wilderness. Waterman wrote dispatches about the challenges faced by the Nature Man, who emerged, a month later, as a fully authenticated fake Stone Age man who would walk into the lights of San Francisco as a man famous for being wild. If that sounded familiar, with a twist, it was no accident: Waterman was part of the story, and the *Examiner*'s articles were written by Philip Kinsley, the same journalist who had written its Ishi articles. Kinsley apparently had the Wild Man beat.[2]

Both Nature Men had pulled a reverse Ishi, acting out a cultural script popular among urban white men anxious about their masculine identity in the modern world. Were they becoming "soft"? Edgar Rice Burroughs, the author of the astoundingly popular Tarzan stories, knew just what the appeal was. He explained, "We wish to escape from not alone the narrow confines of city streets for the freedom of the wilderness, but the restrictions of man made laws, and the inhibitions that society has placed upon us. We like to picture ourselves roaming free, the lords of ourselves and of our world; in other words, we would each like to be Tarzan."[3] Or Ishi.

When Kroeber conceived of the idea of going back to the stream-channeled cañons of Mount Lassen with Ishi, it was in the interest of science. Ishi had come to him in the city, and much ethnographic work could be done there. But it wasn't really fieldwork. To get to really know the culture of the Yahi, it would be better to see it in situ. The anthropologists would need to go there and see the place through Ishi's eyes. They could start with names, the Yahi toponymy, and build their understanding from there. Lobbying to bring Pope along on the trip, too, Waterman promised, "The three of us.... could do the ethnography, ethnobotany, ethnogeography, and ethno-everything else of the Southern Yana."[4]

But the scientists would have been fooling themselves if they believed that their interest in going on a rugged camping trip with Ishi was purely intellectual. The trip was also an adventure, their chance to do what thousands of Americans wanted to do, and were doing, vicariously, through the likes of Buck, Tarzan, or one of the Nature Men, or were actually doing through their involvement in the Boy Scouts, the Sierra Club, or another of the many wilderness and adventure-craving organizations then being formed. Waterman and Kroeber wanted to go. Pope was excited, too. The university couldn't pay his expenses, but that didn't matter. He wanted to hunt with Ishi in his homeland. And he wanted his son to experience it all as well; Saxton Pope Jr. was coming along, too. They were all responding as much to a call of the wild as to a call to duty.

There was only one hitch: Ishi refused to go back. What a crazy idea, he thought. There aren't any chairs, he pointed out. No big houses either. Not much food. The list went on. Ishi spoke up for the comforts of civilization, trying to dissuade the Big Cheap and Waterman and Popey. Kroeber assured him that they weren't going to leave him there, if that was what worried him. But that wasn't it; it was something deeper. Going back to nature would hardly be an escape for him. But the three white men pressed their request, and Ishi finally acceded.

Thrilled, Pope, Waterman, and Kroeber began to assemble their equipment for the expedition. They needed cameras and field notebooks, cooking utensils, machetes, and tents. They needed bows and arrows, too. And though they intended to live partly off the land, they needed to bring a lot of food. The museum's bone room became the staging ground where all of the equipment was gathered. When Ishi found out about it, he was incensed. The food was contaminated, the trip would be a disaster; it was thoughtless to store food so close to the remains of the dead. What were they thinking? Pope assured Ishi that he was a powerful shaman, a *kuwi*, as Ishi already knew. His power would protect the food. Besides, everything was sealed. Ishi was not convinced. It was only after they told him that new food had been bought that he again reluctantly agreed to go.[5]

The band of explorers experienced many things that summer along the streams of Wahganupa. And they took many things with them back to the city: photographic records and mementos, notes, 116 plant specimens, maps, and some of Ishi's old belongings. The trip was secret, but newspapers got wind of the expedition and reported on Ishi taking "the amateur wild men" into his old haunts. When they returned Kroeber delivered a public lecture titled "Ishi in His Old Haunts," illustrated by photographic slides taken on the trip. Some of those images, pictures, and news stories can be assembled into an album and scrapbook through which we can look back at their expedition into the wild.[6]

Photo Album and Scrapbook: Trip to "Ishi's Old Haunts,"
May 13–June 2, 1914

Kroeber, Ishi, Pope, and Pope's son, with all of their gear, boarded a Southern Pacific train on May 13, 1914, heading toward the foothills of Mount Lassen. Stepping off the train in Vina, the now well-traveled Ishi casually gave a twenty-five-cent tip to the black porter in the Pullman car. At the train station they were met by Merle Apperson, the man who had been Waterman's guide when he searched the cañons in vain for Ishi's people back in 1910. Kroeber had made arrangements with Merle and his father, Jack; they would supply horses and pack their gear into Deer Creek cañon. The Appersons were to tell no one that Kroeber and Ishi were coming back.[7]

The Appersons' corral contained several wild horses, and everyone was apprehensive as Ishi approached, fearing that he would spook them. But the horses remained calm in his presence. After Kroeber, Pope, Waterman, and Merle received their mounts, the Appersons found they were one shy. So Ishi rode on a wagon with Jack Apperson and Pope's son, heading east from Vina toward Deer Creek. Eight miles in they stopped at the Speegle ranch and got their last horse for Ishi. Ishi recognized the horse, for it had once been wild in Deer Creek and the Speegles had raised him. They called him Black Bart, after a legendary highwayman from San Francisco who robbed Wells Fargo stage coaches in the mountains and left poems behind. Ishi wanted to ride Black Bart.[8]

Just after leaving the Speegle place, Pope dismounted and ran up ahead, finding a spot to take a photograph. Merle Apperson,

with his signature pointed cowboy hat, held the reins of Pope's horse for the shot. Waterman rode the white horse off to the left, and Pope Jr. and Jack Apperson sat in the wagon behind. Kroeber, eager at the front of the group, pivoted to look back. Ishi, in his coat and tie, was right there on Black Bart, nervous. Mostly he was unnerved not by the horse but by what lay ahead and the company he was keeping.

Jack Apperson had led the party of surveyors that plundered Ishi's camp in 1908. When the party arrived at Deer Creek Flats above the cañon, they had to wait for Homer Speegle to come up with packhorses. To kill time Jack took out his pistol, hoping to get Ishi to shoot it. But Ishi misunderstood: "Are you going to shoot me?" he asked. In 1908 Ishi had shot an arrow at Jack; maybe this was Jack's chance to even the score. When Jack saw that Ishi was frightened, he felt awful. He put the gun away and reached out and touched Ishi on the shoulder, blurting out, "Brother." Ishi, still tense and nervous, replied in kind, "Brother." The scene left such an impression on the Appersons that they later had Ishi and Jack reenact it so that a "memory picture" could be taken. Ishi still looked uncomfortable when his "brother" again touched him on his shoulder.[9]

The Speegles finally arrived, and the party headed down the trail into the cañon. But Ishi was still furtive. The boy Mel Speegle reported that Ishi was "watching on both sides of the trail.... He was looking to the north and he kept watching those cliffs—very nervously." All of the Speegles meanwhile were staring at the Indian and doubting his identity. When Homer first saw him, he exclaimed, "That ain't Ishi. That's a fake." Ishi certainly looked different. He was not the gaunt man they had seen three years before. Ishi, who loved ice cream and coconut pie, had put on weight, some forty pounds. When he decided to take off his Western clothes when they got to the stream at the bottom of the cañon, his body resembled the pudgy Knowles entering the wilderness of Maine more than the lean Yahi who showed up at the slaughterhouse in Oroville three years earlier. The Speegles were convinced that this Ishi was a hoax, just as William Randolph Hearst had been convinced that the Nature Man was a fraud. As far as the Speegles were concerned, he had have to prove he was the real wild man.[10]

But there was a big difference between Knowles and the Indian. Ishi was in fact going home. As the party came down to a spot near the end of the horse trail, a lava wall went almost straight down to the creek below, and you could find narrow footholds to make your way down at that point. Ishi went out ahead of the group. A little way down, he reached into a crack in the wall and pulled out a pole made of pine, bark stripped and smooth. He placed one end into a notch in the wall and then laid the pole across the narrow gorge. He then went across, hand over hand. Speegle's doubts were instantly dissolved: "Nobody but an Indian, nobody but Ishi could do that," he said. The *Chico Record* later reported that Merle Apperson, "who is said to know the maze of rugged hills and steep canyons of Deer creek country better than any living white man, admitted after a few days that Ishi knew it better than he did, knew it like a book, in fact." Back in 1910 Merle had told Waterman that he knew the country "like a book," and Kroeber had been hopeful that with Merle's help the elusive Yahi might have been discovered. But they had come up with only blank pages then. Now it was time to fill them in, to let

Ishi's knowledge of the place pour out of him onto the pages of a book the anthropologists would compose.[11]

They made their way down into the heart of Ishi's homeland and made camp along the stream of Wahganupa, at a place Ishi called *ya'muluk'u*. The anthropologists unpacked their things, including the camera equipment. This would be one of their primary recording instruments, supplementing their eyes, their ears, and the paper they brought along to receive impressions of Ishi's culture and Ishi's world that could later be collected into a book.

Kroeber started by replicating the photo session he had done with Ishi back in September 1911, when he'd taken a set of pictures of Ishi's face and profile. These first shots were meant to record the objective appearance of the man, not be windows on his soul. Placing the right profile photographs from 1911 and 1914 next to one another illuminates Speegle's skepticism. In the first photograph, Ishi has short hair, singed just after he arrived in Oroville as a sign of mourning. In 1914 his hair is long, his leather ear ring is gone, his body is fuller. This photographic set is like the before-and-after images of Indians going to boarding schools, but in reverse. Before, Ishi's hair was short and he wore a suit; after, his hair is long and he is bare-chested.

Could Ishi so easily slip back into another world, becoming the Nature Man again, and turn his back on the modern world? For much of the camping trip Ishi in fact wore a shirt and pants, even shoes. Ultimately Kroeber's first photograph of Ishi at Deer Creek captures nothing of Ishi's identity. It is a pose assumed for Kroeber, the anthropologist. He wants to picture Ishi in his home; he wants to get *as if* images, *as if* Kroeber weren't there. *As*

if white men had never been there. *As if* this were a true picture of aboriginal America, pristine and uncontaminated. Instead of an individual removed from his place and his culture and standing next to a Museum of Anthropology built by mining money, Kroeber now made a picture of a representative Yahi in his natural surroundings. Here understanding Ishi's culture would no longer be abstract, removed, *unheimlich*. It would be explored in place. It is 1914. World war is breaking out. Ishi, a day before, rode the train and tipped Pullman porters. But the storytelling of the photographs invites us to enter another time, a mythical time anthropologists often call "precontact," before contact with white men.

Pope had a camera, too, and his backstage photograph of Kroeber photographing Ishi exposes this carefully constructed form of storytelling. We see Kroeber's careful work with the box camera, setting up his shot of Ishi. At the top right, the result is seen: Ishi attaching the points of a harpoon, just as his people had always done. By 1900 Ishi was using iron nails to point his harpoons; that is not what Kroeber recorded. In a series of photographs, the process of making the harpoon was documented; another series showed Ishi at work on the river as a fisherman. In one photograph he is standing on a stone in the middle of the stream, appearing almost to walk on water, waiting for a salmon to spear.

Kroeber believed that culture was imbedded in the things people made, and now he was revealing not just the object itself—a harpoon, Yahi type, tagged and displayed in a museum—but the process of its construction and the natural setting of its use. Photography is also a process, imbedded in culture and technology. The nail-less harpoon is in Ishi's hands, which is in the box

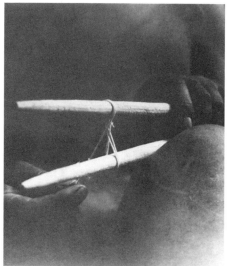

camera in Kroeber's hands, and Kroeber, the camera, Ishi, and the cañon are all in Pope's camera, and Pope is behind it all, but images of Indians and nature are behind Pope's lids and lenses, too, all infinitely nested together, like a Russian doll.

Ishi allowed Kroeber to make a documentary record of a number of the processes by which a piece of wild nature was turned into a tool, a part of Yahi culture: breaking obsidian and then chipping arrows, selecting and honing arrow shafts, making fire by spinning wood shafts. These photos were just like the descriptions of arrow making in the story of Lizard. And they were a world apart from them as well.

If Ishi had been a woman, reed gathering, basket weaving, acorn grinding, and soup making might have been at the center of the story Kroeber recorded in images. But because he was a man the images are mainly scenes of hunting with bow and arrow. Ishi notched a piece of wood out of a juniper tree and cut it into shape, using a metal ax. The best bowman of the Yahi used an ax, too, Ishi explained, but that was a prized possession. It was perfectly natural for him to use one, if one was at hand, and Kroeber dutifully took pictures, with their contaminating object in the frame. Kroeber then took photographs of Ishi's shooting position, both standing and kneeling, and to the casual observer the bow shows no signs of being worked by forged tools. The bow Ishi used on the trip was manufactured in San Francisco, by Ishi, and taken back with him to Yahi country.[12]

Hunting with bow and arrow was Pope's special area of interest. He wanted to learn everything he could about it from Ishi. Ishi removed his clothes and shoes to hunt; they made too much noise.

"He placed every footfall with precise care; the most stealthy step I ever saw; he was used to it; lived by it," Pope observed. Once, when Ishi heard a blue jay sing out, he stopped and gave up the hunt. The blue jay was saying "Here comes man," Ishi explained. Pope believed that Ishi knew the language of the animals. Ishi could call animals to him. When he kissed his fingers to make a plaintive squeak like a rabbit in distress, rabbits would come to see what could be done. Wildcats would show up as well, hopeful that a meal was in the offing. As a test, Pope asked Ishi to repeat the call in twelve different locations. Even with Pope around, the calls worked. Pope shot three arrows at a wildcat whom Ishi had called, but missed each time. Mel Speegle observed that Pope couldn't hit a bobcat or a rabbit because he couldn't gauge speed and distance. But Ishi could, and he didn't miss.[13]

But it wasn't really a wildcat or a rabbit that Pope wanted to shoot; it was a buck. Kroeber had secured special permission from the Fish and Game Service to "take for scientific purposes one male deer," even though it was not the proper season. Ishi would do the shooting (though the permission slip granted that right to Kroeber, Waterman, and Pope). Pope wanted to participate in the hunt, but Ishi found it hard to hunt with him. Pope didn't prepare himself properly. Ishi bathed in the river, fasted, and rubbed himself with the leaves of yerba buena. (San Francisco was originally called Yerba Buena after this plant.) Pope and the guides smoked tobacco. They had to stop that; it was disrespectful to the deer. Besides, the deer would smell the smoke.[14]

Pope might have spoiled his chances in yet another way. One day he saw a rattlesnake and killed it with his machete. They flayed it and cooked it up. It tasted like rabbit or fish, Pope said. Kroeber and

Waterman had some, too, and they said it was good. Ishi thought it was all bad. You didn't kill *kemna*. You respected it and left it alone. You didn't bring it back and cook it up in the camp's pots! For the rest of the trip Ishi refused to eat food cooked in the pots. They had been contaminated. Kroeber thought whites contaminated Indians. Indians didn't think it was whites who contaminated them, but the things they did, their violations of natural rights. Ishi expected the men who ate the snake to sicken and perhaps die.[15]

They didn't, but Ishi still attributed their bad luck in hunting deer to the killing of *kemna*. Patience, careful preparation, and spiritual respect were the keys to Ishi's own success in hunting. With Pope and the others on this trip, each of these was in short supply, even though the whites tried to emulate Ishi. They tried and failed, and their patience wore out. So one of the guides took down a buck with his rifle.[16]

Kroeber brought over his camera, and the work of documenting the Yahi deer hunt for scientific purposes went forward, even though it was all contaminated by the original snake sin. First, Pope asked Ishi to fire arrows into the dead deer. Why should he do this? Pope wanted to test the penetrating power of Ishi's arrows. From forty yards Ishi shot three arrows into the dead buck. The first hit the neck, the second hit the spine, and the third "entered the thorax back of the scapula." Pope asserted that each arrow made a "mortal wound." That is, each arrow would have been mortal, if the deer hadn't already been killed by the cold lead blasted from the factory-made rifle.[17]

Ishi then was asked to remove the arrows, all for the camera. There is no record of Ishi's attitude about this whole experiment. We are left to read his reaction in his face, as he pulls the arrow

from the buck and looks back at Pope with his camera. Kroeber is taking photographs, too, and the whole scene has been carefully staged. Pope's son thought the scene was off-kilter. "I've always felt embarrassed that the deer's head was visibly propped up in the photograph which shows Ishi retrieving the arrow," young Saxton said. He did not share his father's passion for shooting arrows, for killing things, and for scientifically recording it all. When his father and Ishi went out to hunt, he stayed in camp, pretending he was the cook.[18]

Using an obsidian knife, Ishi began the long process of skinning the buck, while Kroeber and Pope took dozens of pictures. If all went well, the buck's spirit would go up through the hole in the high rock. Kroeber had seen the place for himself as the group came into the cañon. They had all climbed up to a lookout on a high rock formation that had been Ishi's lookout post over the cañon. (He would see ranchers coming, and his words described the direction they were coming from and the terrain they were going over, such as *nirigam,* "he comes down the hill from the north.") Ishi drew pictures in the sand of the people he had once spied. Then he pointed to a hole in a rock and said, "Pawn." Kroeber explained to everyone that he meant "deer." This place, between Pine and Deer Creek, was called *hanmā wi.* There was a quartz formation around this hole, and when they got back to the horses Ishi gestured to show how it was like a rope, like this rope on the horse. It was like the rope that Cottontail Rabbit had used to get back over the mountains from the east, after he had set the sun on its course. Here was the spot where the soul of the buck, killed four times—once by bullets and thrice by arrows shot for the camera—would go, if the proper respect had been shown.[19]

The others were having fun and trying to be better guests, better Indians. A portrait taken of the group along the stream's shore includes Pope Jr. and Ishi in their loincloths, Kroeber in his jacket with pockets bulging with tobacco, pipes, pencils, notebooks, a jackknife, and whatnot, and Pope at ease, displaying his long bow, the arrow ready to draw. Pope Jr. recalled that his father "was in the fullness of that physical grace and strength which he never lost. He had graduated to the English longbow and was testing his hunting skill with it against that of Ishi and his shorter bow."[20]

Pope observed that Ishi wore his "improvised breech clout even though his white companions abandoned this last vestige of respectability." The whites went "naked in the wilds" as they imagined Ishi had once done, bathing and swimming in Deer Creek. "The water was cold, the sun was hot and the year moved toward its summer fullness," Pope Jr. remembered. They sat on the bank of the stream and stood on the pebbles of the shore. Pope Sr. captured the scene in another photograph, much less formal than the previous one. His son is playing in the water, and Kroeber sits at the water's edge, his back to the camera. Waterman stands as a vision of strength and beauty. Ishi is lying across the rocks in the foreground, taking it all in. Pope stands behind them all, looking through the camera at the whole scene. He had often noted the perfection of Ishi's body, his feet especially. When he looked at Ishi he saw "grace and strength in every contour" of his body, even though it had lost its litheness. Pope said his stature was "magnificent," that Ishi was "absolutely perfect." Pope Jr. saw grace and strength in his father, and others, women and men, saw this as well. It's as if Pope was mirroring what he saw in Ishi.[21]

Looking on, Ishi probably saw something different. Ishi delighted in Pope Jr., who was just a kid; Waterman and Kroeber seemed like kids, too, and hardly knew how to move gracefully or quietly through this landscape. Pope was strong, but he was hardly graceful or silent in hunting, though he was getting better. Ishi most admired Pope's skill as a magician. Pope often tested his physical strength against Ishi's. The two wrestled. They played the game in which they grasped right hands and then tried to upset the other. Ishi was "strong but awkward," Pope said. Boxing with Pope, Ishi was "deft" but unskilled. He did not like to "exhibit his strength." All of Pope's observations about Ishi's body and strength were a reflection not only of Pope's own interest in exhibiting strength but of his culture's anxieties about the white male body in the machine age.

These worries reached a crescendo for the culture at large when a black man, Jack Johnson, became the boxing champion of the world in 1908. Soon Jack London and others raised a call for some "Great White Hope" to defeat Johnson. Ironically, on the same day that Ishi first traveled to San Francisco, newspapers reported that the latest "great white hope" was a boxer who was half-Irish. The other half was Indian.[22]

Those men who went into the ring with Jack Johnson as the white hope were cultural kin to the Nature Men who went into the woods to prove that civilized man could live in the wild. (Darling and Knowles both fancied themselves boxers.) Even as many leading intellectuals, especially those associated with the growing movement called eugenics, saw the white body and mind as the pinnacle of achievement, a physical inferiority complex gnawed at the self-image of many whites. Indians were confined to reservations or compelled to assimilate to white standards of appearance and culture. African Americans were hobbled in public life by Jim Crow laws that confined them to separate, and unequal, spaces. But at the same time, images of Native American and African American bodies appeared everywhere in movies and photographs. Even as white men saw those bodies as inferior, there was something they saw that they wanted: a wild power and freedom they worried they had somehow lost. Somewhere below consciousness, many white men harbored a tangled and confused desire to both possess and destroy those bodies.[23]

For Kroeber, sitting naked by the river was like going back to his own childhood, to the year he spent in the country under doctor's orders, sent there to reinvigorate his health and body. Those summer months had been spent in the lakes of the Adirondack Mountains, and in the fall he went to a boarding school along the Shepaug River, where he swam naked in its deep pools. Kroeber loved rivers and creeks, finding solace in and along them. As if to capture shadows of his own past, he took several pictures of Ishi swimming in the water, and the light that bounced back from Ishi etched images of joy onto the film in Kroeber's camera.

The group's main camp was on the bank of Deer Creek at a spot Ishi called *Ya'muluk'u*. They kept a campfire going late into the evening, and finally bedded down in their sleeping bags, arranged in a row between the fire and a rock ledge. Kroeber taught young Pope the names of the constellations. Greek and Roman mythology—Aquarius, Pisces, and the strong man Hercules—were reflected down into the cañon. Ursa Major and Minor, the big and little bears, looked down. In the Roman telling of the story, Callisto was a wood nymph who hunted with her bow in the wilds of Arcadia. Jupiter desired her and tricked her into having sex with him. She bore a child, Arcas. Jupiter's infuriated wife turned Callisto into a bear. Later the son came across his mother in bear form. As he drew his arrow back, Jupiter saw what was about to happen and turned Arcas into a bear as well. Ever after, Callisto and Arcas lived in the sky next to one another, Ursa Major and Ursa Minor. Many years later, when Kroeber had a daughter, he would name her Ursula.[24]

Ishi might have had quite a lot to say about bears on the trip. There was the story of Grizzly Bear in the sky. Long ago, during the time of the story people, the children found ashes, and everyone wondered if there was fire around. Grizzly Bear put his hair in a topknot, fasted and prayed, getting himself ready, and then swung himself right up into the air, going up all the way to the hole in the sky. He crawled up and looked out to the West, up and down, and saw nothing. To the East, up and down. Nothing. He turned around, and looked to the North, up and down. Nothing.

But when he looked South, he saw fire, streaming up, blazing. All the creatures, Wood Ducks and Chipmunks and Bears, escaped the blaze by diving into a hole in the ground. All except for Coyote, who got caught in the fire. At the last minute he dived into a hole in Oak Tree, who told him, "I will burn on the outside but not the inside." Coyote scrambled in, but his feet were left sticking out. The fire blazed through. In the morning Coyote looked at his black, charred toes. "Mmm. Look at my Pit River grasshoppers." He ate his toes, as if they were roasted grasshoppers. Coyote then brought back the secret of drilling for fire to the people, and the world was renewed. They all sat around the fire, and the animals were all rec-reated, Deer and Rattlesnake, Panther and Grizzly Bear.[25]

Much of this story was too complicated to fully tell around the campfire, for there was still a language barrier between Ishi and his white companions. (He would carefully tell it in his own language back in Berkeley.) On the trip Ishi spoke of Ursa during the day when they came across the bear's places and stories could be pointed out on the ground.

Back in San Francisco Ishi had already conveyed to Kroeber much of what they would find. In 1913 he had drawn a map of his homeland, laying out the main streams, Deer Creek and Mill Creek, and Battle Creek to the north and Butte Creek to the south, all flowing west to Daha, the "Big Water" of the Sacramento River. He indicated historic village sites, trails, and the heads of the salmon run on each waterway. Kroeber had asked him about tribal boundaries and was able to pencil in the territory of the Yahi, bounded by that of the Wintu to the west, the Maidu to the south, the Southern Yana to the north, and others beyond.

Kroeber reproduced the lines Ishi had drawn out and filled in the place-names he pointed out, completing it with a legend. He noted that Indians in California "usually refuse point blank to make any attempt of this kind." But Ishi's map "proves the California Indians to have been not totally devoid of faculty in this direction." In fact map making was a tool Ishi frequently used. In San Francisco he had drawn a map for young Fred Zumwalt of the places around Mountain Lake from which soil samples had been taken. During the 1914 trip he drew maps in the sand for the young boys and explained how once when he was young he had traveled south with his mother, possibly into Maidu country near Yankee Hill, where a "candy man" had given him sweets.[26]

On the trip Ishi drew another map for Kroeber, tracing Deer Creek from the Sacramento River and Balèxa, a large Wintu village with a sweat-house, that had been located near Vina, all the way up to Bopmayu'wi, the high place at the head of Deer Creek. Kroeber noted that these "places were *mapped* by [Ishi], *not* pointed out." It was important to Kroeber to establish that Ishi could abstractly represent his own landscape. The map, densely packed with numbers corresponding to more than thirty place-names, makes it clear that this was an intimately known landscape. Ishi looked across the water at places he knew, at history. Kroeber shared Ishi's rock with him for a moment, precariously standing amid the flow of water, as if standing on the rock in this stream were a time machine, allowing him to perch himself for a moment in Ishi's Stone Age world and see the geography that he knew by heart. When they all traveled the land and water together, the intimacy and knowledge seemed to grow and grow.[27]

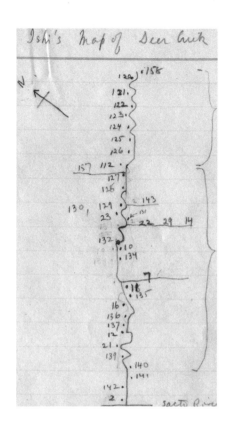

Despite Waterman's ambition to do an "ethno-everything," ethnogeography became the center of Kroeber's attention. But even this job could not be completed. After the trip Kroeber wrote to the linguist Edward Sapir, "[We] have just returned from three weeks in his old home with Ishi. We did not try to get much from him except geography, but...were very successful. We were also hampered by the fact that he knows a larger tract than we were able to cover. We may be able to complete the job some other time, but have enough now to serve as a framework for myths and history."

Though Kroeber had earlier described Ishi's civilization as "puny," the depth and range of his landscape proved to be vaster than the anthropologist imagined. Perhaps by looking at Ishi's land only in maps Kroeber had underestimated it, or got his scale wrong.[28]

Kroeber's painstaking work on geography, filling up many note pages with hundreds of place-names, is remarkable. He knew that Yahi myths and history were interwoven with place, so geography, as much as language, provided the framework for understanding Ishi and his culture. Kroeber drew his own maps and made panoramas of the cañons of Deer Creek and Mill Creek, which each looked like small-scale versions of the Grand Canyon. Caves, villages, trails, wagon roads, cabins, stream crossings, cliffs—all had names, and Ishi shared many stories about them. One place was where the deer souls went after death; at Kiticú'wi Indians from the West had once come and killed a doctor; a mile or two up from the group's main campsite was Bāxāni, a cave used by the Yahi for storage and refuge. Back in 1906 Ike and Marse Speegle happened upon that cave. Stumbling over stone metates used to grind acorn meal, the intruders went into the dark cave, struck a match, and built a fire. The Speegles saw some dead animals, a pile of overalls and other clothes, a small cache of coins (some of them of Mexican mint), and a bearskin. Ike thought the skin was "one of the finest" he had ever seen, and he took it.[29]

When Ishi showed the cave to Kroeber and the others, he started to cry as if from cold. He then looked at Marse, and indicated that he had stolen his *samani*, his bear rug. Ishi and five others had watched, hidden in the brush, as the Speegles made off with their belongings eight years ago. Without the *samani*, they had suffered in the cold that winter. The Speegles had been using it as a lap blanket. Later in the trip, when they were exploring Mill Creek to the north, Ishi stopped one day at a large boulder. He dug in the earth next to it and uncovered a bear claw. This place had a name, Wamoloku, which might mean "Bear Claw's Place." It might have been the place where Ishi had killed the black bear for the *samani*, first shooting it with an arrow and then stabbing it with an obsidian knife. Marse promised to return the bearskin on their way out. When Marse gave it back to him, Ishi, delighted, turned it over to show them where the arrow and the knife had gone through the bear's hide.[30]

Wamoloku, the bear *samani*, the cave Bāxāni—all of these were bound to Ishi, a part of his identity. Their loss was felt deeply; their return appreciated immensely. Kroeber was now, in an intimate way, seeing for himself Ishi's sense of place. Now, instead of seeing this land as "the utterly wild cañon of Deer Creek," as he had described it in 1912, he was beginning to experience it as Ishi's homeland, a place filled with stories. Still, this was only a partial sense of the Yahi landscape. To fully appreciate it, you would need more time, at least the full round of seasons. And you would need more voices, not just one Yahi returning as a guide to men who did not even fully comprehend his language.[31]

His companions told Ishi stories, too, but they were not of this place. During an intense rainstorm, when the party was holed up in a cave along Mill Creek, Pope entertained Ishi and the others with dramatic performances of Rudyard Kipling's poem "Mandalay." It is told from the perspective of a British imperial soldier, back in London but dreaming of a woman he met in Mandalay. Living in hazy industrial London, the soldier says, "I am sick o' wastin' leather on these gritty pavin'-stones, / An' the blasted Henglish drizzle wakes the fever in my bones." Ultimately the soldier rejects English women and English life, with the explanation, "I've a neater, sweeter maiden in a cleaner, greener land!" Kipling, an apologist for English empire, eroticized the East and inspired Burroughs's Tarzan with his stories of Mowgli in *The Jungle Book*, the boy raised by wild animals in India.[32]

When the United States took possession of the Philippines in the Spanish American War in 1898, Kipling, who was born in India but had moved to the United States in 1892, wrote a poem to instruct his adopted countrymen about the costs and responsibilities of imperialism:

> Take up the White Man's burden—
> Send forth the best ye breed—
> Go bind your sons to exile
> To serve your captives' need;
> To wait in heavy harness,
> On fluttered folk and wild—
> Your new-caught, sullen peoples,
> Half-devil and half-child.

White men were part of Ishi's burden. He even bore the weight of Kipling, for the Yahi man had been described as "the Mowgli of the California jungle." Whites saw the real American Indian Ishi through the lens of Kipling's Indian raised by animals. Ishi bore Pope, and Waterman, and Kroeber, too. To be sure, he enjoyed the companionship of the three men, but the trip was hard. He was weighed down by their dreams. And he was weighed down by history and loss.[33]

Ishi took them all up to see the village of Wowunupo'mu tetna, Grizzly Bear's Hiding Place. This was the secluded village

that the surveyors had broken into in 1908. Ishi had shot his arrow at Jack Apperson in warning, and left behind his mother, wrapped up in a quilt. Jack had looked at the old woman, gave her *agua,* and then cleaned the village of the Yahi's possessions. Now there were only remnants to look over in the Wowunupo'mu tetna ruins: the houses falling back into the earth, some boards and rusty tools, a tin of log cabin syrup. No people. Ishi stood for a photograph beside one of his old houses and remains. During his "wild Indian expedition" back in 1910, Waterman had taken photographers here to prove that the elusive Indians existed. When he met Ishi in Oroville, Waterman showed Ishi a photograph of himself. When they got to San Francisco, Waterman showed Ishi a photograph of his raided *wowi* to see how he would react, to show how much the white man knew. Taking more pictures now was taking what was left, and holding on to it.

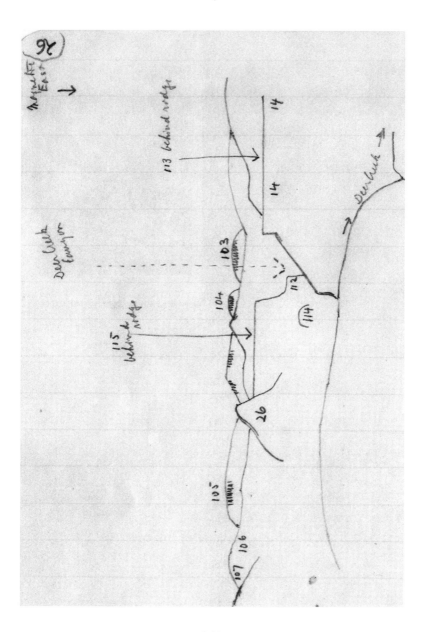

Kroeber drew panoramas from Wowunupo'mu tetna and from the trails above Deer Creek, identifying all of the places you could see, with numbers that corresponded to place-names he took down from Ishi. On the heights Ishi protected his eyes from the sun and looked out over the emptied landscape. He walked the land below with Kroeber and the others. He stood in open meadows and pointed out the sites of old villages, abandoned and all but erased from this widowed land. What was it like to stand in this terrain of ghosts? They went to the cave where Ishi's mother, who had survived the surveyors' raid, had later died, and Ishi wept. Another day, Ishi came back to camp, disturbed, and told Pope Jr. that he thought he heard his sister and mother calling to him along the trail. Recall the German word *unheimlich*,

the familiar made strange, your home turned into a place that chills you to the bone. For Ishi, there must have been a sense of *unheimlich,* of being "alone in the wilderness." This is what Knowles, Nature Man No. 2, had called his book. It was what the Nature Man was looking for, an escape into nature away from the crowded city, the madding crowd. For Ishi, being alone here, with no other Yahi, turned his home into a wilderness, howling and haunted. He shared his geography with Kroeber, but it was a geography of loneliness.[34]

Ishi was eager to break camp and happy to get on the trail back to Vina. Along the way Marse Speegle returned the bearskin. Kroeber purchased for the museum a number of Ishi's other things in the Appersons' possession. At the train station at Vina, Ishi and Pope entertained the gathered crowd by shooting arrows. Ishi invited others, even ladies from the audience, to shoot a cracker box. Ishi had no trouble hitting the target. He even backed up and shot an arrow over a house, and still hit the target. Geese flew overhead, and Ishi exclaimed, "Go, go t-tee, go, go t-tee." Someone gave him paper and a pencil, and he drew the geese. Not satisfied, he crossed the picture out and laughed along with the onlookers. He gave arrowheads to women, and when the train pulled in he was the first to board. From the train he gave a very short whistle-stop speech: "Ladies and Gentlemen, good-bye!"[35]

Kroeber was less eager to leave the streams of Wahganupa. He walked at the rear of the pack train going back to town. Even then, he was still writing down place-names. The train ride from Vina brought him back to San Francisco and his many responsibilities at the university and the museum. His own home was empty; Henriette was gone. Every time he returned to San Francisco after her death, as he would later confess to an intimate friend in New York, he was filled with "the prison gate sense." It was a reflection

of his own state of mind, and a mirroring of Ishi's unwild place in his own museum.[36]

From the train station the party could see smoke hanging over the landscape, which they believed had come from a forest fire. In fact, they were told, Wahganupa had erupted while they were in the cañons camping, a reminder that the whole world was first made of rock and fire and then shaped by the streams of history.

Illustration Captions

p. 209: Nature Man No. 1: Ernest Darling with Jack London in Tahiti. From Jack London, The Cruise of the Snark *(New York: Macmillan, 1928), 188.*

p. 211: Nature Man No. 2: Joseph Knowles entering the wilderness of Maine, 1911. From Joseph Knowles, Alone in the Wilderness *(Boston: Small, Maynard, 1913).*

p. 216: On the journey tot Deer Creek. Photograph by Saxton T. Pope, 15-25486. Courtesy of the Phoebe A. Hearst Museum of Anthropology and the Regents of the University of California.

p. 220 (top): Ishi, September 1911. Photograph by Alfred Kroeber, 15-5410. Courtesy of the Phoebe A. Hearst Museum of Anthropology and the Regents of the University of California.

p. 220 (bottom): Ishi, 1914. Photograph by Alfred Kroeber, 15-5771. Courtesy of the Phoebe A. Hearst Museum of Anthropology and the Regents of the University of California.

p. 222 (top, left): Ishi ready with harpoon. Photograph by Alfred Kroeber, 15-5744. Courtesy of the Phoebe A. Hearst Museum of Anthropology and the Regents of the University of California.

p. 222 (top, right): Ishi binding points on salmon harpoon. Photograph by Alfred Kroeber, 15-5729. Courtesy of the Phoebe A. Hearst Museum of Anthropology and the Regents of the University of California.

p. 222 (bottom): Kroeber photographing Ishi binding points on salmon harpoon. Photograph by Saxton T, Pope, 15-5835. Courtesy of the Phoebe A. Hearst Museum of Anthropology and the Regents of the University of California.

p. 224 (top, left): Ishi making a bow. Photograph by Alfred Kroeber, 15-5683. Courtesy of the Phoebe A. Hearst Museum of Anthropology and the Regents of the University of California.

p. 224 (top, right): Ishi calling rabbits. Photograph by Saxton T. Pope, 15-5815. Courtesy of the Phoebe A. Hearst Museum of Anthropology and the Regents of the University of California.

p. 224 (bottom): Ishi shooting, kneeling. Photograph by Alfred Kroeber, 15-5689. Courtesy of the Phoebe A. Hearst Museum of Anthropology and the Regents of the University of California.

p. 227 (top): Ishi with shot deer. Photograph by Saxton T. Pope, 15-5825. Courtesy of the Phoebe A. Hearst Museum of Anthropology and the Regents of the University of California.

p. 227 (bottom, left): Ishi skinning deer. Photograph by Saxton T. Pope, 15-5831. Courtesy of the Phoebe A. Hearst Museum of Anthropology and the Regents of the University of California.

p. 227 (bottom, right): Saxton Pope Jr., Ishi, Alfred Kroeber, and Saxton Pope Sr. Donor Alfred Kroeber (photographer unknown, probably Waterman), 15-5783. Courtesy of the Phoebe A. Hearst Museum of Anthropology and the Regents of the University of California.

p. 230: Ishi, Alfred Kroeber, and Thomas Waterman. Photograph by Saxton T. Pope, 15-5838. Courtesy of the Phoebe A. Hearst Museum of Anthropology and the Regents of the University of California.

p. 235 (top): "Sketch J: Copy of a Map Drawn by Ishi." Alfred Kroeber, Yahi Place Names, Reel 161, A. L. Kroeber Papers, BANC FILM 2049. Courtesy of the Bancroft Library, University of California, Berkeley.

p. 235 (bottom): Ishi on rock in river. Photograph by Saxton T. Pope, 15-5839. Courtesy of the Phoebe A. Hearst Museum of Anthropology and the Regents of the University of California.

p. 236: Ishi at river crossing of his 1909 camp. Photograph by Saxton T. Pope, 15-5856. Courtesy of the Phoebe A. Hearst Museum of Anthropology and the Regents of the University of California.

p. 240: View of location of Ishi's 1909 camp. Photograph by Saxton T. Pope, 15-5871. Courtesy of the Phoebe A. Hearst Museum of Anthropology and the Regents of the University of California.

p. 241: "Panorama Sketch I," Alfred Kroeber, Yahi Place Names, Reel 161, A. L. Kroeber Papers, BANC FILM 2049. Courtesy of the Bancroft Library, University of California, Berkeley.

p. 242 (left): Ishi with specimens from the remains of his 1908 camp. Photograph by Saxton T. Pope, 15-5854. Courtesy of the Phoebe A. Hearst Museum of Anthropology and the Regents of the University of California.

p. 242 (right): Ishi standing at main hut at his 1909 camp with Waterman. Photograph by Saxton T. Pope, 15-5862. Courtesy of the Phoebe A. Hearst Museum of Anthropology and the Regents of the University of California.

p. 243: Ishi at old village site on north side, one-half mile below the mouth of Sulphur Creek. Photograph by Saxton T. Pope, 15-5867. Courtesy of the Phoebe A. Hearst Museum of Anthropology and the Regents of the University of California.

p. 244: Returning to Vina. Photograph by Saxton T. Pope, 15-5845. Courtesy of the Phoebe A. Hearst Museum of Anthropology and the Regents of the University of California.

· *Eight* ·

DEATH MASK

✻

End of the Trail

The posters for the Panama Pacific International Exposition pictured Hercules muscling the earth apart, creating the Panama Canal. He looked just like the muscle-bound Erick Sandow, the popular body builder. Everyone could take part vicariously in feeling the power of American civilization to remake the earth. "THE HUMAN RACE AND THIS AMERICAN NATION ESPECIALLY HAVE SCORED A GREAT VICTORY OVER NATURE," William Randolph Hearst's paper announced in a full-page spread. The canal was a wonder of the modern world, and San Francisco had won the right to celebrate its construction with an enormous fair. More than six hundred acres, much of it created out of the sea at the marina with landfill, were sculpted into an architectural celebration of modernity and manifest destiny.[1]

The Panama Pacific Expo was "an encyclopedia of modern achievement," one guidebook proclaimed. "This is the first time in the history of man the entire world is known and in intercommunication.... In speaking of the earth, the qualification

'The known world' is no longer necessary. For the first time all the world is known." No place was "wild"; every place was interconnected. Standing in Washington, D.C., President Woodrow Wilson pushed a gold button that sent a radio wave westward to San Francisco that opened the fair at noon on February 20, 1915. Wilson's transcontinental signal triggered the lighting of the spectacular Tower of Jewels and opened the fair's gates. More than three hundred thousand people streamed through into the fairgrounds that day, a new world's record.[2]

U.S. Secretary of the Interior Franklin K. Lane was Wilson's man on the spot, charged with giving a speech to open the celebration. Lane, who two years before had been presented with two arrowheads by Ishi, bemused by the Big Cheap's bald head, chose to highlight one of the fair's scores of sculptures. He might have chosen Auguste Rodin's masterpiece, *The Thinker*. Instead he invoked the mythology of westward expansion by singling out Solon Borglum's action figure, *The American Pioneer*. "Here he stands at last, beside the western sea, the incarnate soul of his insatiable race," Lane proclaimed. It was the pioneer spirit that had "slashed God's work as with a knife" to create the canal. "The long journey of this slight modest figure that stands beside the oxen is at an end. The waste places of the earth have been found." But there was a new frontier, the spreading of "the gospel of an advancing democracy—strong, valiant, confident, conquering." A pamphlet added, "All hail to the white-headed, noble old pioneer who, with gun and axe, pushed his way thru the wilderness."[3]

Yet it was another sculpture, tragic rather than triumphant in mood, that received most of the "popular applause." It was an "an Indian brave, utterly exhausted, his strong endurance

The Pioneer, *by Solon Borglum. From Juliet James,* Sculpture of the Exposition Palaces and Courts: Descriptive Notes on the Art of the Statuary at the Panama-Pacific International Exposition San Francisco *(San Francisco: H. S. Crocker, 1915).*

worn through by the long, hard ride, storm-spent, bowed in the abandon of helpless exhaustion, upon a horse as weary as he, [who] has come to the end of the trail, beyond which there is no clear path." James Earle Fraser, who two years earlier had designed the new Indian head nickel for the U.S. Mint, created the noble sculpture. One observer concluded, "The symbolism of the 'Pioneer' and 'The End of the Trail' is...a very fine expression of the destinies of two great races." A visitor was to experience a moment of pathos and pity in front of Fraser's plastered elegy, followed by eight days of exuberance over the wonders of the modern world at the Golden Gate of America's empire, all bequeathed to the citizens of the present and future by the old pioneer.[4]

The End of the Trail, *by James Earle Fraser. From Juliet James,* Sculpture of the Exposition Palaces and Courts: Descriptive Notes on the Art of the Statuary at the Panama-Pacific International Exposition San Francisco *(San Francisco: H. S. Crocker, 1915).*

The year before, Ishi participated in a ceremony unveiling a monument to American Indians at Lincoln Park near Berkeley. The Daughters of the American Revolution sponsored the monument, and Ishi and Waterman were the entertainment for the group's fundraising event. The DAR also prevailed upon Ishi to unveil the monument in a formal ceremony. The bronze tablet set into a granite boulder was meant to honor the place of the Indian in American history; in particular, it

Unveiling of the Daughters of the American Revolution Indian Monument in Lincoln Park; Ishi in background. Photograph by Robert Heizer, 15-21019. Courtesy of the Phoebe A. Hearst Museum of Anthropology and the Regents of the University of California.

commemorated the site of a burial mound, containing the remains of 450 Indians as well as stone tools and shell ornaments, that had been razed and exhumed so that railroad tracks could be laid through.[5]

Across the Bay San Francisco also had a Lincoln Park, situated on a bluff above the Pacific Ocean at Land's End. The Pacific symbolized a beginning and an end in 1915. It was the beginning of a new America for whites, a new Empire, many thought, especially as the canal connecting the Atlantic and Pacific had been punched through. But many whites also believed that the Pacific was the end of the trail for Indians. It was time to put up monuments to their passing, with the last Stone Age man on hand to lend living poignancy to the commemoration. But Ishi wore a suit and tie to these events, not yet ready to ride off into the sunset oblivion.

San Francisco's Lincoln Park was quite literally the end of a brand new trail: the first transcontinental road for automobiles, the Lincoln Highway. Conceived in 1913, the highway ran from New York's Times Square to its terminus in the park. It was built by subscription, not financed by the U.S. government. Individuals contributed, many of them famous, including Theodore Roosevelt, Thomas Edison, and Woodrow Wilson. Even a group of Eskimos in America's territory of Alaska chipped in; their contribution arrived with the note "Fourteen pennies from Anvik Esquimaux children for the Lincoln Highway." Pictures of the Natives' pennies appeared in the press, serving as seed money to inspire others to give. Much of the route followed the old California Trail of the Gold Rush. Now Americans could drive their favorite piece of twentieth-century technology to nostalgically retrace the old route, completed just in time for the Panama Pacific Exposition.[6]

Though cars had been sputtering around the country for many years, the 1915 fair served as an inaugural ball for the horseless buggy. The Palace of Transportation featured "the greatest automobile show in the history of motordom." Hundreds of cars were on display. Automobile races thrilled crowds. Henry Ford even set up a scaled-down version of his assembly line, the key innovation behind modern mass production and the new wave of industrialization that swept over the nation in the early years of the new century. Visitors could witness a car being assembled before their eyes in just ten minutes; it was almost like stop-action photography. Each worker put one standardized item onto the frame, building up the mechanical contraption piece by piece until its full form took shape and it seemed almost alive.[7]

Though you could use the machines for transportation around your town or city, the auto show also showed you how you could see "the wilds" through your windshield. Huge relief maps, "the most wonderful of their kind ever erected," displayed the Lincoln Highway and other auto routes of the country, with attractions lit up by tiny bulbs. Automobiles could now travel from San Francisco directly into the Yosemite Valley, and water and power from Hetch Hetchy was now going to hydrate and electrify the city. John Muir grudgingly conceded, "These useful, progressive, blunt-nosed mechanical beetles will hereafter be allowed to puff their way into all the parks and mingle their gas-breath with the breath of the pines and waterfalls."[8]

Kroeber and Ishi, who had first toured the city together by automobile, had mixed feelings about the machines. Ishi liked them but preferred the trolley and thought the reason whites got sick was because they spent too much time in their cars. Kroeber played pranks on car drivers, tying strings across roads just to see if drivers would stop. When asked by a writer for the California automobile club if he ever had any dangerous encounters with Indians, Kroeber quipped, "In all my years of exploring I never had any narrow escapes from anything. The dangers we encounter are not in the wilds but right at our front doors. Speaking of savages, there's the reckless automobile driver...."[9]

Ishi arrived at the Exposition in a new car on the day he was to be the guest of honor of the Blackfeet delegation. The Blackfeet were being paid by the Great Northern Railroad to promote tourism in Glacier National Park. These Blackfeet, now barred from hunting in the park lands, were earning a living on the road. In the *Overland Monthly* the Blackfeet and other Indians who came to the fair were depicted as movie-like images of the past coming to stand on the sidelines as witnesses to "America's greatest achievement." "That the latest Americans should be given an opportunity to draw near the heart of this sorrowful race, whose moccasined feet are marking time in the land of shadow, is a matter for rejoicing," mused the magazine. Indians standing by as mute witnesses to white-driven progress was a familiar trope in American literature and painting. The *Overland Monthly*, born in 1868 just before the golden spike completed the transcontinental railroad, saw Indians in elegiac terms as part of a vanishing frontier. Their presence at the fair, these writers and artists thought, foreshadowed their imminent absence in a way that made American-made progress more manifest and more profound.[10]

A photograph of the Blackfeet shows them standing on the beach below the Cliff House, literally on the edge of Pacific oblivion, as if they had stepped into John Mix Stanley's painting *The Last of Their Race* (1857). Another photograph, though, undermined this message of vanishing. It showed the Blackfeet, in full regalia, lined up to make a bank deposit at a branch opened for business on the Exposition grounds. The teller may have been ready to accept their cash, but, as the article concluded, presumably quoting an unnamed Blackfeet, "The door of the Indian's yesterdays opens to a new world—a world unpeopled with red men, but whose population fills the sky, the plains, with sad and specter-like memories....We have come to the day of audit— a swift-gathering of all that is life, in the gloaming, after the sunset." The picture shows Indians putting money in the bank for their future, just as Ishi put his money in Kroeber's safe. But the accompanying story insisted that Indians were fading away in some apocalyptic "audit."

Ishi received an invitation to appear with the Blackfeet as their guest of honor. He wanted his young friend Fred Zumwalt to accompany him. Fred's mother drove the two to the fair in the family's "bug," a new green car. Ishi preferred the old red Buick, but the new car had a self-starter and electric lights. At the Exposition the Blackfeet performed dances in Ishi's honor. They had apparently planned to initiate him into their tribe, just as they had done with two white children when the Great Northern Building was dedicated. Ishi respectfully declined. Nonetheless, as Fred remembered, "I can recall how proud he was that day to receive some sort of honor from the other Indians and to be my host." The Great Northern Building's movie theater held a special screening of the university's movie about Ishi. Ishi sat next to Fred in the auditorium, apparently not seeing the images as "specter-like memories."[11]

Along with cars, movies were the big new thing at the fair. As the *Los Angeles Times* observed, "The world's amazing advance in science…is shown at San Francisco chiefly and most effectively though the medium of the cinematograph, a miracle which previous expositions lacked, but which is the most telling device employed to narrate and display the growth and spread of civilization.…It is the voice and the picture of the speeding world." Cars, planes, electricity, radio—all were part of this sped-up world, in which there were no places unknown, even to those who never left home, for all places had been captured on film.[12]

Ishi and Blackfeet at the Panama Pacific International Exposition, 1915. Courtesy of the Phoebe A. Hearst Museum of Anthropology and the Regents of the University of California.

Films were made about the fair, including one featuring Mabel Normand, the star of what might have been the first film Ishi saw. She teamed up with the comic actor Fatty Arbuckle to make a silly documentary. We arrive at the Ferry Building, starting off our tour of San Francisco from essentially Ishi's P.O.V. We are shown the streetcars and automobile taxis and are taken on a tour down the streets of San Francisco. One of the sights they highlight is the towering St. Francis Hotel. Ironically a few years later Fatty Arbuckle held what newspapers called a "wild party" in that very same hotel. When one of the young female party-goers died a few days later, Arbuckle was implicated in a sex scandal, luridly covered by Hearst's papers. Though he was finally acquitted—the jury even apologized to him because they felt he had been smeared—his films were banned. After the Arbuckle scandal, many Americans began to wonder if movies represented the advancement of Western civilization, or were leading to its decline and fall.

Americans also began to wonder if the war raging in Europe would lead to the end of civilization, with technological advancement turned lethally against humanity on a scale never seen before. The Panama Pacific's official story was of worldwide progress, spurred on by America's manifest destiny and led by whites. On the last day of the fair visitors were given badges emblazoned with a picture of the Indian's "end of the trail" and heard about how the Panama Canal opened up a new pathway to progress for whites.

But according to one of the Blackfeet Indians, the Exposition might have turned out to be the end-of-the-world party for whites instead. Two years earlier, he reported, a fellow tribesman was "walking about the earth hunting a black-tailed deer" when he heard a great noise. Two Angels whisked him away to heaven, where the Great Spirit came out of a tepee to give him a message for Indians: "Tell them all to wear feathers in their hair, because there are many people on earth, and I want to know which are Indians." The Great Spirit then told the Blackfeet about the great war that was coming and that only a few whites would be left living after it was all over. Then the land would be given back to the Indians.[13]

In all of San Francisco it would have been hard to find anyone who greeted the coming of the Exposition with as little enthusiasm as Alfred Kroeber. For Kroeber the relationship between world fairs and Indians was vexed and troubling. There was a long and unillustrious history of formally putting Indians on display. Kroeber's mentor, Franz Boas, had organized the displays for the Chicago Fair in 1893, but it was a bitter experience, as he felt he was expected to act like a circus impresario. Kroeber had no intention of joining such a circus. In 1911 he had written to the museum's board of directors that ethnographic displays at the fairs were really "amusement concessions...too often of the cheap show variety, thus being without educational significance." This fair would sponsor no official ethnographic displays. But in the Zone, a section just outside the official fairgrounds, given over to amusements, a simulated village of Zunis and Hopis was erected. Kroeber would much rather have gone off to study Zuni in situ in New Mexico; indeed he would leave San Francisco at the height of the fair to do just that. In New Mexico he would tell his prospective Native hostess that he was willing to eat beans three times a day if she would take him in for the summer. She thought he was so "cute" and "distinguished," with his well-trimmed beard, that she accepted. She found Kroeber, enjoying the simplicity of life away from the great city showing itself to the world, to be a friendly and helpful guest.[14]

But if anthropology did not have a high profile at the fair, race certainly did. In fact after a low-profile anthropological conference was held, an official Race Betterment Week opened at the fair, to much fanfare. David Starr Jordan, president of Stanford University, jumped at the invitation to promote eugenics, the movement devoted to "improving" the human race by promoting reproduction among those deemed fit and preventing it among those seen as unfit. An elaborate Race Betterment

Exhibit received a bronze medal for "illustrating evidences and causes of race degeneration and methods and agencies of race betterment."[15]

Jordan explained to fairgoers that war was a threat to this "race betterment." War worked against the principle of the survival of the fittest: it killed off the best men of every nation. Eight million had been killed or wounded in the world war, Jordan said; they were "the flower of their country's manhood, and the degenerate and unfit are left behind to repopulate the warring nations." Jordan had written to Kroeber before giving his speech, fishing for more evidence to support his thesis. He wanted to know if warfare killed off the strongest Indians in any tribe. Kroeber couldn't help him, and wouldn't even if he could. He wrote back that many tribes in California did not militarily resist the Spanish or the Americans. But "those that did suffered most from indiscriminate massacres, in which strong and weak, old and young, men and women, were sacrificed together." He must have been thinking about the Yahi. Ishi had survived, but he was certainly no "degenerate"; he was a man of strength and intelligence. Warfare had left children and women dead along with men, weak or strong, and Kroeber's distaste for Jordan's way of thinking seeps through the letter he sent him. Kroeber would give Jordan no arrows for his eugenicist quiver.[16]

The prominence of eugenics at the San Francisco Exposition must have dismayed Kroeber, for he had been battling this movement ever since it reared its superior head. He even risked ridicule to challenge the plainly racist assumptions built into the seemingly scientific cause. In a public lecture in February 1914 covered by the Associated Press, Kroeber said, "Eugenics today has become a joke." Hereditarian thinking, the belief that human beings and human culture fundamentally sprang from a racial genetic endowment, was "the greatest snare of modern thought." "Scientists have run riot with the idea," Kroeber complained, but they failed to distinguish between "heredity, which comes from the inside, and inheritance, which, like a fortune, comes from the outside." Some people are endowed with treasures; others aren't. But beneath it all, people are essentially the same the world over. "Civilization is an inheritance, pure and simple, not caused in the slightest degree by heredity."[17]

Kroeber was using civilization as a synonym for the anthropological idea of culture. For Kroeber culture was not shaped by one's genes. Indeed it existed on an entirely different plain, above the physical; it was "superorganic." Furthermore he challenged the way race was understood by proponents of eugenics. "So far as civilization is concerned," he argued, "there is no such thing as an Anglo-Saxon breed or a white man's burden. Kipling...has fundamentally false ideas of national psychology. He does not know what a race is or what civilization means." It would be fun to be entertained by Pope's telling the Kipling poem in the cave above Mill Creek later that summer, but the writer's view of race was a serious matter—a matter of serious error, Kroeber thought. "The cave-man of the ice age possessed the same mental capacities of the Anglo-Saxon of today, and until this fact is recognized all history will continue to be misunderstood." Finally Kroeber shot back at the moral superiority assumed by the eugenicists, with their calls to sterilize those they saw as unfit and encourage those they saw as of higher intelligence to intermarry and protect their finer genes. "It is easier to talk of breeding improved human beings than to begin by improving oneself and training one's children better," he declared. "The future of the human race can only be enhanced by individuals and by courageous adherence to ideals by nations."[18]

As Kroeber hammered home in several academic papers, eugenics rested on a false analogy between culture and nature. Until proved otherwise, he said, one must believe in "the absolute equality and identity of all human races." "All men are totally civilized"; no group of people is any lower than any other group of people. "A stage of civilization is merely a preconception made plausible by arbitrarily selected facts." Those scientists who believed otherwise believed in myth and magic, he charged, cleverly reversing modern scientists' tendency to see "primitive" peoples as beholden to irrational, mythical thinking. Eugenics was voodoo, a "dragon of superstition," a "mirage," a "fallacy."[19]

A writer for the *Los Angeles Times* responded, "It is a free country and the worthy man has a right to ridicule eugenics, but he should not feel sore if others laugh at instead of with him." Indeed eugenics was a widely held article of faith at the time and at the Exposition. At San Diego a small sister exposition was held coinciding with the one in San Francisco, and one of its central exhibits was on anthropology. Aleš Hrdlička was in charge. He assembled an exhibit of skeletons and skulls arranged into racial groupings. In at least one case, a collector had robbed a grave in the Philippines in order to supply specimens for the exhibit. The order and presentation of the "'thoroughbred' white American" next to the Indian and the "full-blood American negro" strongly suggested different evolutionary paths for each group, resulting in different intellectual capacities of these so-called races. As such, Hrdlička's anthropology flew in the face of the cultural relativism and belief in fundamental human equality espoused by Boas and Kroeber. Kroeber insisted there were no actual "stages" of civilization, but you could make such prejudice "plausible by arbitrarily selected facts," such as arranging skulls in an exhibit to make viewers think that brain size had something to do with intelligence, which in turn had something to do with race.[20]

By taking evolution into their own hands, eugenicists argued, Americans could create essentially a master race. But while Indians may be fading and vanishing, new immigrants from Mexico and southern Europe were viewed as a threat. The "thoroughbred" had the best brain, Hrdlička implied. Mixing with new immigrants might lead to what eugenicists called "race degeneration." Eugenicists raised the alarm about "the prevalence of brains of a doubtful or undesirable quality among the immigrant population."[21]

Hrdlička was *the* expert on brains. In fact he was the anthropologist who studied the remains of Qisuk after he died of tuberculosis, which he reported on in "An Eskimo Brain." Kroeber had done his first anthropological work with this group, when they were alive. His interpreter had been Esther Eneutseak, an Eskimo woman from Labrador whom Boas had brought to the 1893 World's Columbian Exposition. When Esther gave birth to a baby girl at the Exposition, she named her Columbia. Twenty-two years later, during the Panama Pacific Exposition, Columbia served as the bridesmaid at a traditional Eskimo wedding, but with a twist: it was performed on a beach in southern California. With her mother and several others, they were then living in an "Eskimo village" in Ocean Park. Having attended several world's fairs over the years, they were now making their living starring in Hollywood films about Eskimos and performing for tourists.[22]

What had gone around was coming back around. Eskimos were giving birth on a beach in California, not being pushed into the ocean; they were collecting pennies to pave the Lincoln Highway to Land's End in San Francisco, participating in American "progress" rather than being left behind. They were acting in movies. The tangled web of relations between anthropologists and Native peoples stretched across the globe and put people in weird positions and places. Even the anthropologists found themselves with strange bedfellows. Kroeber and Hrdlička, for instance, looked at people in entirely different ways, but now they were drawn together into an enigmatic life-and-death partnership. Kroeber's relationship with Ishi was recapitulating his earlier relationship with Qisuk and the Smith Sound Eskimos, and Hrdlička would come into the picture as well.

The Eskimos were still in the news and still on Kroeber's mind. In December 1909 he wrote a newspaper article on "the explorer's Eskimo." When he looked at Ishi, he worried that the Yahi would succumb to tuberculosis, like nearly all of the group Peary brought to New York City. Like his wife, Henriette.[23]

One of the two survivors had been the child Minik. Minik had grown up in America, like Columbia. He discovered that his father had not been buried after all, that Boas had tricked him. Kroeber might have seen the *San Francisco Examiner*'s sensational feature about the scandal: "Pathetic Appeal of Little [Minik], Who Was Brought to New York, 'in the Interest of Science,' Turned Adrift after His Unhappy Relatives Had Died Here and He Had Seen Father's Skeleton Grin at Him from a Glass Coffin in the

New York Museum of Natural History and Who Has Abandoned 'Civilization' Because He Cannot Get Justice." Minik went back to Greenland, and like Columbia got married. Just before he left New York the *Times* reported that someone said that he "should bequeath his brain to science for anthropological purposes." Shocked, Minik said, "You're a race of scientific criminals. I know I'll never get my father's bones out of the American Museum of Natural History. I am glad enough to get away before they grab my brains and stuff them into a jar!"[24]

"Science Can Go to Hell"

Kroeber had longed to take leave of San Francisco for some time. As it turned out, the Exposition provided his ticket out of town. At first, though, it looked as if he would put off his long-delayed sabbatical yet again. His responsibilities teaching and running the museum mounted. Moreover he did not feel right about leaving Ishi behind. When Pope looked at his friend Kroeber he may have seen a man on the verge of nervous exhaustion. In any event, the doctor's orders were firm: Kroeber should take his sabbatical. Ishi would be in good hands. So Kroeber let himself go, which was at the same time letting Ishi go.[25]

Though Kroeber trusted the doctor, he was worried about the health of Ishi and disconcerted that so much of his culture yet remained unrecorded. Kroeber had been too busy with other responsibilities to fully immerse himself in the difficult task of learning Yahi; Ishi had learned a few hundred words of English, but it was not enough for the deep ethnography they wished to do. Kroeber had always hoped that Edward Sapir, the one anthropologist who knew the related Yana language well, would do this work with Ishi. Indeed just two days after Ishi first arrived in San Francisco, Kroeber telegraphed Sapir in Ottawa, "Have totally wild southern yana at museum....Do you want to come and work him up?" But Sapir was tied down with his position with Canada's geological survey; he could not come. The next four years saw repeated invitations from Kroeber and repeated rejections from Sapir. In February 1914 Kroeber wrote again: "Is there any likelihood of your making the trip here in connection with the Exposition?" Kroeber was organizing a small anthropological conference to coincide with the Exposition and invited Sapir to give a paper.[26]

Sapir was honored by the invitation, though he was puzzled by the topic he was assigned, "Correlations in Time." Kroeber explained, "The average American anthropologist...treats his data with the most scrupulous attention to geography, but with an almost punctilious avoidance of the factor of time." He hoped Sapir would "break through [that] tradition and inject a new point of view." Sapir graciously put together a paper on the topic, but it was really one that Kroeber himself should have written. It was he who was most interested in thinking about history in relation to anthropology. After Sapir accepted, Kroeber wrote back with another offer: Could he stay after the meeting and work with Ishi? If so, he would be put on the university's payroll. Sapir agreed to do the work. Kroeber was ecstatic. And relieved. He told Sapir, "[I am] anxious to have you get ahold of Ishi as soon as possible." Ishi had been in the hospital that winter. Though some doctors diagnosed him with tuberculosis, others, Pope in particular, rejected that diagnosis. Kroeber noted that Ishi had "come around in good shape" and so "those who denied [the diagnosis] were apparently right." Still, Kroeber was alarmed: "The moral is to get from him what we can while he is well instead of trusting that he will last indefinitely." He assured Sapir, "You will find Ishi bursting with mythological, ethnological, tribal, and geographical information, which he is delighted to impart."[27]

Kroeber thus handed two of his own responsibilities to Sapir, whom he regarded as the country's most brilliant linguist. In effect he had designated Sapir his better half. While Sapir came to work with Ishi at Berkeley, Kroeber would be free to escape. So desperate was he to get away that he did not even stay for the conference in early August, though he was officially the chairman. (Waterman stood in for him.) Kroeber left on a Santa Fe train bound for fieldwork among the Zuni in New Mexico. From there he headed to New York City and then Europe, a land torn by world war. Eight million people were already dead, wounded, or missing in action. Western civilization was in shambles.

Kroeber visited family in Germany, Henriette's and his own. He met with anthropologists whom he knew only through correspondence. And he spent hours in the cafés of Vienna, still a vibrant city of ideas even in the midst of war, talking about the world, talking about Freud, Jung, and psychology. All the while he was sending postcards and souvenirs to his friends, including Ishi. Waterman or Gifford would read them to Ishi, and they wrote down his replies. Kroeber was back in New York by February, refreshed and inspired. "[It was] a trip I would not have missed for anything," he said. Then he began putting together all of the fieldwork he and others had done among California Indians and turning it into his indispensable volume, *The Handbook of the California Indians*.[28]

Ishi went on a journey as well, across the San Francisco Bay to live with the Waterman family that summer. He slept on the outdoor porch with Waterman; the anthropologists and Pope felt that being outdoors would be good for his health. Almost every day he walked along Strawberry Creek to the anthropology building and sat down to work with Sapir. Sapir found him bursting, all right; it was hard to slow him down enough so that Sapir could take in what he was saying, write it down in his notebooks, and then, through whatever means available—English, Yana, gesture, pantomime—find translations for the words in Ishi's texts. He was slow, though, in telling Sapir the Yahi words for *mother* and *father, galsi* and *ganna*. He hadn't needed to use them in a long time, Sapir surmised.[29]

The work wasn't easy. Sapir groused to Kroeber, "At first it seemed perfectly hopeless, for reasons you know better than anyone else." But with time, and through "brute memory of stems and grammatical elements" of Yana, Sapir was able to obtain texts from Ishi and begin interpreting them, It was taxing work, though, and Sapir couldn't take out his frustrations on the good-natured Ishi. But Waterman, a notoriously irascible man equipped with a short fuse, did get under Sapir's skin. Kroeber wrote to Sapir from Europe, advising him, "The only way to handle Waterman … is to keep your temper and give him some of his own rough-house." Sapir threatened to quit, but he kept at his work with Ishi, and the two made slow but valuable progress.[30]

The anthropology conference was held in August. Waterman chaired the meeting, Sapir gave his paper, and other anthropologists presented their work. Hrdlička was even part of the program, though because he could not be there in person a colleague read his paper on "human eugenics"; it was much less skeptical of the movement than was Kroeber. Ishi posed in his suit for a photograph with Sapir, Waterman, and the visiting anthropologists Paul Radin and Robert Lowie. The only thing that distinguished him from the anthropologists was his lighter suit, darker skin, and longer hair. Summer classes were also being held at Berkeley, and Ishi would go as a guest. One of the students was Esther Watson, visiting that summer with her Reed College professor, William Ogburn. Ogburn was living with Waterman that summer along with Ishi, so Esther was invited over on several occasions. On one occasion she sat down on the rug before the fireplace with Ishi and played a stick game with him. One stick, marked, represented man; an unmarked stick was woman. He put one in each hand and chanted his game song: "Oo å hay nay; Oo å nay hay nay! over and over again until I designated which hand I chose." If she chose the marked stick, Ishi won the round. She went with Ishi and the anthropologists to see a shell mound, the refuse of Indians along the Bay from times past that could be studied by the anthropologists. She often saw Ishi making arrowheads beneath the pepperwood tree next to the anthropology building, and she saw him in Waterman's class when he came to demonstrate fire making with sticks.[31]

A newspaper reported tongue in cheek that Ishi, once a "cave man," had become an anthropology professor: "[He is] a gentleman now, and in his 'store clothes' and with his top hat he's very proud of himself—all except his feet. He won't wear shoes because he says they hurt his feet, and besides, what's the use of being a professor if one has to wear shoes." Ishi had become "one of the notables of the University of California" and was teaching

California's sons and daughters how to make fire from sticks and about "the mode of life of his people." Although the reporter dead-panned the story, it was meant as a joke. But in a sense the story was accurate: Ishi was the professor, and Waterman, Sapir, and Kroeber were the instruments through which he expressed his knowledge. Ishi constructed the official anthropologists to be carriers of Yahi culture, laboriously chipping and notching and assembling with sinew or glue or whatever was at hand until the stories might fly straight.[32]

Ishi poured into Sapir six forty-five-page notebooks, each packed with Yahi words and many with Sapir's own glosses in between lines of Yahi text, though much remained obscure to him and many words he found impossible to "unravel." There were 3,296 lines of Yahi text, composed of some thirteen thousand words. At the end of the summer Sapir wrote to Kroeber, "I think I can safely say that my work with Ishi is by far the most time-consuming and nerve-racking that I have ever undertaken. Ishi's imperturbable good humour alone made the work possible." The modest Sapir, admitting that his texts were not as abundant as one might hope, reported to Kroeber that he felt he had succeeded in getting "material of value" from Ishi. Waterman concurred, telling Kroeber that although Sapir "beefed right up to the last" he "was quite successful with his work." Though Waterman later worried that he had let Sapir "ride him too hard," Ishi seemed indefatigable in relating his stories. Sapir, though, was spent. He never fully translated and published the texts Ishi had given to him, and it was only the dedicated and loving work of a later generation of anthropologists who discovered what Ishi was bursting to say that summer.[33]

Ishi told of Cottontail and how he put the sun into its path in the sky; about Grizzly Bear going up into the hole in the sky to search for fire; about Coyote and his scorched feet, eating his toes as if they were roasted grasshoppers. He told the story of tricky, lusting Coyote and his sister, Coyote Woman, and how she dressed herself up for the dance, wearing her wildcat skin blanket, and Coyote told her to paint her face, and she did, brightening it with red paint. Coyote dressed up in disguise and went to the dance in secret; there his sister grabbed him and took him aside, not recognizing him. Why are you alone, Coyote-in-disguise asks. My brother is back home, sick, she says. He is too sick to eat, she says. Is he really, Coyote-in-disguise asks. He certainly isn't sick enough to die, he says. Certainly he is, she says; so it is with him.[34]

Although, as Pope noted in his "medical history of Ishi," Ishi had been living that summer in "Waterman's home under most hygienic conditions with plenty of outdoor recreation, sleeping, proper food, and diversion . . . his health suddenly began to fail." It was really not so sudden. Kroeber had seen it coming, while Pope had been "over-optimistic" about Ishi's full recovery from earlier illnesses. In fact Kroeber had demanded reports from Waterman and Gifford about Ishi's health: "It's our responsibility and we ought to live up to it." He wanted them to keep track of Ishi's weight and take his afternoon temperature. An elevated temperature in the afternoon was a sign of tuberculosis, the dreaded disease that had claimed Kroeber's first informants, Qisuk and the other Eskimos, as well as his father and his wife.[35]

In August Kroeber learned from his mother-in-law that Ishi had a bad cough, and she complained that Gifford had not given him exact figures on his weight. Ishi was admitted to the university hospital in San Francisco on August 22, 1915. Under the heading "physical examination," his chart read, "Medium sized, well built, dark skinned Indian, fairly well nourished, with long black hair in 'pigtail' down back, prominent cheek bones, broad features, large, long nose. Patient lying in bed comfortable; not especially sick looking, coughing frequently very hard."[36]

In late August, just before his boat left for Europe, Kroeber wrote to Waterman with a heartfelt set of instructions: "We have got to handle the case. The physicians go by the book and rule, and it's up to us to apply our knowledge of the individual and our judgment to their findings and advise." This approach was diametrically opposed to the one Kroeber followed in almost all of his own anthropology. He believed that anthropologists, because they try to understand culture, should "refuse to deal with either individuality or individuals." But in talking about Ishi's medical care, he said, "Pope has the only right idea, which is to handle him as a person, not a hospital case." Modern medical science robbed patients of their individuality, Kroeber knew; it turned them into a collection of bones and organs, mechanical pieces fit together into a complex whole. But this view took no account of Ishi's background, nor of his Indianness, which Kroeber insisted must enter the diagnostic and therapeutic picture. Kroeber believed the physicians were correct in their diagnosis, but he insisted, "They didn't understand the Indian. Nor did they know what to do with him. All they could dope up was the usual prescriptions for a typical American case without money. Pope has the right imagination what to do, but I'm confident he's over optimistic, and when the Indian got better was ready to let things slide." If

Ishi recovered, Kroeber said they should treat him as they had before, giving him air, exercise, and distraction. If he became weaker and tuberculosis ensued, he suggested sending him to Guinda to live with the museum's former watchmen, who himself had been suffering from tuberculosis for ten years. Or even to Vina to live with Merle and Jack Apperson, who'd once stolen from Ishi but now called him brother.[37]

On August 24 the doctors reported that Ishi's skin tests for tuberculosis were positive. His coughing and hiccups continued; the doctors gave him morphine, which stopped them for a few hours. His condition improved slightly in late September, and the decision was made to move him "to a room in the Museum where he can get more fresh air and sunshine with special arrangements for supplying him food more suitable to his taste." Finally Dr. Moffitt recommended that after becoming stronger, Ishi should "return to the country and mountains and live more as he formerly did." In the doctors' judgment, civilization had spent Ishi, and all that could be done for him was to send him away from the city, back to the wilderness.[38]

If Ishi had been white, the recommendation would probably have been the same. Henriette had been sent to Arizona, with its dry air and sunshine, to recover. People at the time drew a connection between landscape and health. Since the mid-nineteenth century California physicians had been keenly interested in what they called "medical topography," the effect of geography, climate, hydrology, and meteorology on health. The job of the physician was to understand the effect of climate on the human body and prescribe the right kind of nature to cure ailments that were afflicting their patients; their role was to be "the assistant of nature." In turn, "nature" could be sold to patients as a cure, and that is precisely what boosters in the Southwest were doing, proclaiming that its "flood of sunshine at all seasons" could cure consumption.[39]

After Ishi's discharge from the hospital in October, the anthropologists worked hard to set him up in the best environment the city could afford. Waterman informed Kroeber that the Pacific Island exhibit room, "the brightest and sunniest" in the building, had been cleared out for Ishi. "I think we are doing as well for him as is humanly possible; and he is fairly cheerful and is getting his strength back slowly. He seems to spend a large part of his time in bed; and it would be impossible to send him away yet if we wanted to." But Waterman wanted to. In November he worried about having Ishi's "death on our consciences," telling Kroeber, "I feel quite sure that San Francisco's climate will get him in the long run if he stays."[40]

Kroeber agreed with the desirability of sending Ishi away, but worried about its practicality. What would happen to Ishi if he were separated from the people who cared the most for him, his friends? And how would the matter of his support be worked out? The university would not keep paying his salary if he went away. Kroeber himself was broke; he had gone deeply into debt paying for the treatment of Henriette over the years. They hoped that Interior Secretary Lane, the recipient of Ishi's gift of two arrowheads, might furnish a stipend to help this victim of "the pioneer" he so venerated. But hopes of gathering together the funds to send Ishi off to a sanitarium in Tucson or Denver seemed far-fetched. Kroeber apparently did not consider bringing Ishi with him to New Mexico in the summer of 1915, perhaps because his health was still good and Sapir was coming to "work him up." Kroeber did suggest some practical plans to get him to what everyone agreed would be a more salubrious environment than San Francisco, to Guinda or to the Appersons. Still, he worried that the "adverse psychic factors would...outweigh the purely physiological benefits." Nonetheless "tentative arrangements were made with responsible caretakers," Pope reported. But then Ishi never got strong enough to travel. Every time his condition appeared desperate enough to warrant sending him away, he was in no condition to travel, but when he was doing better everyone around him felt less compelled to send him away, perhaps being "over optimistic."[41]

Kroeber must have been skeptical of the curative power of climate; it hadn't worked for Henriette. Native Americans seemed even more vulnerable to the ravages of tuberculosis than white Americans. On one Nevada reservation, 36 percent of everyone who died succumbed to this one disease; in South Dakota in 1885, it was 65 percent. Though tuberculosis is one of the few diseases known to be present in Peru and perhaps other parts of the Americas before Europeans arrived, Europeans introduced or reintroduced it to all parts of the hemisphere. Native Americans were hard hit by the disease, in part because their bodies were made even more vulnerable to infection through crowding on reservations and poor nutrition. The Navajo called tuberculosis "the fading away of the heart." Though there was some hope that tuberculin (an extract from tubercle bacilli first discovered in 1890) could cure the disease, its use had largely proven ineffective by the 1910s. Doctors could treat tuberculosis only by prescribing what one physician called a "dietetic-hygienic *régime*":

better nutrition, exposure to sunlight, and relocation to climates thought to be more salubrious.[42]

Pope was often at Ishi's side as he convalesced in the Pacific Island room of the museum. He was probably Ishi's best friend. The city water that the Spring Valley Water Company piped into the museum did not please Ishi, and he asked for fresh spring water, "sweet water," he called it. Pope did his best to get some fresh water for his ailing friend. From his bed Ishi spent hours looking out his window at the steelworkers putting up the frame for the new hospital. "All a same monkey-tee," he said. They were just like monkeys, he meant, using Chinese American slang ("all a same"), English ("monkey"), and a Yahi suffix ("tee") to get his idea across.[43]

Pope once asked Ishi what he thought made men sick in San Francisco. His first reason was "Sacko mahale," women who were menstruating. Women should go into their own space then and have no contact with men, not to mention food or utensils. This was a time for women to be on their own and live in a lodge separate from the main village, refrain for working, and pursue other things, maybe pay more attention to their dreams. His second and third reasons had to do with modern life. Too much *wowi:* they spent too much time in their houses, inside. Pope agreed with this viewpoint, and was a consistent advocate of the salutary effects of fresh air, sunshine, and outdoor living. Ishi also identified "too much automobile" as a culprit.

Finally he mentioned "Coyote doctor," which Pope interpreted as the "evil spirit" but may have referred to *kuwi,* who used their powers to cause sickness in people rather than cure them. Good *kuwi* would blow smoke and ashes in certain directions around patients to protect them. Or they sucked small pieces of "obsidian or cactus thorns from their clients, averring that these were the etiological factors of sickness." All sorts of "pins"—cactus thorns, bee stings—might get lodged in a person's body, causing pain and sickness. The *kuwi* would suck them out, and then place them safely into a small container, often made from the trachea of birds. Such sucking doctors, who had worked among many California tribes, were already becoming rare. But their powers, augmented with their repertoire of healing songs, were known to be extraordinary.[44]

Kroeber knew of some sucking doctors, called *kegeior,* among the Yurok, and they were happy to treat patients if the price was right. There is no record of any attempt to seek out one of them to treat Ishi. Pope considered such doctoring sleight-of-hand magic, of no real value, and Kroeber probably agreed. Ishi's uncle had probably been a *kuwi;* he kept his healing powers even after his foot was crippled in a steel bear trap. Ishi himself may have been a *kuwi,* or a *kuwi* in training. The young Frank Day saw Ishi trying to heal his companion outside of Oroville. And he did make the rounds at the hospital, singing songs that brightened the spirits of patients. Ishi probably would not have trusted an Indian doctor he did not know, for he could just as well be a coyote doctor. We can only wonder what Ishi thought of all the pins that were stuck into him, a new vaccine from Pope administered early on and hypodermic needles shooting morphine into his body full of pains.

In mid-November Waterman reported to Kroeber that Ishi's afternoon temperature was almost normal: "He seems quite cheerful, is filling out, and in every way gives signs of getting on his feet." He "summoned enough strength to make a few arrows or to talk about his life in the wilds," Pope reported. But Ishi's cough persisted. He could no longer eat without suffering great distress. "Even water caused him misery," Pope said, impressed that Ishi never complained. In January Pope remained optimistic and wrote to Kroeber about possibly moving him to a "forest range, later on." "I think there is a chance for recovery...if he could be put in the proper environment."[45]

Ishi was making a few arrows, but mostly was confined to his bed. Pope brought him a .22-caliber rifle "to interest him." Ishi dragged himself out one day with the rifle in tow. "His eyes lighted with joy as he told me of his adventure," Pope told Kroeber. But Ishi's condition worsened. Pope wanted to take one last picture with Ishi, and so he coaxed him to get out of bed. "He was always happy to be photographed and accommodated me," Pope said. In the picture Pope stands erect behind Ishi, his bow drawn and aimed up and to the right; Ishi, bare-chested and emaciated, kneels before Pope, holding his bow with an arrow notched but undrawn on its sinew string. "It was only after the picture was developed that I recognized to what a pitiful condition he had been reduced," Pope confessed remorsefully. "Had this been apparent before, I should not have asked this exertion of him." Apparently even Pope could not see the man before him. It was only after the photographic representation did not meet his expectations that he realized the extent of Ishi's consumption. Later Pope wanted to include the image in his article "Medical History of Ishi," to be published in the anthropological journal Kroeber edited. It would make manifest Ishi's "tragic fate." But Kroeber had it removed. He had strong objections, considering the picture "too mournful and unesthetic" (as the managing editor explained to a complaining Pope). In other words, it was in bad taste.[46]

On March 18, 1916, Ishi's condition was so bad that he was taken back to the hospital, entered as patient 11032. He was "vomiting and retching occasionally, evidently in great distress." He was coaxed to eat, but he couldn't keep anything down. An attempt to feed him through a tube into his stomach failed, and the "patient was greatly irritated."[47]

Gifford wrote to Kroeber, alerting him to Ishi's desperate state and informing him that everyone expected Ishi to die within a week or two. He reported, "[Pope] wants to make a cast of his face and hands after death; also to perform an autopsy." Gifford also inferred that "the hospital would like to have his body." He told Pope that Kroeber, and Ishi, wanted to have a "proper burial," but his words seemed to have no impact. Upon receiving Gifford's letter, Kroeber wrote back furiously, with ammunition to help Gifford beat back the plans for an autopsy and general dissection. He charged, "The prime interest in this case would be of a morbid romantic nature":

> I must ask you as my personal representative on the spot in this matter, to yield nothing at all under any circumstances. If there is any talk of the interests of science, say for me that science can go to hell. We propose to stand by our friends.[48]

The letter was uncharacteristically passionate, venting rage against science and its determination to turn Ishi into a laboratory specimen. The *Examiner's* story on Minik had juxtaposed the "interests of science" and the terrible fate of the Eskimo in

New York at the beginning of Kroeber's career. Now Kroeber wrote, *If there is any talk about the interests of science, say for me that science can go to hell.* These searing words began their journey across the country while Ishi was on his deathbed, coughing up blood. Kroeber also sent a telegram, instantly traveling from New York to the Western Union office in downtown San Francisco: "URGE COMPLETE ADHERENCE ORIGINAL PLANS. POPE WILL HONOR MY WISHES." It was received there at 6:17 a.m. on March 25. At noon that day Ishi suffered a massive pulmonary hemorrhage, and Pope was called to his bedside. Pope found him "very weak and faint": "With stoic calmness [Ishi] looked at the great quantities of blood that poured from his mouth and nose. I administered a large does of morphia. He died soon after, at 12:20 p.m., March 25, 1916."[49]

A few hours later the autopsy Kroeber tried to prevent went forward. "A compromise between science and sentiment" was made, Gifford defensively told Kroeber. The doctors took possession of the body they had once described as perfect. Dr. J. V. Cooke, who with Pope had learned from Ishi how to use a bow and arrow, presided. His postmortem report for "Ishi. Hospital Number 11032," begins, "The body is that of a considerably emaciated Indian 168 cm. in length. There is no rigor mortis. The body is still warm." It describes what Cooke saw inside Ishi's body, with sections on the "Abdominal Cavity...the Heart... Lungs...Spleen...Liver...Gallbladder...Kidneys...Adrenals," and so on, ending with "Brain.—Weighs 1300 grams. It is removed and shows no gross abnormalities with the exception of some increase in fat beneath the pia. The skull is small and rather thick."[50]

Pope made the death mask, pouring plaster over Ishi's face to produce a mold that would capture his features, and then Ishi's body was taken to Mount Olivet Cemetery in Colma. In mourning Pope shot arrows from Ishi's bow until he had bested the Yahi archer's mark by fifteen yards and was satisfied. Waterman, Gifford, and Pope visited the embalmed body in the parlor and, as Pope reported, "reverently placed in his coffin his bow, a quiver full of arrows, ten pieces of dentalia or Indian money, some dried venison, some acorn meal, his fire sticks, and a small quantity of tobacco." These things would accompany him on his journey to the land of the dead. Pope thought that the Yahi cremated their dead, but he was mistaken, confusing the fire that illuminates the journey to the other world with the fire that consumes a dead body. Just before the coffin was sent into the blaze, Pope slipped his own arrow into Ishi's quiver, revealing the way he loved the dead man.[51]

> To tell about the dead, the dead,
> They see, the dead,
> They see a little at a time....
> So many dead,
> Dead people, rolled up,
> Their bodies rolled up, flexed, stiff and cold.
>
> They go south,
> They jump through the hole (into the other world)
> Make fire, make firelight....
> They stop and talk by the fire
> Then they go through,
> Go right through the door.
> The fire is put out.

He takes one person at a time.
They shut the door and climb up the sky.
They don't believe it.
They go back down, go down and walk, the dead.
Walk around the ground.
Then they whirl,
A whirlwind, people say,
They go up through the sky on a rope, the dead....

Then they are done.
The people, they are all done.
Look north, look west, look east.[52]

By the time Kroeber received Gifford's letter explaining what happened after Ishi died, he knew that, according to Ishi's beliefs, his six-day journey to the land of the dead had already been completed. In New York Kroeber shaved his beard, creating a stir among his anthropological friends (who had nicknamed him "the Beard" after his iconic whiskers), and continued his work on *The Handbook of California Indians*. In the summer he traveled again to New Mexico for more fieldwork among the Zuni. Years before, a Hopi potter from the area had made a clay jar that was taken into Kroeber's collection at the museum; it had been selected to hold Ishi's ashes. When the summer was over Kroeber returned to San Francisco, probably afflicted again with "the prison gate sense" of confinement.[53]

Ishi's ashes had been placed in the Hopi pottery jar south of the city in Colma, but there were still remains of the man lying about the museum. In his office Kroeber found a container holding Ishi's preserved brain. It took him two months to decide what to do with the brain he had never wanted removed from his friend. How to make it right? There was no way. He looked in all directions. He looked east, and offered it to Aleš Hrdlička at the Smithsonian Institution in Washington, D.C.: "I find that at Ishi's death last spring his brain was removed and preserved. There is no one here who can put it to scientific use. If you wish it, I shall be glad to deposit it in the National Museum collection."

Hrdlička didn't respond until December, explaining that he had been away in Florida "running down another 'ancient man'": "I hardly need to say that we shall be very glad to receive and take care of Ishi's brain, and if a suitable opportunity occurs to have it properly worked up." Following Hrdlička's detailed instructions, Kroeber had Ishi's brain packed in soft excelsior in a moderate-size box and surrounded by absorbent cotton soaked with the liquid in which the brain was preserved. After receiving the package, Hrdlička's secretary, Ms. Rosenbusch, wrote back to Kroeber, asking if the brain was a gift, or if it was being deposited. If a gift, who was it from? In his response Kroeber avoided taking personal ownership of the brain, giving it away instead to a larger organization:

Dear Madam:

Ishi's brain was sent to the National Museum as a gift with the compliments of the University of California. I believe there would be some question as to who was the legal possessor before it was sent to Dr. Hrdlicka. If you will enter as donor the Department of Anthropology of the University of California, I think your record will be as accurate as you can make it.

The contents of Ishi's skull were put in a vat for safekeeping in the Smithsonian, in the same container as the brain of John Wesley

Powell, once the head of the U.S. Geological Service and the Smithsonian's Bureau of Ethnology.[54]

Still in the university museum was the death mask Pope had made, the plaster likeness of Ishi's face. A mask conceals and reveals. A mask has power; it both sharpens and upsets identity. When Kroeber published Pope's "Medical History of Ishi," he had to photograph the mask to accompany the article. He had to confront the white mask, small and rather thick. He focused in on it with the camera. The alabaster image was all he ever really had.

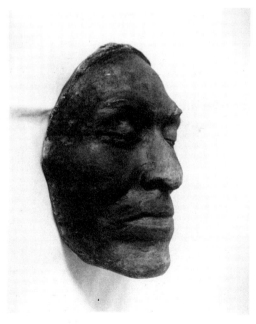

Ishi's death mask. Courtesy of the Phoebe A. Hearst Museum of Anthropology and the Regents of the University of California 15-6404.

What was beneath his own mask, his professional persona, his status as a widower and a mourner of a friend whose wholeness had been violated by the very science of man to which he had dedicated his life? Kroeber began to feel his own cracked face, his splitting skull, the nausea, headache, and vertigo.

He walked down the street somewhere in San Francisco. He thought he was going straight but was listing badly, bumping into people, finally stumbling down into the gutter in front of the saloon. The saloon keeper and a policeman found him there. When they stood him up, they could see that the well-dressed man wasn't just some bum on the street, drunk out of his mind. They took him to a backroom and gave him coffee. The man came to and seemed perfectly sober, solemn even. So they put him in a five-cent taxi and sent him home. At the end of the journey Kroeber had to reach into his pocket for a nickel to cover the fare for crossing the city, which had a buffalo on one side and the head of an Indian on the other.[55]

Epilogue

THE HEARTH OF PROMETHEUS
AND THE WILDERNESS OF ISHI

ALFRED KROEBER FELL INTO THE GUTTER FOR PHYSIOLOGICAL, not psychological, reasons. The professor thought that he might be going crazy, or that he had a brain tumor. In fact he was suffering from Ménière's disease, caused by an organism that attacks the inner ear and makes its victim experience dizziness, nausea, headache, and vertigo.

Though he knew that the disease is organic in origin, Kroeber believed that his own vertigo, his sense of disequilibrium, manifested a troubled past and his current psychological state. His interest in Freudian psychoanalysis had been piqued when he visited Vienna, and he underwent psychoanalysis himself in an effort to get at his own basic, "primitive" levels of personality. Psychoanalysis is a technique of looking below the surface of one's character—a surface put in place by culture and history perhaps—and finding what lies beneath, in a more wild state. Asked years later what he got out of psychoanalysis, Kroeber said that he "learned to not be so solemn."

After Ishi's death Kroeber questioned his own profession of anthropology, and even took a leave from his teaching duties at Berkeley in order to become a psychoanalyst himself. He called this period his "hegira," alluding to the time when Mohammed left Mecca and wandered until he found a home again in Medina. Kroeber confessed that he was "overtaken" by a feeling of "Sturm und Drang."[1]

German for *storm and stress,* Sturm und Drang also refers to a literary movement led by two of Kroeber's heroes, Schiller and Goethe. Those Romantic writers sought to throw off the controlling societal norms governing a young man's personality and unleash emotion and passion. Goethe's poem celebrating the man who stole fire from the Gods, Prometheus, opens with the defiant fire snatcher taunting Zeus. Prometheus celebrates the home and hearth he has constructed himself despite the gods:

> Cover your heaven, Zeus,
> With cloudy vapors
> And like a boy
> beheading thistles
> Practice on oaks and mountain peaks—
> Still you must leave
> My earth intact
> And my small hovel, which you did not build,
> And this my hearth
> Whose glowing heat
> You envy me.

Kroeber even began writing stories of his own, and he shared his budding literary output with Sapir, whom he saw as his better half; Sapir reciprocated by sending his own poetry to Kroeber. Each fearlessly critiqued the other; Kroeber, like a young Goethe, wanted to see more passion, more "intensity of feeling," in Sapir's poems—in himself. Kroeber's stories, such as "Twelve Brothers," drew on elements of the culture and mythology of California Indians. But to Sapir they also revealed parts of Kroeber's personality: sadistic or masochistic tendencies, neuroses, repression. Kroeber squirmed, and responded honestly to Sapir's "cool, painstaking analysis." "I often wonder people don't see more of the repressions," he replied. "It's only lately I've begun to realize how successfully I disguise myself.... In other words, I feel the mask as a mask, and usually sense it as wrinkled and obvious." He knew people thought him "cool and impersonal," but beneath the mask he was emotional and wild. He "admired recklessness": "[I am a man] relieved when I can escape beyond morality." He bowed to morality in his life, but confessed to Sapir, "I carry it as a fetter."[2]

After this last letter was sent to Sapir in 1920, the conflicted and shattered Kroeber finally began to become whole again, with the help of his new wife, Theodora; a new home in Berkeley with gardens designed by John McLaren, the Golden Gate Park superintendent who gave Ishi the plaid shirt; a retreat for family and friends in the Napa Valley they called Kishamish; and continued contact with California Indians. When Kroeber was first dating Theodora, who had lost her first husband to an illness worsened by his service in the Great War, they went to a faculty dance. Afterward Theodora, Kroeber, and another professor were sitting silently before a fire. Finally the other professor interrupted the silence, asking, "What do the wild flames say?" Their wordless reverie abruptly ended, Kroeber replied sharply, "The point is, they do not *say* anything."[3]

Kroeber was returned to the hearth. He and Theodora were married, she bringing two children from her first marriage, Theodore and Clifton, into the new family. They later had two children together: Karl, who would become an important scholar in his own right, and Ursula, who would gain fame as a brilliant writer of fantasy novels grounded particularly in their imagined landscapes. Kishamish was a restorative place of imagination, nature, and culture for the whole family. Indians, anthropologists, and other friends visited them there in the summer. And Kroeber continued his scholarship and fieldwork. He cowrote a book recounting Yurok stories with a Yurok man named Robert Spott. Once Spott's nephew questioned why he spent so much time with the anthropologist. "White men hurt so much. We have to help him," Spott replied. Help Kroeber got. The landscape and the people restored him.[4]

His children do not remember their father as a solemn man, but as "almost continuously good-humored, full of fun, focusing on and enjoying the amusing aspect of everything." A few times, just for fun, Kroeber found something on a walk, string that a dog was chewing or a ribbon left from a party, and decided to stretch the thin barrier across a street, just to see how many cars would stop in respect at this trickster's boundary line. As Theodora said, this was "social protest within the absurd, a weapon for which he had a lifetime preference."[5]

Kroeber became one of the leading American anthropologists of the twentieth century, writing scores of important articles and books. Everyone always thought he would write, or should write, a book about Ishi. But Kroeber wrote little about Ishi, the fire maker. A few words were devoted to him in his massive *Handbook of the California Indians*. It was uncharacteristic of the book as a whole to deal with individuals, but Ishi appears under a section on the Yahi entitled "The Last Survivor." Two paragraphs are given to Ishi, the first detailing his appearance in Oroville and the second his adaptation to modern life in San Francisco. At the end of the second paragraph Kroeber wrote about the man himself: "He was industrious, kindly, obliging, invariably even tempered, ready of smile, and thoroughly endeared himself to all with whom he came in contact."[6]

Kroeber could not bring himself to tell Ishi's story in full; instead he placed that trust in Theodora's hands. He served as "principal informant" as she embarked on this most precious task. While she was working on it, the couple took one last trip to Europe, in 1960, where Kroeber participated in a conference on "anthropological horizons." He himself was about to slip over the horizon. In Paris he tired one night on the walk back to the hotel after dinner at Le Vernouil, and for the first time he leaned a little on Theodora's arm. Kroeber died that night of a heart attack. After the doctor pronounced him dead, Theodora sat with him "through those shadowed hours between life and death when, as the California Indians put it, the Spirit lingers, concerned for the living." She remembered their life together, and she made sense of what was happening through the worldview of California Indians. By morning "his Spirit had taken leave of the body, of the world of the living, to find its way to the Trail down which it must journey, to the Land of the Dead."[7]

Theodora sent a telegram the next day conveying the sad news: "Alfred died quietly during the night in Paris. Saturday. I am returning Lufthansa Monday tenth. Ashes will follow by air." The *San Francisco Chronicle* printed his obituary the following day, October 6, 1960, hailing Kroeber as the man who "shaped the science of anthropology." Some people in Indian country were saddened by the news. Mary Dornback, a Yurok woman whose family had hosted and helped Kroeber when he first went out to do fieldwork along the Klamath River, wrote her own remembrance for the California Council of Indians newsletter. She was especially grateful for the contribution Kroeber made by speaking on behalf of California Indians for the federal Indian land claims case in the 1950s: "Members of the [Council of California Indians] feel that they express the conviction of every California Indian when we say, that we will be forever grateful to the Great Spirit, who must have guided Dr. Alfred Louis Kroeber from Hoboken, New Jersey, to California where he soon became our friend and in later life, our greatest hope for long delayed justice." Though some anthropologists spoke on behalf of the government in the land claims cases, Kroeber stood by the Indians, and he helped win the legal battle. Of course the war had already been lost, and winning the case led to a settlement that settled nothing: in 1968, eight hundred dollars was paid to qualified Indians as compensation for their inestimable losses of land and life.[8]

Only a few people in the courtroom heard Kroeber's testimony in the case. But through her beautifully written book, *Ishi in Two Worlds: A Biography of the Last Wild Indian in North America*, published a year after Alfred died, Theodora shared the story of this great loss with a much larger circle. It soon became a best-seller, along with Harper Lee's *To Kill a Mockingbird*. Each book was about an epic failure of the American promise of "life, liberty, and the pursuit of happiness." Each offered its readers a chance to reckon, deeply, with that failure. *Mockingbird* spoke to the African American experience, evoking the legacy of slavery and the racial prejudice that continued to keep people apart and put some people down. *Ishi in Two Worlds* spoke to the Native American experience, conjuring the dark side of American expansion and the legacy of genocidal policies, whether they aimed at a physical or a cultural extinction.

Ishi in Two Worlds struck a chord. There were many heartfelt reactions by white readers. One man incarcerated at Folsom Prison, situated along the American River, a few watersheds south of Ishi's homeland, wrote to Theodora, telling her he read seven hundred books a year and *Ishi in Two Worlds* brought him "more reading enjoyment than any others." Johnny Cash sang at that same prison a few years later, sympathizing with those wild men who were walled up along the river but could hear the railroad train passing by.[9]

Other readers wrote to Theodora, asking what they could do for American Indians. Environmentalists were inspired by her respectful re-creation of the Yahi world before contact with whites. Reviewing the book in the *Sierra Club Bulletin,* Kenneth Brower wrote, "To reconstruct for ourselves the Yahi life would of course be impossible and undesirable, but certain values of their existence are to be had in our diminished wilderness, even with the population what it is." Wilderness, Brower believed, could give modern Americans a sense of another way of life and provide an antidote to the urban condition. We may not be able to go back to Ishi's Stone

Age nature, but "we can turn again to the wilderness as the hope for America. Its therapeutic silence, immensity, and simplicity would perhaps slow down our thinking until we are really thinking."[10]

For Ishi, his world was silenced only when he and the other Yahi survivors were compelled to live as fugitives. As reverent as Brower was in his regard for Ishi, there was a disjuncture between the wilderness he hoped for, a refuge for modern Americans from the hustle and bustle of their lives, and the homeland Ishi and the Yahi had once made for themselves along the streams of Wahganupa. That landscape had always been vibrant with the sounds of voices, often singing. But the Wilderness Act of 1964, passed just two years after the appearance of *Ishi in Two Worlds*, enshrined the idea of nature as a place where people did not live, but were temporary, recreational trespassers. The act states, "A wilderness, in contrast with those areas where man and his own works dominate the landscape, is hereby recognized as an area where the earth and its community of life are untrammeled by man, where man himself is a visitor who does not remain." As powerful as the act has been in protecting areas from development, it expresses a dualistic view of people and nature alien to many Native Americans. As the Laguna Indian writer Leslie Marmon Silko says, "The land, the sky, and all that is within them—the landscape—includes human beings."[11]

In Ishi's name—or more accurately, in the nickname given to the Yahi survivor by Kroeber—a campaign was started to designate part of the Yahi homeland as an official wilderness. The Mother Lode Chapter of the Sierra Club mailed out a flyer describing the Ishi Wilderness Proposal: "We now have a chance to preserve for generations to come the Ishi Wilderness in a still untouched and primitive condition." Further into the proposal one sees that the human presence, Ishi's presence, was what drove the desire to preserve that land as official wilderness. "The wealth of Ishi and his people was destroyed before the true value of that society was known," the proposal argues. "We cannot let the fate of the land follow the same path." The schizophrenic split between people and land that characterizes the wilderness idea is manifest in the proposal's desire to preserve Deer Creek in its still "untouched and primitive condition." Of course many feet had touched that landscape, many hands had been laid upon it, and blood had seeped into it, much of it spilled as the new American empire expanded to the Pacific and beyond.[12]

The Ishi Conference was held in Chico in May 1979. Dennis Banks, one of the founders of the American Indian Movement, which marked the cultural and political resurgence of Native peoples in the 1960s, delivered the opening address. Gary Snyder, described as "a noted poet, environmentalist, and warrior-lover of Mother Earth, [who] will share his love and dedication," delivered the keynote. Of all the leading non-Native environmentalists of his generation, Snyder had done most to place humans into the revered landscape he called wilderness. Snyder did not see wilderness as uninhabited and unstoried. Perhaps that is because this Pulitzer Prize–winning poet and outdoor hero of the Beat Generation began his serious scholarship as an anthropologist, writing his undergraduate thesis at Reed College on a Haida story. Later in his life Snyder witnessed a Bear Dance performed by Maidu and others on Mount Shasta, Wahganupa's taller brother to the north. As the grounds were being readied for the dance and just as the pole for the dance was raised up, Snyder overheard a conversation in which a Maidu man said, "Science went up so high that now it's beginning to come back down. We're climbing up with our old-ways knowledge, pretty soon we'll meet science coming down." After witnessing the Bear Dance, Snyder was moved to write an essay in which he retold a Tlingit tale about a woman who married a bear.[13]

In that story a woman is out gathering berries when she sees a handsome man among the bushes. She falls in love with him, but it turns out that he is a bear. She marries him anyway and goes to live with him in his cave. One day her people show up at the cave, seeking revenge. The bear wants to fight them off, but the woman-bear does not want her people to die. The bear at last agrees to give up his own life to the human hunters, but on one condition. The woman-bear is to teach them the proper way to treat his remains, how to pay respect to the dead.

White environmentalists paid respect to Ishi by getting forty-one thousand acres of his homeland designated wilderness in 1984. Indians paid respect, too, in a variety of ways. The Konkow Maidu artist Frank Tuttle created a mixed-media image of the man from whom he drew inspiration. Calling the work *What Wild Indian?* Tuttle wanted to "ignite viewers to ask themselves this question and momentarily make note of their gut reaction." On the central panel Tuttle reproduced one of the first photographic images of Ishi from Oroville; Tuttle saw in him a survivor, a preserver of his identity in the midst of madness. To symbolize rebirth and continuity, Ishi holds in one hand a flame and in the other a rosebush. Tuttle could not have known it, but the Smithsonian secretary who handled the original bequest of Ishi's brain was named Rosenbusch.[14]

The matter of Ishi's remains was remembered as well. Pope and the others believed that they had respectfully treated the remains of Ishi in 1916, but in fact they fell far short. Art Angle, a Maidu Indian living in Oroville and a member of the Butte County Native American Cultural Committee, wanted to return Ishi's ashes to his homeland and conduct a proper ceremony. "I am not his blood relative, but I am a Native American," Angle explained to a reporter. "We are determined to perform this duty according to Native American ritual. We need to look at what we can do for him in the best way we can, to put him to rest in a proper way." Angle saw it as a matter of completion and respect. "It is very important that he be returned here as a complete person, a complete spirit," he said. "If you look at the native country where he came from— the open streams, the brush, the animals, and then you go to this Colma cemetery where he is interred..." Angle paused a moment, then completed his thought: "It just doesn't fit."

"Ishi himself is not completely together," Angle pointed out. "He is incomplete because he is not in his homeland. And the Yahi tribe is not complete because he is out of the homeland." But Ishi was incomplete in another way. Angle was troubled by a story he had heard: that Ishi's brain had been removed and pickled in a jar and was being held in a museum somewhere. When he asked the University of California about it, he was told that the brain had been cremated along with the rest of Ishi's remains. Angle wasn't so sure, and he asked Orin Starn, a Duke anthropologist who was writing a book about Ishi, to look into the matter. Nancy Rockafellar at the University of California at San Francisco had been looking into the issue as well. Starn finally got to the bottom of the mystery when he found the letters between Kroeber and

Hrdlička at the Bancroft Library. (He tells the saga in his marvelous book, *Ishi's Brain*.) He discovered that Ishi's brain was in the Smithsonian Institution.[15]

The University of California and the Smithsonian were called on the carpet for their neglect and the apparent cover-up, and for the legacy of colonialism their collections embodied. Kroeber's ethics were called into question as well, as Indians asked what right he had to turn Ishi into a museum piece in the first place. Angle requested that the Smithsonian return Ishi's brain. Mickey Gimmell of the Pit River and Redding Rancheria said, "We believe that it is right that whatever remains the national museum has of Ishi, they should be returned and properly reburied." The Smithsonian agreed to return the brain; indeed it was compelled to do so under the Native American Graves and Repatriation Act. But to whom should they return it? The law mandated that it should go to a relative or to the tribe, yet Ishi was supposedly the last of his tribe.

Ultimately the brain was returned, not to Angle and the Maidu, but to the Pit River Tribe and Redding Rancheria Indians, whom the Smithsonian deemed to be closer culturally to the Yahi than the Maidu. The whole process of return and supposed redemption was built on bureaucratic fictions and ignored the secret history of how Yana and Yahi Indians survived by seeking refuge among neighboring tribes. To Ron Morales, a Honey Lake Maidu, the claim that Ishi was the last of the Yahi was erroneous and damaging. He took issue with people "saying there are no more Yahi": "It's just not true. We're their neighbors...we should know. It seems like, how could people *be* so damn wrong?"[16]

In the fall of 2000 the clay pot engraved "Ishi, Last of the Yahi, 1916" was taken from the Colma cemetery to the streams of Wahganupa. Pit River and Redding Rancheria Indians brought the pot, and the brain wrapped in bearskin, to an undisclosed location in Ishi Wilderness. The burial site would be concealed, like the old Yahi village at Wowunupo'mu tetna. Cemented shut, the Hopi pot had to be cracked open with a stone. Leslie Marmon Silko says that to the Hopi, the "rocks and the clay are part of the Mother. They emerge in various forms, but at some time before, they were smaller particles or great boulders. At a later time they may again become what they once were. Dust. A rock shares this fate with us and with animals and plants as well."[17]

The remains—the ashes, the brain, the melted obsidian from the arrowheads, pieces of bone, an unread note someone had put in the pot back in 1916, the shards of the clay pot itself—were all placed carefully into a beautiful old Pit River woven basket. Ishi did not fall through. His new old friends stood by him in the restored landscape, weeping and singing through the night.[18]

Afterword

Google Earth, Earthquake Weather

❋

Whe when I was growing up in California's Sacramento Valley, *googol* was the word we kids knew stood for a very large number, something way beyond billions, trillions, and zillions. It tickled our imagination, as it was meant to do. A googol (1 followed by 100 zeros) was a number invented by a mathematician, named by his nephew, useful for charting very large space—the dimensions of the universe, or the amount of subatomic particles it holds. Now everyone knows Google (rendered this way because of a spelling error) as the name for a search engine, something you use to explore the seemingly infinite data contained within that place called the virtual world. As I was researching this book, the California-based company went online with a new product, something it called Google Earth. Using this tool you could take a trip anywhere on the planet—almost no place was offline, wild—and you could do it all, as they say, from the comfort of your own living room.

The first place I visited was Ishi's so-called wilderness. Adopting the perspective of Kroeber, I started in Vina as he had done when

Ishi took him back into his homeland. I ventured east across the plane of the Sacramento Valley and along Deer Creek, following the stream up into the cañon. At the touch of the track pad, I would move from the cañon bottom up to a bird's-eye perspective, and as my navigation skills were undeveloped I often spun out of control, almost like Cottontail and his whirlwind travels in the story-time of the Yahi. I "walked" along the Moak Trail, trying to find those vantage points from which Kroeber drew panoramas of the cañons. I looked, but found no link indicating Wowunupo'mu tetna, Grizzly Bear's Hiding Place, Ishi's hidden village whose location has remained secret to this day. Even as I was amazed by the cartographic power of Google Earth, I had to respect the fact that there were some places about which even Google knew nothing.

By the time I made the virtual journey, I knew something about this territory. I had a sense of a portion of its history, and that helped me understand both what the satellite images of the cañon could see and what they could not. I had the beginnings of a sense of place. Before Boas, most anthropologists were "Google earthers," scholars who studied people around the world from the comfort of their own living room. These armchair anthropologists relied on the accounts of explorers, traders, or missionaries to see the world. For most historians, pretty much all we have is the armchair, or a chair in the archives. The past is foreign territory, and we can't actually visit it; we come to know it only through the traces left behind: documents, oral histories, firsthand accounts. But because this book was to be about place as well as history I wanted to actually visit the old haunts of Ishi and Kroeber.

Afterword

Place is more than its location or representation (as on a map). A place—as opposed to simply space, some location on the planet defined by latitude and longitude—is one part its unique ecology (its community of life arranged on the landscape) and one part history (the things said and done and experienced in the location). In my armchair, reading letters in the archives, newspaper accounts, memoirs of Indian hunters, translations of Yahi stories, I was learning about those events that made the Deer and Mill Creek areas into places full of vibrant and tragic memories. But to get a fuller sense of place in all of its dimensions, I needed to go there.

Instead of riding a horse I drove my car along rutted forest roads, some of them built on the old Lassen Trail, to the trailhead in Ishi Wilderness. I walked into the cañons of Mill and Deer Creeks, and it was only then that I really began to sense this place. My eyes were opened to its beauty. Having read so many descriptions of these cañons as barren, rugged, and inhospitable, I was surprised to walk through the grassy savannahs with their acorn-laden blue oaks and native wildflowers, through the cool ravines with trickling side streams, next to the main creeks themselves, roaring in places, which support one of the last wild Chinook salmon runs in the state, and to scramble down to the shady water's edge and breathe in the smell of damp soil and plants all around. Most of the grasses were invasive, as were the yellow thistle and medusa's head. But there were still the narrow-leaf mule's ear, the nettle-leaf horsemint, white yarrow, and dozens of other plants the Yahi knew.

When the trail went high up on the cañon walls, in among the manzanita and redbud, I had a stunning view of this water and lava-shaped landscape, grand and beautiful. It certainly wasn't as big as the Grand Canyon, yet the rugged rims and towering lava outcroppings bordered a spectacular green world around the streams. This place was a grand cosmos unto itself. As I walked I began to get an embodied sense of place; you learn the geography by using muscle to get your body down, or up, the trail. You feel the sun on your forehead; you hear the sounds of birds; you taste the water (but only after filtering it, for the cattle in the area have contributed giardia to the streams). The trail itself is a record of humans walking this landscape; each foot falls on ground already trodden countless times by humans. And now my footsteps were layering this earth, too, put down here, like that of other brief visitors like Kroeber, to mingle among the many footfalls of Ishi and the other Yahi.

Wilderness adventurers often try to imagine that they are entering landscapes untouched and unseen by humans; they like to take on the role of explorer, like a latter-day Meriwether Lewis or William Clark. Joining such imaginings is the conceit that one can, for a moment, experience and see the place as its Natives did, when the continent was truly free. Because I was coming into this place from my historical perspective, it didn't really cross my mind to look at it as an uninhabited wilderness. I did indulge in a thought experiment, trying to see it through the eyes of Kroeber. Pretending that I was a Yahi would have been too much of a stretch, and a disrespectful act of dispossession to boot. But the ethical and mental barriers between being myself and playing at being Kroeber did not seem as high. Like him, I was a university professor and a white scholar of Native American history and culture. Kroeber and I were both the same age when we walked into Ishi's homeland. I even had a beard like his. Separated by ninety years, I was following his ghost down the trail.

As I walked on I came to know how great the chasm was between my being here and Ishi's being here. When Waterman went looking for the elusive Yahi in these cañons, he was helped by Merle Apperson, who knew the country "like a book." I did not know it like a book, but knowing it that way, someday, was what I was after. Ishi knew this place not like a book, but like a story. There is a world of difference in those two ways of knowing—the textual and the oral, the abstract and the embodied, the one who relies on map, compass, and dumb luck and the one who relies on experience, history, and one's senses to know where one is.

I knew how to get back to the trailhead and my car, but I was basically lost in this landscape. I watched the stars at night. In the morning I saw the great drama of the sun glinting onto the cañon walls, and appreciated its warmth and life as it glazed across my skin at my camping spot. I thought of Ishi greeting the sun every day, hand on his heart. I could hear birds, but I had no idea what they were saying. I certainly couldn't call out to any creature, except perhaps another human being (though they were still a rare sight). When the trail ended I wanted to descend to the edge of the creek, but there was no path and the terrain was steep. I had to scamper or slide down, sometimes grabbing onto any vegetation along the way. (No doubt this is when I accidentally grazed most of the poison oak that would remind me for weeks of this trip.) At water's edge I was struck by the sound of the stream. It roared as if a thousand voices had come together into a torrent, as if the landscape was clamoring to be heard.

As a historian, it is impossible for me to imagine a landscape without stories. The historian William Cronon says, "In the beginning was the story. Or rather: many stories, in many voices, pointing toward many ends." Stories are entangled with the places we inhabit, and it is those stories that turn raw space into meaningful place. There is always a question of where the stories come from: if they are imposed on the landscape, if they grow out of experiences there, or if the place somehow communicates its stories to people attuned to listening. It is this last perspective that many Native Americans take, insisting that their stories about place have come by listening closely to the world around them, from long observation and being within the landscape. Stories come out of the landscape to those whose attention is undivided by the dualistic thinking that places nature and wilderness off to one side of a chasm, and culture and civilization on another side, and usually higher up.[1]

Historians are storytellers, too. Within the greater clan of historians who write about the history of the United States, it has been two groups, environmental and western historians, who have paid the most attention to the stories told about the relationship of people to place. For a long time the perspectives of white Americans dominated their stories about the relationship of people to nature in North America. It was a young historian from the University of Wisconsin who first fixed that storyline in the national imagination. Speaking at the World's Columbian Exposition in 1893, the same place were Esther the Inuit from Labrador and Franz Boas were working, Frederick Jackson Turner described a place he called "the frontier" as "the meeting point between savagery and civilization." In his story the frontier was a not merely a place but a force of nature requiring Americans to adapt to new conditions. In meeting the challenges of "winning a wilderness," whites were transformed as they first "descended" into primitive conditions and worked their way up out of them. At first, Turner said, "The wilderness masters the colonist. It finds him a European in dress, industries, tools, modes of travel, and thought. It takes him from the railroad car and puts him in the birch canoe. It strips off the garments of civilization and arrays him in the hunting shirt and the moccasin." In effect whites became Indians, stripped of the cultural baggage of Europe, then reinvented as sturdy, can-do Americans, people who would stop at nothing to make progress. Turner assumed Indians were incapable of advancing; they were simply the backdrop or temporary tutors in wilderness ways until the whites were ready to take great strides forward. Farms, towns, and eventually cities replaced wilderness in Turner's evolutionary version of American history.[2]

Others before had told much this same story, of how a landscape viewed as raw or wild was wrested from Indians and then turned into a garden landscape, eventually dotted with bustling cities. But Turner turned the tale into an explanation of why America and Americans were also unique and destined to conquer the continent. Turner's American origin story undergirded national expansion. It is like a trestle made of words that has enabled the national train to head into ever expanding horizons, while the passengers, riding steady, do not worry about the varied landscape they are steaming through or the people and communities they are tearing asunder. They seem to be making progress, steady progress.

It is perilous to question the foundational myth of a nation, but that is just what the new western historians began doing in the 1980s. Instead of seeing western history as the mechanism through which a distinct, democratic nation was formed and a path to political and economic leadership was forged, instead of emplotting that past as a triumph for democracy and America itself, perhaps that history could better be appreciated as a tragedy, a story of decline instead of ascent. But describing the new storyline simply as an inversion of the old narrative—turning progress into decline, triumph into tragedy—fails to do justice to what these new western historians were trying to do. They wanted to write the story of the landscape inclusively, taking into account the competing narratives of many actors whose different perspectives and experiences were now being conveyed.[3]

But looking at the story from either side of a divide, white or Indian, still posits a kind of absolute isolation between two sides of the story, black or white hats on one side, feather headdresses adorning fierce or noble Indians on the other side. Had there been cultural crossings on the frontier? Could Indians at once adopt parts of white culture—whether horses, guns, cars, or Christianity—and still remain Indian? Could Indians both accommodate and resist whites and modernity at the same time? Were there times and places where Indians controlled as much power in shaping interactions as whites did, or more?[4]

In many times and places middle grounds between natives and newcomers opened as they crossed each other's physical and cultural borders and made contact. Some of the contacts precipitated horrible acts of violence, but some were more tranquil and unexpectedly peaceful. Think of the party of whites and Indians among the Ponderosa Pines that Hi Good and his band of Indian hunters barged into. Think of Ishi taking a discarded beer bottle and turning it into an arrowhead or sharing a meal with the half-Yana Indian and his white friend from San Francisco, who had taken leave from their work on a steamboat plying the waters of the Sacramento River into Ishi's homeland. And think of Kroeber, Waterman, and Sapir pushing their powers of comprehension to the limit so that they might hear one of Ishi's stories whole. Failing that, they got as much of it as they could on wax cylinders, the new recording devices of the modern age.

Such thoughts ran through my mind as I began to piece together a new narrative about the lives and landscapes of Kroeber and Ishi. Their origins and outlook offered an opportunity to write the kind of multiperspectival history the new western historians championed. And yet there was a limit to just how far I could go in representing the point of view of each man. It's hard—as well as perilous and presumptuous—to get inside the head of another, especially when the other is a real person who lived in the past. Doing so involves a kind of violation, and I was particularly sensitive about this with regard to Ishi. After all, there is a long and troubled history of whites imagining that they knew what it was like to be Indian; sometimes they thought they were more Indian than Indians themselves. And the possession of his brain was at the heart of the mistreatment Ishi endured.

But conveying the perspectives of others is one of the great humanistic contributions of history and narrative, for it allows us to deepen empathy and understanding. Kroeber left many words behind, so I used them whenever possible to convey his thoughts and perspectives. Ishi had many of his words recorded as well, though his thoughts were certainly filtered through the recording media and imperfect translations. No trace of the past, no document is completely transparent to what happened in the past, let alone how people experienced those events. But there was enough information for me to reconstruct many scenes and suggest the feelings each actor experienced, from Ishi's train ride to San Francisco to Kroeber's ultimate crisis of conscience about his profession. Moreover the scenes were important: the context in which Ishi and Kroeber met helped tell the story, and it was that context I also hoped to illuminate. Key areas of that contextual landscape were the frontier, the city, modernity, and wilderness.

The encounter between these two men in some ways embodied the whole story of the American frontier, but I knew I'd be looking at that frontier in a light very different from Turner's. It would be a story of exchange and adaptation as much as a story of courageous resistance and tragic loss. The frontier would be a porous border of intercultural exchange more than a distinct line between two groups fighting over land and livelihood. It would be, as a later group of anthropologists and literary critics saw it, a "contact zone." That contact zone shifts in the course of our story, from the cañons below Wahganupa to the streets of San Francisco.

Turner's frontier, where "wilderness" met "civilization," was always at the same time a story of urban America, whether he admitted it or not. After all, he'd given his speech in Chicago, America's second city, and only after the U.S. census had proclaimed that a frontier no longer existed in the United States. His story ended with the building of cities and looked back with an inescapable nostalgia to wilderness as the beginning of America's greatness. For fin de siècle Americans, Ishi embodied wilderness and frontier life, an idea particularly fascinating for urban Americans. That wilderness in the shape of a man should come directly into the city was a story that, if it weren't true, would have to have been invented. When Ishi came to San Francisco he was seen as *the last* in order to bring into relief *the new*. Ancient and modern, an epochal ending and beginning, seemed to be present in the same place at the same time. But for some Indians, their continued presence in cities was more confirmation of a cyclical view of history, and of their insistence on remaining, surviving, and making a place for themselves in the new urban world.

The encounter between Ishi and the Stone Age on one hand and San Francisco and urbane modernity on the other had always been central to the way whites told his story. San Francisco newspapers delighted in drawing images of Ishi as a primitive caveman touring the sights of the modern city. Though he rejected such journalistic sensationalism, Kroeber himself portrayed Ishi as a pure representative of aboriginal America suddenly thrust under the lights of modernity. Ishi as noble representative of the beginning of mankind coming face to face with the most advanced humanity was also essential to how Theodora told Ishi's story. She held up Ishi's intelligence and good humor, his physical as well as inner strength as reasons to question just how advanced modern man really was. For her, and for those of her contemporaries who worshipped the primitive, Ishi was important precisely because he served as a window into a bygone America, one that existed before contact with Europeans. In fact Ishi's story has inevitably been the story of modernity, of urbanizing America constructing a vision of itself and its other.

San Francisco of a hundred years ago was a perfect place to experience the rush of the new urban-industrial-consumer order. I think of Kroeber first arriving in San Francisco with the birth of the twentieth century, feeling the excitement of the citizens (though the bustle was nothing new to the New Yorker). All the lights suddenly went out with the earthquake in 1906, and Kroeber walked through the city turned dark, as if nature was objecting to its domination. As he walked up Market Street that black day, Kroeber passed by the Emporium, once "the most beautiful store on earth," featuring a "grand display of a million-and-a-half dollars worth of all good kinds of merchandise." The neoclassical building was seven stories tall, with fifteen acres devoted to shopping and set aglow by ten thousand electric lights. (The building had its own power plant.) The fires destroyed the store's stock, but it was quickly rebuilt and reopened. A blind man sold lavender in front of the store for decades, perhaps inspiring Charlie Chaplin's *City Lights,* which featured a blind girl who sold flowers. By the time Ishi arrived at the Ferry Building in 1911, San Francisco, preparing for the great Panama Pacific Exposition, was alive again. Commerce was booming, and so was consumerism.[5]

You can still take a ferry into San Francisco from Oakland, as I did one day in the midst of researching this book, but it's certainly the route less traveled today. (Most people either go under the Bay, on BART, or over it, on the Bay Bridge.) The Ferry Building, which survived the great quake, still stands, and it presents a wonderful view as you glide close to shore on the ferry. It's been converted into shops mostly dealing with cooking and food and a farmer's market, a place to go in the city to reconnect with nature. As I walked up Market Street, feeling the stone and brick and the blasts of sound and light, nature seemed to fade away and an energizing force field of activity took over. There was the rush of people, trolley cars, bikes and SUVs, billboards and illuminated signs. It is still a financial center, but on street level it's also a consumer's paradise. Eight blocks up, where the old Emporium once stood, is the new nine-story Westfield San Francisco Shopping Centre. When the new store was erected, one San Franciscan expressed no nostalgia, saying that she was excited by the new store that would "rise from the bones of the old Emporium. There are no ghosts here. After all, everything does change."[6]

Sometimes the more things change, the more they stay the same. What if Alfred Kroeber, when he walked by a hundred years ago, somehow entered a time portal and was moved a century ahead? The Shopping Centre has more lights and video, but it is still a shopping center. He would stop in his tracks at the sight of one hip new store on Market, Anthropologie, which stocks CC Outlaw apparel and invites its customers to "sift through time" and "nap like an Egyptian queen" on the Mamello chaise. The contents of Kroeber's museum on Parnassus Heights seem to have been weirdly brought down here and reproduced as simulacra. Anthropology the science has been turned into Anthropologie the store, something Kroeber would have hated to see. Yet he probably would have appreciated the irony. He would have writhed and smiled and been intrigued. Of course in his day, anthropology was bowdlerized for circus-like entertainment at the Orpheum and at world's fairs.

A century later Market Street is still Market Street. A hundred years ago grand department stores like the Emporium were developing the marketing stagecraft they would employ to turn America into what one historian calls a "Land of Desire." The rise of consumer culture was an integral component of the rise of industrial capitalism, and thus a key dimension of modernity.[7]

Modernity is a word that has carried many meanings. For my purposes it means a new period in American history taking shape in the two or three decades before and after 1900. It involves a complex and overlapping set of economic, technological, social, and cultural changes that attended America's transformation from a preindustrial to an industrial world— or, in shorthand, a change from the culture of the countryside to the culture of the city. Of course not everyone lived in the city (though according to census returns a majority of Americans would live in cities for the first time in 1920), and the countryside was still there. But it was transformed, becoming industrialized and ever more tightly linked to urban and global markets.

Different historians date the advent of modernity to different periods and debate just what it involves. I see it as comprising several interdependent elements: the ascent of corporate capitalism, the increased pace of global trade and communication facilitated by new steam- and electric-driven technologies, a large-scale shift in social identity from the local community to to the abstract nation, a faith in human progress and human domination of nature, accelerated urbanization, the rise of scientific positivism, the disenchantment of nature, and a yawning distance between the mass of humanity and the source of their food and fiber: the countryside, or more generally, nature. The experience of modernity was acutely felt in the city, and many cultural observers experienced the fast pace, anonymity, commercialism, and secularism of the modern world as a kind of weightlessness. Nothing seemed fixed and solid; everything seemed fake or illusory; all was in motion, floating, flying, speeding by.[8]

Ishi served as an imaginary mooring mast, as Americans drifting weightless and volatile like hydrogen airships threw down anchors to connect to something solid. Here was "ancient man." Pure, unadulterated man. Tribal man. A strong man of the earth. Wild man.

Indians had always served as a screen on which Euro-Americans projected images created deep within their cultures and minds. Ishi's wildness was not something inside of him, inherent, some kind of genetic or racial endowment, but a laminate, something applied to him. The ones who layered wildness on him were the wild ones. Molly Gloss, a writer mentored by Alfred Kroeber's daughter, Ursula Kroeber Le Guin, explored this dynamic in her novel *Wild Life*. The main character is a female novelist living along the Columbia River in turn-of-the-century America. She begins hearing stories about a mysterious creature in the wilds of the northwest forests of the Cascade Mountains at precisely the moment that Kroeber was actually looking for the rumored last band of wild Indians living on the watershed of the southern end of the Cascades. Gloss's character goes out in search of Bigfoot, but she is skeptical. She thinks that if wild men exist, they live only as a projection:

> It seems to me men have always endowed the Indian, the Negro, the Hottentot with savagery and a strong reek, with apelike looks and movements, and with a taste for white women, and my own belief is that it's not a matter of other races but a matter of fear. There is a bestial side to human nature, basic and primitive impulses in the bodies of men which clamor for satisfaction, and it must be a Christian comfort to ascribe such things not to oneself or one's tribe but to hairy giants and savages. It may be the Wild Man of the Woods is but a ghost of the wild man within.[9]

Whereas earlier Americans may have wanted to deny or exorcize this ghost within, turn-of-the-century Americans desperately wanted to reclaim it. Contemporary crazes for hunting, camping, and wilderness trekking and the creation organizations such as the Sierra Club were largely about rekindling the wildness within that Americans believed was being extinguished by modern life. They sought instruction from Indians, and their children became Boy Scouts, Girl Scouts, and Woodcraft Indians. Charles Eastman, a Santee Sioux man, shared with whites some of the ways Indians had lived in reverence of nature, and they tried to listen to what he said. Whites flocked to camps where they played Indians, dressing up in feathers and bestowing on themselves names they thought sounded Indian.

But there was always a gap between playing Indian and being Indian. For whites, playing Indian amounted to an escape from history, yet history could not be denied in Indian communities. In playing Indian, whites were stepping into an image they themselves had projected from a split personality. They wanted to escape civilization as they knew it and venture into its antithesis, wilderness. To Indians, of course, the wilderness sought by whites was not a void, but the height of civilization as they knew it, which included the more-than-human world in which every member was bound to other people and other creatures in webs of care and respect. Luther Standing Bear, the Sioux man who played in the band that paraded over the Brooklyn Bridge on its opening day, explained:

> We did not think of the great open plains, the beautiful rolling hills, and winding streams with tangled growth, as "wild." Only to the white man was nature a "wilderness" and only to him was the

land "infested" with "wild" animals and "savage" people. To us it was tame. Earth was bountiful and we were surrounded with the blessings of the Great Mystery. Not until the hairy man from the east came and with brutal frenzy heaped injustices upon us and the families we loved was it "wild" for us. When the very animals of the forest began fleeing from his approach, then it was that for us the "Wild West" began.[10]

The wilderness was created in two ways by modern Americans. It was an idea, and it was an effect of their ideas and their presence on the landscapes of the continent, which were unsettled or shattered by the impact of westering American civilization. Through wars of dispossession, and later wilderness policies, whites removed Indians from their close relationship with the land. As many Indians saw it, without people to manage and know it, the land fell out of a civilized state and became wild. James Rust, an elder from the Southern Sierra Miwok tribe, lamented, "The white man sure ruined this country. It's turned back to wilderness."[11]

Kroeber sensed the problem of whites' romantic views of Indians. He wanted to dispel the notion that Indians were wild, for that perception went hand in hand with the idea that Indians had no culture or civilization. It was that culture Kroeber was dedicated to documenting and understanding. He did not want to become Indian in the way of some of his contemporaries. But like them, he also felt trapped by the urban world. He was a punctual and responsible professional, a consummate museum director and well-trained anthropologist. Yet he also champed at the bit of his modern life; he described a "prison gate sense" infusing his San Francisco existence. There was something about himself that he believed had been locked away.

There was always something of the Sturm und Drang in Kroeber, a passion that he wanted Edward Sapir to put into his poems, as if Sapir's writing could express his own wild side by proxy. Kroeber could not find an outlet for his stormy feelings by playing Indian. Studying Indians was part of his profession, his controlled life. By being with Indians, however, Kroeber could come to terms with his internal schism. As a professional he valued the role of culture; individuals were merely vessels and expressions of cultural patterns. But it was his friendship with Ishi that inspired him to rail at his profession and the modernist quest for the absolute knowledge that he himself pursued. "Say for me that science can go to hell," he cried when Ishi was to be dissected. For Kroeber, this was a wild outburst, and that was precisely the point. The Yurok man Robert Spott understood the anthropologist's pain and tried to heal him. "White men hurt so much," he said. "We have to help him."

Kroeber staked his professional career on practicing salvage anthropology among Native Californians. But Ishi and Spott and other Indians just may have salvaged Kroeber's life. Thus each man at the center of my story is wild in different ways. For Ishi, wildness is imposed upon him from without by another culture. For Kroeber, wildness is something that dwelled within, repressed by his own culture and his chosen profession of anthropology.[12]

Wild Men is ultimately about two individuals and two worlds intimately mixed together in ways that turned out to be at once inspiring and tragic. Each man stood looking at the other from the opposite edge of a chasm. They reached out in the hope of keeping the other from falling in.

Modernity was like an earthquake, and people in all places were shaken by it. Sometimes the effect was an unmooring, a rolling weightlessness as the earth liquefied and then resolidified; sometimes it was catastrophic. Everywhere new places were built up and over old domains.

Despite the disruptions and disconnections of modernity, there had always been powerful stories told about its salutary effects for humanity, citing growing populations, rising standards of living, technological progress in communications and transportation, and democratization of political systems. But every seeming advance has a shadow, and modernity has been a paradox. It has promised much: material abundance, wealth, the breaking down of barriers, the expansion of knowledge, the liberation of humankind from the limits of malevolent nature as well as all kinds of political repression. Yet modernity has not always delivered what it has promised and sometimes has used that promise to legitimize regression and repression: colonialism and dispossession, the routinization of labor and the exploitation of working people, the commodification of plants, animals, water, the earth itself, and even the sky.

In the 1970s a number of so-called postmodern critics began to question the storytelling roots of modernity, laying bare what they called "the metanarratives of legitimation" that had been used to justify the sweeping changes to people and the planet. These metanarratives, highlighting the growth and unification of knowledge, economic and technological progress, political liberalization, and liberation from the limits of nature, were the word trestles of the new age, just as manifest destiny was the metanarrative undergirding America's colonial expansion westward in the nineteenth century. Postmodern critics dissected each of the metanarratives, pointing to the instability and power plays behind knowledge; instead of humans being liberated from nature, nature had been dangerously exploited. Human power over nature put power into the hands of the few, while the many were compelled to work flat out, in farm or factory, to transform nature into commodities for the profit of others.[13]

Critics of the metanarrative were not against storytelling—far from it. To one big story they preferred many stories that reflected the knowledge and experience of local peoples. Some even celebrated indigenous stories and looked to them as a source of hope. To these critics modernity is like the vacuum-mouthed monster pictured in the Beatles' film *Yellow Submarine,* sucking in every creature and object in sight, and then the entire scene itself, and at last its own body, leaving oblivion behind.

Ishi was and continues to be so fascinating in large part because his story seemed to represent an alternative to the modern world. And though certainly Ishi was partially a screen on which to project such colonial nostalgia, the truth is that Ishi, and many other Native Americans, did offer an alternative. They had another bundle of stories to tell, ones that countered modernity and its metanarrative of progress.

Native Americans have been keeping their stories alive, feeding them during all of the disruptions and periods of indifference. Together they form something of a metanarrative of their own, one very different from the metanarrative that has been told to explain and justify modernity. The message from Indian country, the big story, is something like this: Everything is alive. All life is sacred and mysterious. Everything, every life, is interwoven, the warp and weave of a precious basket. The basket holds all we are and can hope to be.

The stories Indians told did get through, even though at times Kroeber seemed oblivious to them. (As when the Yurok man Re'mik told him why the big earthquake had hit San Francisco: "Earthquake is angry because the Americans have brought up Indian treasures and formulas and taken them away to San Francisco to keep.") Years later Alfred's daughter, Ursula K. Le Guin, wrote an essay titled "The Carrier Bag Theory of Fiction" that in its way celebrated the stories Indians had been telling all along against modernity's boosters. Most Western stories, she noted, were the stories of *the stick,* sagas of clubs and spears and swords and progress by the male as hero. Repressed and almost forgotten were stories of *the basket,* of gathering, of care, community, perseverance, and love. Le Guin cast her lot in with the bag people, those who carefully gather and preserve rather than strike out. I found myself quite taken with her position (especially so given my family name, Sackman).[14]

If narrative is a sack or basket, the storyteller is a gatherer collecting things and placing them within it. Fortunately many others had gathered and preserved in books many of the things I would find to put in this basket, beginning with Alfred Kroeber, Thomas T. Waterman, Saxton Pope, and Edward Sapir, later with books by Theodora Kroeber, Robert Heizer, Richard Burrill, Orin Starn, and Clifton and Karl Kroeber. Jean Perry, Herbert Luthin, Leanne Hinton, and others involved in the Yahi Translation Project have brought out English translations of the stories Ishi told to Sapir in Yahi in 1915. Other elements were preserved in the archives, particularly at the Bancroft Library, where Alfred and Theodora

Kroeber's papers are held, along with those of the Phoebe Hearst Museum of Anthropology and the Department of Anthropology at Berkeley. Other stories could be gleaned from newspapers. My gathering basket was overflowing.

The book would be another, smaller basket, one that could be used for cooking. I selected ingredients from the gathering basket. A lot of what went into it was drawn from what Ishi and Kroeber had said or written. A lot came from what others observed about Ishi and Kroeber. A lot came from each of the men's cultures. Again, the basket overflowed. It had to be cooked down. That is the art of history. Its facts are never raw; the historian always cooks them. Everything that went into my basket came from the lives and landscapes of Ishi and Kroeber, but then it was stirred and heated into something new and different. I hoped to make something that would taste of the worlds Kroeber and Ishi inhabited, maybe the Pacific crab Kroeber ate at Fisherman's Wharf or the acorn soup the surveyors discovered in Ishi's village of Wowunupo'mu tetna, still warm.

In doing this cooking, I had the guidance of other historians. I also listened to the voices of California Indian artists, writers and painters and basket makers, who continue to gather stories that reveal and honor a world different from the one celebrated by the metanarrative of progress. I think of the art and writing of contemporary California Indians with roots near Ishi country, of the portraits and landscapes supersaturated with color, irony, and history created by Judith Lowry (whose ancestry is Konkow Maidu, Hamawi Pit-River, Washo, Scots Irish and Euro-Australian); of the exquisitely etched memoirs of Daryl Babe

Wilson (of the Achumawe and Atsugewi), who grew up on the other side of Wahganupa/Mount Lassen from Ishi; and of Janice Gould (mixed-blood European and Konkow Maidu) and her collection of poems called *Earthquake Weather*.[15]

Janice Gould's background is decidedly mixed. Both of her maternal great-grandmothers were Koyangk'auwi (or Konkow) Maidu Indians, from the Yankee Hill area. The Konkows are the Yahis' neighbors to the south, the same Indians who may have left food for Ishi at Yankee Hill. Art Angle, the man who spearheaded the drive to return Ishi's remains, is also Konkow. Both of Janice's great-grandmothers married white men, one an Irishman, the other a Frenchman named Jacques Osier, who worked as a railroad engineer planning the iron horse's route down the Feather River. Instead of speeding by, Osier married and stayed behind. When Janice's grandmother Nellie died of cancer, her mother, Vivian, was adopted by a white woman named Beatrice Lane, who lived in Berkeley. As Janice explains, "[I began writing as a] way to record what it means for me to be a Koyangk'auwi mixedblood." Her poems were testimonies from "a member of a disrupted Indian family."[16]

Vivian married a white man, too, and the couple lived in San Diego until Janice was nine years old. In 1958, when her father lost his job, the family moved back to Berkeley to move in with Beatrice, the woman who had adopted Vivian as a child. So Janice grew up just a few minutes from the Kroebers' house as Theodora was writing *Ishi in Two Worlds: A Biography of the Last Wild Indian in North America*. She often played in the ravines on the university campus where Kroeber, though retired, was still a presence. Though unrecognized, an Indian presence was still on the campus, too, as it was across the state.

Janice's adopted grandmother, Beatrice, had originally moved with her family to California just before the earthquake of 1906. Like Kroeber, they lost many of their belongings in the fire, but some things were salvageable. Janice ate cereal in the morning from Beatrice's "ceramic bowls patched and glued together, with brown, resinous seams—survivors from the wreckage of that earthquake."[17]

One of the messages of this book is about the earthquake that was the colonization of California by whites and modernity, an upheaval that shook and fragmented families, communities, and landscapes. Another message is how Indians have been picking up the pieces and putting their vessels back together. In *Mabel McKay: Weaving the Dream*, Greg Sarris, a Cache Creek Pomo, relates the biography of the world-famous shaman and basket maker Mabel McKay. When in the 1970s plans were made to build a dam that would submerge the place where she had traditionally gathered reeds for her baskets, McKay joined with others to protest. The dam dream was the same one that had brought the surveyors to Deer Creek in 1908, the very people who plundered Grizzly Bear's Hiding Place. Though McKay thought the damming was inevitable (for she had dreamed of it years earlier), she nonetheless stood with others against the construction. A photograph shows the basket weaver standing pat before an enormous earthmover, equipped with tires that towered over her. The dam was built and the gathering grounds were submerged, but not before the sedges were transplanted to another place, where native basket weavers would continue to gather materials for their baskets. The California Indian Basketmakers Association now works to preserve access to traditional gathering sites and "to provide a healthy physical, social, cultural, spiritual and economic environment for the practice of California Indian basketry."[18]

Against overwhelming odds, Native Californians have again and again taken the steps that have ensured sustainability, cultural and ecological. They have told the little stories that have survived the onslaught of modernity and its propulsive metanarrative promising earthly salvation if everyone would simply sacrifice their old values, their traditions, and their homelands to the greater cause of progress. Indian survivors from "that earthquake" have found ways to put the bowls and baskets back together.

In a prose poem called "Easter Sunday," Janice writes about the transformation of the California landscape, visible in all the introduced plants, in the army's rifle range, and in the old mission in the Coast Range. It is a story of linked ecological and cultural conquest, and yet of resilience, too, for she is there to witness it all on an Easter Sunday. Driving to see the old mission grounds at Los Padres, she writes:

> This spring the sturdy flowers have opened, and my mother reels off the endless list of names as we pass by: lupine, California poppy, clarkia, larkspur, Indian paintbrush, owl's clover, buttercup, vetch, trillium, forget-me-not, columbine, fairy's lantern, pearly everlasting. The species are so mixed we hardly know the indigenous from the introduced, the native from the volunteer, the survivor from the parasite populations that have sprung up in the friendly habitat. This is California with its rich, false history.[19]

I am part of that history, rich and false, a history of loving and abusing people, animals, and the land itself. Like Janice, there are Frenchmen in my ancestry. Half of my family are French immigrants who came to California between the 1880s and the 1920s. One branch owns a ranch on those very fields and slopes with the military's firing range and the old mission Janice observed on that Easter Sunday. My mom grew up far to the south in Los Angeles but spent wonderful summers there "on the ranch." When I was growing up, the extended family would reunite on this land. There was card playing, bacon making by the women, wine drinking by the men.

And there was hunting. Unfamiliar with guns, I was a reluctant participant, but I went along. I remember driving up in trucks into the hills above the ranch, the men and all of us on the lookout for deer. I never saw one, but then we stopped abruptly on a ridge, and getting out we spied faint brown specks among the brown brush and oaks—deer, they said. It seemed as though they were a mile off. The rifles had powerful scopes; aim was taken and shots cracked the air. A buck was hit, and we all packed back fast into the truck for the chase. When we got to where the bullet had hit its target, the deer was gone, having fled into the woods. I remember being amazed at the hunters' ability to track the wounded animal, finding "sign," a drop of blood on blades of grass or branches. We finally caught up with the prey, its strength slowly draining away. We kids were kept away and off to the side. Soon we heard a splattering of shots from a .22-caliber pistol, followed by more shots, then still more, until the deer hung its head down at last, dead from the sloppy execution. Something must have gone wrong: this was not how hunting was supposed to end. The ethical relationship my relatives and many modern hunters have with their prey was broken that day. I don't think the soul of that deer went up and out through the portal in the rocks. The deer was carefully cleaned and butchered and turned into venison, but I never learned to appreciate the meat and the hunt.

Years later I did learn to appreciate the way California Indians hunted deer and related to nature more generally. Gail Kelly, the legendary anthropology professor at Reed College, had assigned my class to write papers on the symbolic nature of food in some culture. I happened upon the Yurok and found a wealth of information, mostly recorded by Alfred Kroeber or his students, about deer and salmon in Yurok life and mythology. I learned that the Yurok believed animals were related to them, kin; that the animals were always watching; that when a deer fell to a hunter's arrow, that deer had given itself up and expected to be appreciated and honored. When the opportunity came to propose a book for the *New Narratives in American History* series, I knew I wanted to go back to that world, to discover more about the anthropologist's relationship to California Indians, and about California Indians' relationships to the landscape on which I was born and grew up. And I wanted to know more about the great upheaval of the gold rush, about the man-made earthquakes that have transformed the landscape and have profoundly shaken Indian communities. About all of the killing.

Today when I walk the woods and the beautiful golden hills of California, the killing haunts me, it all haunts me, as well it should. In her essay "Haunted America," Patricia Limerick points out that "the landscape bears witness to the violent subordination of Indian people." History cannot exorcize ghosts from the landscape, and I don't believe that would be a good thing to try, even if it could. History can help us acknowledge the ghosts, acknowledge the terror that befell Indian communities in America. Many of those communities have somehow found ways to live on. We, Indians and immigrants alike, have inherited a landscape that has been shaped and disrupted by the past. We have inherited a set of stories, too, and they can teach us how to turn this country back from a wilderness into a homeland.[20]

Notes

Prologue: One Small Step

1. A. L. Kroeber, "The Elusive Mill Creeks," *Travel Magazine,* August 1911, in Robert Heizer and Theodora Kroeber, eds., *Ishi, the Last Yahi: A Documentary History* (Berkeley: University of California Press, 1979), 80.

2. Alfred Kroeber, "It's All Too Much for Ishi, Says the Scientist," *San Francisco Call,* 8 October 1911, in Heizer and Kroeber, *Ishi, the Last Yahi,* 111; A. L. Kroeber, "Ishi, the Last Aborigine," *World's Work,* July 1912, 304.

3. Letter from Kroeber to Phoebe Hearst, 11 May 1906, Reel 67, George and Phoebe Apperson Hearst Papers, BANC MSS 72/204 c, Bancroft Library, University of California, Berkeley.

4. Theodora Kroeber, *Alfred Kroeber: A Personal Configuration* (Berkeley: University of California Press, 1970), 71–72, 76.

5. A. L. Kroeber, "The Indians of California," *Transactions of the Commonwealth Club of California* 4 (December 1909): 430–31.

6. A. L. Kroeber et al., "Notes on California Folk-Lore," *Journal of American Folklore* 19 (October–December 1906): 322–25; A. L. Kroeber, *Yurok Myths* (Berkeley: University of California Press, 1976), 418.

7. Philip Fradkin, *The Great Earthquake and Firestorms of 1906* (Berkeley: University of California Press, 2005), 265–66.

8. Theodore Winthrop, *The Canoe and the Saddle* (Tacoma, Wash.: J. H. Williams, 1913), 19; James Swan, *Almost out of the World* (Tacoma: Washington State Historical Society, 1973), 15.

9. Saxton Pope, "The Medical History of Ishi," *University of California Publications in American Archeology and Ethnology* 13, no. 5 (1920), reprinted in Heizer and Kroeber, *Ishi, the Last Yahi*, 234; Kroeber, "Ishi, the Last Aborigine," 306.

10. Pope, "Medical History," 225; A. L. Kroeber, *Handbook of the Indians of California* (1925; New York: Dover, 1976), 343; Ishi, "Long, Long Ago," in Jean Perry, "When the World Was New: Ishi's Stories," in Karl Kroeber and Clifton Kroeber, eds., *Ishi in Three Centuries* (Lincoln: University of Nebraska Press, 2003), 275–92.

ONE: THE YAHI IN THREE WORLDS

1. Ishi, "Long, Long Ago," in Jean Perry, "When the World Was New: Ishi's Stories," in Karl and Clifton Kroeber, eds., *Ishi in Three Centuries* (Lincoln: University of Nebraska Press, 2003): 275–92.

2. A. Kroeber, *Handbook*, 336–46; Alfred Kroeber, Ishi field notes, Reel 161, A. L. Kroeber Papers, BANC FILM 2049, Bancroft Library; Jerald Johnson, "Yana," in Robert Heizer, ed., *Handbook of the North American Indians* (Washington, D.C.: Smithsonian Institution Press, 1978), 8: 361–69; Theodora Kroeber, *Ishi in Two Worlds: A Biography of the Last Wild Indian in North America* (Berkeley: University of California Press, 1961), 11–39; Orin Starn, *Ishi's Brain: In Search of the Last "Wild" Indian* (New York: Norton, 2004), 64–79, 244; M. Kat Anderson, *Tending the Wild: Native American Knowledge and the Management of California's Natural Resources* (Berkeley: University of California Press, 2005); Steven Schoonover, *Before Ishi: The Life and Death of the Yahi: A book under construction correcting a chapter of Northern California history, being written with nerve-wracking transparency;* www.norcalblogs.com/yahi/ (accessed 18 January 2009).

3. J. Goldsborough Bruff, *Gold Rush* (New York: Columbia University Press, 1949).

4. Louise Clapp, *The Shirley Letters from California Mines in 1851–1852* (San Francisco: T. C. Russell, 1922), reprinted in Library of Congress, *California as I Saw It: First-Person Narratives of California's Early Years, 1849–1900,* http://lcweb2.loc.gov/cgi-bin/query/r?ammem/calbk:@field (DOCID+@lit(calbk146)) (accessed 20 May 2008).

5. *The Butte Record*, 1854.

6. *The Butte Record*, 1854.

7. "Worldmaker's Trail," www.indianvalley.net/maidu.html (accessed 20 May 2008).

8. Michael Gillis and Michael Magliari, *John Bidwell and California: The Life and Writings of a Pioneer, 1841–1900* (Spokane: Arthur H. Clark, 2004), 249–310; James Rawls, *Indians of California: The Changing Image* (Norman: University of Oklahoma Press, 1984), 86–108; Albert Hurtado, *Indian Survival on the California Frontier* (New Haven, Conn.: Yale University Press, 1988), 128–30; Richard Burrill, *Ishi Rediscovered* (Chester, Calif.: Anthro, 2001), 16–17.

9. H. H. Sauber, "Hi Good and the 'Mill Creeks,'" *Overland Monthly* 30 (1897): 122–27, in Heizer and Kroeber, *Ishi, the Last Yahi*, 19–25.

10. R. A. Anderson, *Fighting the Mill Creeks* (Chico, Calif.: Chico Record Press, 1909), in Heizer and Kroeber, *Ishi, the Last Yahi*, 39–41.

11. A. Kroeber, *Handbook*, 336–346; Johnson, "Yana," 361–69; Schoonover, *Before Ishi*.

12. Rawls, *Indians*, 181–83.

13. Rawls, *Indians*, 185–86; R. A. Anderson, *Fighting*, 33, 50.

14. Rawls, *Indians*, 141–42.

15. Rawls, *Indians*, 143–47.

16. Rawls, *Indians*, 147–54.

17. Rawls, *Indians*, 152.

18. William Kibbe, *Report of the Expedition Against the Indians in the Northern Part of This State* (Sacramento: State Printing Office, 1860), in Heizer and Kroeber, *Ishi, the Last Yahi*, 14–19.

19. Starn, *Ishi's Brain*, 132–33; Kibbe, *Report*, 19.

20. Thankful Carson, *Captured by the Mill Creeks* (Chico, Calif.: n.p., 1915), in Heizer and Kroeber, *Ishi, the Last Yahi*, 25–32.

21. Rawls, *Indians*, 163.

22. Frank Baumgardner, *Killing for Land in Early California: Indian Blood at Round Valley* (New York: Algora, 2005), 211–12.

23. R. A. Anderson, *Fighting*, 55, 52.

24. R. A. Anderson, *Fighting*, 57–58.

25. Sim Moak, *The Last of the Mill Creeks, and Early Life in California* (Chico, Calif.: n.p., 1923), 23, in Library of Congress, *California as I Saw It* http://lcweb2.loc.gov/cgi-bin/query/r?ammem/calbk:@field(DOCID+@lit(calbk173)) (accessed 20 May 2008).

26. Moak, *Last*, 23; R. A. Anderson, *Fighting*, 58.

27. Moak, *Last*, 24.

28. T. T. Waterman, "The Yana Indians," *University of California Publications in American Archeology and Ethnology* 13, no. 2 (1918), in Heizer and Kroeber, *Ishi, the Last Yahi*, 149.

29. Waterman, "Yana," 149; T. Kroeber, *Ishi in Two Worlds*, 88–90.

30. Stephen Powers, *Tribes of California* (Washington, D.C.: Government Printing Office, 1877), 280–81.

31. R. A. Anderson, *Fighting*, 58–59; Moak, *Last*, 31–32.

32. Moak, *Last*, 33.

33. R. A. Anderson, *Fighting*, 59; Moak, *Last*, 33.

34. Ishi, "The Journey of the Dead" in Jean Perry, "When the World Was New: Ishi's Stories," reprinted in Karl Kroeber and Clifton Kroeber, eds., *Ishi in Three Centuries* (Lincoln: University of Nebraska Press, 2003), 278–80.

35. Ishi, "Long, Long Ago."

36. Ishi, "A Story of Lizard," in Herbert Luthin and Leanne Hinton, "The Story of Lizard," reprinted in K. Kroeber and C. Kroeber, *Ishi in Three Centuries*, 293–317.

37. Luthin and Hinton, "Story of Lizard," 298.

38. Waterman, "Yana," 150–51.

39. Waterman, "Yana," 151.

40. Burrill, *Ishi Rediscovered*, 107.

41. Ben Frost testimony, Box 10, Folder 3, Theodora Kroeber Papers, mss 69/145, Bancroft Library.

Two: The Anthropologist in Three Worlds

1. Gustave Koemer, ed., *Opening Ceremonies of the Brooklyn Bridge, May 24, 1883* (Brooklyn: Press of the Brooklyn Eagle Job Printing Department, 1883), 99, 43–45; Luther Standing Bear, *My People the Sioux* (1928; Lincoln: University of Nebraska Press, 1975), 171; "An Indian Chief in New York City," *American Missionary* 39, no. 4 (1885): 114–15.

2. Carl Alsberg, "Alfred L. Kroeber: Personal Reminiscences and Professional Appreciation," in Robert Lowie, ed., *Essays in Anthropology: Presented to A. L. Kroeber in Celebration of His Sixtieth Birthday, June 11, 1936* (Berkeley: University of California Press, 1936).

3. Elizabeth Blackmar and Roy Rosenzweig, *The Park and the People: A History of Central Park* (Ithaca, N.Y.: Cornell University Press, 1992), 131, 443.

4. Alfred Kroeber, "Reminiscences" (1955–56), Reel 183, Alfred Kroeber Papers, BANC FILM 2049, Bancroft Library.

5. Alsberg "Kroeber"; A. Kroeber, "Reminiscences"; T. Kroeber, *Kroeber;* 22–23; G. Stanley Hall, *Adolescence* (New York: D. Appleton, 1904), 361.

6. A. Kroeber, "Reminiscences."

7. G. Stanley Hall, *Youth: Its Education, Regimen, and Hygiene* (1906; Whitefish, Mont.: Kessinger, 2004), 3–4, 23.

8. A. Kroeber, "Reminiscences."

9. T. Kroeber, *Kroeber,* 29–34.

10. "Two More Vandals Caught," *New York Times,* 6 December 1892; Alsberg, "Kroeber."

11. T. Kroeber, *Kroeber,* 42–52.

12. A. Kroeber, "Reminiscences"; Harold Carew, "They Learn about Indians from Kroeber," *Touring Topics* 21 (June 1929).

13. A. Kroeber, "Reminiscences."

14. Alsberg, "Kroeber."

15. Franz Boas, "Poetry and Music of Some North American Tribes," *Science* 9 (1887): 383–85; Franz Boas, *The Mind of Primitive Man*

(New York: Macmillan, 1938), 17; "No Race Is Inferior, Says World Authority," *Los Angeles Times,* 26 June 1914.

16. Franz Boas, letter to the editor, *Science* 9, no. 228 (1887): 589.

17. Alfred Kroeber, *Anthropology,* 2nd edition (1923; New York: Harcourt Brace, 1948), 2, 11, 841, 849.

18. David Hurst Thomas, *Skull Wars: Kennewick Man, Archaeology, and the Battle for Native American Identity* (New York: Basic Books, 2001), 78, 80–83.

19. Thomas, *Skull Wars,* 60; T. Kroeber, *Kroeber,* 47–48; Kenn Harper, *Give Me My Father's Body: The Life of Minik, the New York Eskimo* (1986; South Royalton, Vt.: Steerforth Press, 200), 85–94.

20. Alfred Kroeber, "The Eskimo of Smith Sound," *Bulletin of the American Museum of Natural History* 12 (1899): 316.

21. Harper, *Give Me My Father's Body,* 88.

22. Aleš Hrdlička, "An Eskimo Brain," *American Anthropologist* 3 (1901): 454–500.

23. A. Kroeber, "Reminiscences."

24. As Kenn Harper notes in his history of this tragic saga, "Of all the scientists involved with the Eskimos, he was in human terms the warmest." *Give Me My Father's Body,* 36.

25. A. Kroeber, "Eskimo."

26. A. Kroeber, "Reminiscences."

27. T. Kroeber, *Kroeber,* 53–54.

28. T. Kroeber, *Kroeber,* 54–57; Mary Gist Dornback, "Anthropologist, Educator: UC's Alfred Kroeber Dies," Council of California Indians, Inc., newsletter, 15 December 1960, in Kroeber Papers, Reel 183; A. Kroeber, *Yurok Myths,* 419–36.

29. A. Kroeber, *Handbook,* 1.

30. A. Kroeber, *Yurok Myths,* 1; T. Kroeber, foreword, in A. Kroeber, *Yurok Myths,* xiv, xvi.

31. T. Kroeber, *Kroeber,* 2.

32. T. Kroeber, *Kroeber,* 54–63.

33. *Los Angeles Times,* 10 October 1903.

34. A. Kroeber, *Handbook,* 219; Alfred Kroeber, "California Place Names of Indian Origin," *University of California Publications in American Archeology and Ethnology* 12, no. 2 (1916): 31–69.

35. A. Kroeber, *Handbook,* v.

36. A. Kroeber, "Indians of California," 430–37.

37. A. Kroeber, "Indians of California," 437.

38. Cornelia Taber, "Remarks," *Transactions of the Commonwealth Club of California* 4 (December 1909): 438.

39. Alfred Kroeber letter to C. E. Kelsey, 30 October and 8 November 1906, CU-23, Box 14, Anthropological Papers of the University of California, Bancroft Library.

40. Luther Standing Bear, *Land of the Spotted Eagle* (1933; Lincoln: University of Nebraska Press, 2006), 38. See also Mark Spence, *Dispossessing the Wilderness: Indian Removal and the Making of the National Parks* (New York: Oxford University Press, 1999); Karl Jacoby, *Crimes against Nature: Squatters, Poachers, Thieves, and the Hidden History of American Conservation* (Berkeley: University of California Press, 2003).

41. A. Kroeber, *Handbook,* ix.

42. Powers, *Tribes,* 277; *Chico Record* and *Oroville Daily Register,* 10 November 1908, reprinted in Burrill, *Ishi Rediscovered,* 70–71.

Three: "Worlds of Stuff"

1. Nels Nelson, "Flint Working by Ishi," in *Holmes Anniversary Volume* (Washington, D.C.: n.p., 1916), in Heizer and Kroeber, *Ishi, the Last Yahi,* 168–72; Saxton Pope, "Yahi Archery," *University of California Publications in American Archeology and Ethnology* 13, no. 3 (1918): 104–52, in Heizer and Kroeber, *Ishi, the Last Yahi,* 172–201.

2. Ishi, "Story of Lizard." Herbert Luthin suggests the connection between Ishi and Lizard in his introduction, "Story of Lizard," 298.

3. Steven Shackley, "The Stone Tool Technology of Ishi and the Yana," in K. Kroeber and C. Kroeber, *Ishi in Three Centuries,* 159–200.

4. Waterman, "Yana," 153–55; "Indians in Wild State Live on Deer Creek," *Oroville Daly Register,* 11 November 1908, in Burrill, *Ishi Rediscovered,* 71–73; Eva Marie Apperson, *We Knew Ishi* (Red Bluff, Calif.: Walker Lithograph, 1971), 53; Starn, *Ishi's Brain,* 231–48.

5. Dorothy Hill, "A Trip to Ishi's Cave: As Told to Dorothy Hill by Mel Speegle, January 28, 1971," *Dogtown Historical Quarterly,* Winter 1992, Folder 5, Dorothy Hill Special Collections, Meriam Library, California State University, Chico; Edward Sapir and Leslie Spier, "Notes on the Culture of the Yana," *University of California Anthropological Records 3,* no. 3 (1943): 282.

6. Sources for the camp raid include Robert Hackley, "An Encounter with the Mill Creek Indians in 1908," Box 10, Folder 4, ms 69, Theodora Kroeber Papers, Bancroft Library; "Camp of Wild Indians Reported," *Chico Record,* 10 November 1908, and "Indians in Wild Sate," *Oroville Daily Register,* 11 November 1908, both reprinted in Burrill, *Ishi Rediscovered,* 70–73; Apperson, *We Knew Ishi;* Burrill, *Ishi Rediscovered,* 39–77.

7. Telegram from Elsbeth Kroeber to Alfred Kroeber, 26 April 1911, Reel 33, Alfred Kroeber Papers, Bancroft Library; Kroeber, "Elusive Mill Creeks," 87.

8. Letter from Waterman to A. Kroeber, 11 November 1910, CU-23, Box 20, Anthropological Papers of the University of California, Bancroft Library; Burrill, *Ishi Rediscovered,* 86.

9. Letter from A. Kroeber to Waterman, 29 October 1910, CU-23, Series 4, Subseries 1, Volume 12, Anthropological Papers, Bancroft Library.

10. Letter from Waterman to A. Kroeber, 26 October 1910, CU-23, Box 20, Anthropological Papers, Bancroft Library.

11. Letter from Waterman to A. Kroeber, dated Saturday, CU-23, Box 20, Anthropological Papers, Bancroft Library.

12. Letter from Waterman to A. Kroeber, 29 October 1910, CU-23, Box 20, Anthropological Papers, Bancroft Library; letter from A. Kroeber to Waterman, 8 November 1910, CU-23, Series 4, Subseries 1, Volume 12, Anthropological Papers, Bancroft Library.

13. Burrill, *Ishi Rediscovered,* 56.

14. Letter from Waterman to A. Kroeber, 26 October 1910.

15. Alfred Kroeber, "The Superorganic," *American Anthropologist* 19, no. 2 (1917): 189, 192.

16. Kroeber, "Elusive Mill Creeks," 85.

17. Kroeber, "Elusive Mill Creeks."

18. Adolph Kessler interview, 18 July 1973, by Steve Morehouse, Phonotape 828 with transcripts, Bancroft Library.

19. Florence Boyle, "Ishi," *California Herald,* February 1962, reprinted in Burrill, *Second World,* 151–53.

20. Burrill, *Second World,* 286–88.

21. *Oroville Daily Register,* 29 August 1911, in Heizer and Kroeber, *Ishi, the Last Yahi,* 92–93.

22. *Oroville Daily Register,* 31 August 1911, in Heizer and Kroeber, *Ishi, the Last Yahi,* 94–95.

23. Ernest Hopkins, "Cave Man, Beware," *San Francisco Bulletin,* 5 September 1911, reprinted in *Chico Record,* 7 September 1911, reprinted in Burrill, *Second World,* 256.

24. *Oroville Daily Register,* 29 August 1911.

25. Letter from Waterman to A. Kroeber, 2 September, 1911, CU-23, Box 20, Anthropological Papers, Bancroft Library; *Oroville Daily Register,* 2 and 4 September 1911, reprinted in Burrill, *Second World,* 231–32, 262–64.

26. Telegram from A. Kroeber to Sheriff, Butte County, 30 August 1911, CU-23, Box 10, Anthropological Papers, Bancroft Library; *Sacramento Union,* 2 September 1911; T. Kroeber, *Kroeber,* 79–80.

27. "Least Civilized Man Tells His Tale by Signs," San Francisco *Call,* 31 August 1911.

28. Burrill, *Ishi Rediscovered,* 193–200.

29. Burrill, *Ishi Rediscovered,* 204; T. Waterman, "The Last Wild Tribe of California," *Popular Science Monthly,* March 1915, in Heizer and Kroeber, *Ishi, the Last Yahi,* 130.

30. Letter from Waterman to A. Kroeber, 2 September 1911, CU-23, Box 20, Anthropological Papers, Bancroft Library.

31. Letter from Waterman to A. Kroeber, 2 September 1911.

32. Letter from Waterman to A. Kroeber, n.d. [1 September 1911], CU-23, Box 20, Anthropological Papers, Bancroft Library.

33. *Marysville Appeal*, 2 September 1911, reprinted in Burrill, *Second World*, 223.

34. Letter from Waterman to A. Kroeber, n.d. [1 September 1911], CU-23, Box 20, Anthropological Papers, Bancroft Library.

35. Letter from Waterman to A. Kroeber, n.d. [1 September 1911], CU-23, Box 20, Anthropological Papers, Bancroft Library.

FOUR: MAKING TRACKS

1. Burrill, *Second World*, 246.

2. Burrill, *Second World*, 247; Sigmund Freud, *The Uncanny* (1919; New York: Penguin, 2003).

3. Marshall Berman, *All That Is Solid Melts into Air: The Experience of Modernity* (1982; New York: Penguin, 1988), 18.

4. Burrill, *Second World*, 265–66.

5. Philip Deloria, *Indians in Unexpected Places* (Lawrence: University Press of Kansas, 2004), 85–87.

6. *Oroville Daily Register*, 5 September 1911, reprinted in Burrill, *Second World*, 156.

7. Alan Trachtenberg, *Shades of Hiawatha: Staging Indians, Making Americans, 1880–1930* (New York: Hill and Wang, 2004), 170–210.

8. Lynn Kirby, *Parallel Tracks: The Railroad and Silent Cinema* (Durham, N.C.: Duke University Press, 1996); Burrill, *Second World*, 265.

9. Adolph Kessler interview.

10. Telegram from Kelsey to Waterman, 2 September 1911, 10:42 a.m., CU-23, Box 23, Anthropological Papers, Bancroft Library; Burrill, *Second World*, 270.

11. Rebecca Dobkins, "The Healer: Maidu Artist Frank Day's Vision of Ishi," in K. Kroeber and C. Kroeber, *Ishi in Three Centuries*, 388–93.

2. Burrill, *Second World*, 253, 271.

13. Burrill, *Second World*, 275–84; *Sacramento Union*, 5 September 1911.

14. Letter from Waterman to A. Kroeber, 2 September 1911; *San Francisco Bulletin*, 5 September 1911.

15. Burrill, *Second World*, 297–320.

16. Deloria, *Indians in Unexpected Places*.

17. Deloria, *Indians in Unexpected Places*, 155. On Kroeber and Angulo, see Robert Brightman, "Jaime de Angulo and Alfred Kroeber: Bohemians and Bourgeois in Berkeley Anthropology," in Richard Handler, ed., *Significant Others: Interpersonal and Professional Commitments in Anthropology* (Madison: University of Wisconsin Press, 2004), 158–95.

18. *Oakland Tribune*, 5 September 1911.

19. Burrill, *Second World*, 310; Waterman, "Yana," 157; T. Kroeber, *Ishi*, 118–19.

20. Susan Danly and Leo Marx, *The Railroad in American Art* (Boston: MIT Press, 1988), 21; Richard White, *It's Your Misfortune and None of My Own* (Norman: University of Oklahoma Press, 1993); Andrew Isenberg, *The Destruction of the Bison: An Environmental History, 1750–1920* (New York: Cambridge University Press, 2000), 159–60; Elliott West, *The Contested Plains: Indians, Goldseekers, and the Rush to Colorado* (Lawrence: University Press of Kansas, 1998).

21. Sheridan quoted in Winona Laduke, *All Our Relations: Native Struggles for Land and Life* (Cambridge, Mass.: South End Press, 1999), 141.

22. T. Kroeber, *Ishi*, 119; Frank Norris, *The Octopus: A Story of California* (1901; New York: Penguin, 1986), 50, 288–99; William Deverell, *Railroad Crossing: Californians and the Railroad, 1850–1910* (Berkeley: University of California Press, 1994), 168.

23. Adolph Kessler interview.

24. Leo Marx, *The Machine in the Garden: Technology and the Pastoral Ideal in America* (New York: Oxford University Press, 1964), 260; Nathaniel Hawthorne, *The House of the Seven Gables: A Romance* (1851; New York: Houghton Mifflin, 1913), 304.

25. Sheriff John Webber, receipt issued to T. T. Waterman, 4 September 1911, Bancroft Library.

26. Douglas Sackman, *Orange Empire: California and the Fruits of Eden* (Berkeley: University of California Press, 2005).

27. Chiori Santiago and Judith Lowry, *Home to Medicine Mountain* (San Francisco: Children's Book Press, 1998).

28. David Wallace Adams, *Education for Extinction: American Indians and the Boarding School Experience* (Lawrence: University Press of Kansas, 1995).

29. Santiago and Lowry, *Home to Medicine Mountain;* Alley, Bowen, and Co., *History of Sonoma County* (Oakland, Calif.: Pacific Press, 1879), 104; Bret Harte, editorial, *Overland Monthly* 1 (1868): 99–100, quoted in Tracy Storer and Lloyd Tevis Jr., *California Grizzly* (1955; Berkeley: University of California Press, 1996), 281; Allan Schoenherr, *A Natural History of California* (Berkeley: University of California Press, 1992), 386.

30. Adams, *Education for Extinction,* 155.

31. Burrill, *Ishi Rediscovered,* 99.

32. Letter of transfer of custody of Ishi to the University of California from the sheriff of Butte County, Oroville, California, 4 September 1911, Reel 36, University of California, Berkeley, BANC FILM 2216, Bancroft Library.

33. David Klehn, *Broncho Billy and the Essanay Film Company* (Berkeley: Farwell Books, 2003).

34. Kroeber, "Ishi, the Last Aborigine," 119.

35. Alfred Kroeber, "The Only Man in America Who Knows No Christmas—Ishi," *San Francisco Call,* 17 December 1911, in Heizer and Kroeber, *Ishi, the Last Yahi,* 112–16.

36. Pope, "Medical History," 231; T. Kroeber, *Ishi,* 124; letter from A. Kroeber to Sam Batwi, 1 June 1911, CU-23, Series 4, Subseries 1, Volume 13, Anthropological Papers, Bancroft Library.

37. Mary Ashe Miller, "Indian Enigma Is Study for Scientists," *San Francisco Call,* 6 September 1911, in Heizer and Kroeber, *Ishi, the Last Yahi,* 99; A. Kroeber, "Ishi, the Last Aborigine," 120; Philip Kinsley, "Untainted Life Revealed by Aborigine," *San Francisco Examiner,* 6 September 1911.

38. Gerald Vizenor, "Ishi and the Wood Ducks" (play), in Gerald Vizenor, ed., *Native-American Literature: A Brief Introduction and*

Anthology (New York: Harper Collins, 1997): 299–336; Gerald Vizenor and A. Robert Lee, *Postindian Conversions* (Lincoln: University of Nebraska Press, 2003), 73–74. See also Louis Owens, "Native Sovereignty and the Tricky Mirror: Gerald Vizenor's 'Ishi and the Wood Ducks,'" in K. Kroeber and C. Kroeber, *Ishi in Three Centuries*, 373–93.

39. *Sacramento Union*, 6 September 1911; *Marysville Appeal*, 31 August 1911; Vizenor and Lee, *Postindian Conversations*, 73–74.

40. "Lone Aborigine Who Is Deep Problem to Anthropologists," *Los Angeles Times*, 10 September 1911.

FIVE: CITY LIGHTS

1. *San Francisco Bulletin*, 5 September 1911.

2. *San Francisco Call*, 6 September 1911, in Heizer and Kroeber, *Ishi, the Last Yahi*, 99.

3. *Los Angeles Times*, 6 September 1911.

4. Philip Kinsley, "Untainted Life Revealed by Aborigine," *San Francisco Examiner*, 6 September 1911; *Los Angeles Times*, 6 September 1911.

5. *San Francisco Call*, 6 September 1911; *Los Angeles Times*, 10 September 1911; *San Francisco Examiner*, 6 September 1911.

6. *San Francisco Call*, 6 September 1911.

7. *San Francisco Call*, 6 September 1911.

8. Kroeber, "Ishi, the Last Aborigine"; *San Francisco Bulletin*, 6 September 1911.

9. *San Francisco Bulletin*, 5 September 1911; *San Francisco Examiner*, 6 September 1911.

10. Kroeber, "Ishi, the Last Aborigine," 121.

11. Gray Brechin, *Imperial San Francisco: Urban Power, Earthly Ruin* (Berkeley: University of California Press, 199), 13–70.

12. J. E. Van Hoosear, "'Pacific Service' Supplies the World's Largest Baths," *P.G.&E. Magazine*, September 1912, Virtual Museum of the City of San Francisco, www.sfmuseum.org/hist2/baths.html (accessed 4 June 2008).

13. Brechin, *Imperial San Francisco*, 71–120.

14. Waterman, "Yana," 157; Kroeber, "Ishi, the Last Aborigine," 121.

15. A. Kroeber, "Ishi, the Last Aborigine," 121; T. Kroeber, *Ishi*, 139.

16. Alfred Kroeber, "Ishi Reading Lessons," Reel 161, A. L. Kroeber Papers, BANC FILM 2049, Bancroft Library.

17. "Show Relics from Ancient Haunts," *Oakland Tribune*, 24 March 1912.

18. T. Kroeber, *Ishi*, 129–30.

19. Rachel Adams, *Sideshow U.S.A.: Freaks and the American Cultural Imagination* (Chicago: University of Chicago Press, 2001), 46; Roselyn Poignant, *Professional Savages: Captive Lives and Western Spectacle* (New Haven, Conn.: Yale University Press, 2004), 215–16.

20. Grant Wallace, "Ishi, the Last Aboriginal Savage in America, Finds Enchantment in a Vaudeville Show," *San Francisco Call*, 8 October 1911, in Heizer and Kroeber, *Ishi, the Last Yahi*, 107–111.

21. A. Kroeber, "Ishi, the Last Aborigine," 121; A. Kroeber, "It's All Too Much," 111.

22. A. Kroeber, "It's All Too Much," 112.

23. A. Kroeber miscellaneous correspondence on 29 August 1911, CU-23, Series 4, Subseries 1, Volume 13, Anthropological Papers of the University of California, Bancroft Library; T. Kroeber, *Ishi*, 133–36; *Oakland Tribune*, 5 October 1911.

24. Letter from Waterman to A. Kroeber, 2 September 1911.

25. Alfred Kroeber, museum press release, 13 October 1911, CU-23, Series 4, Subseries 1, Volume 13, Anthropological Papers of the University of California, Bancroft Library.

26. *Modesto News*, 16 October 1911; letter from Mrs. Ralph Amendlola to Theodora Kroeber, 20 May 1962, Box 10, File 11, Theodora Kroeber Papers, mss 69/145, Bancroft Library; A. Kroeber, "Only Man," 115.

27. Letter from A. Kroeber to Mr. Green, 10 July 1912, CU-23, Box 21, Anthropological Papers, Bancroft Library; Vernon Armand DeMars, "A Life in Architecture: Indian Dancing, Migrant Housing, Telesis, Design for Urban Living, Theater, Teaching," an oral history conducted in 1988–89 by

Suzanne B. Riess, Regional Oral History Office, Bancroft Library, University of California, Berkeley, 1992, 30.

28. "Ishi Refuses to Perform Until Paid," *Oakland News Tribune,* 15 January 1912.

29. Letter from Hauke to C. Kelsey, 27 October 1911, and letter from A. Kroeber to Kelsey, 24 November 1911, CU-23, Box 13, Anthropological Papers; A. Kroeber, "Ishi, the Last Aborigine," 121; letter from Kelsey to commissioner of Indian affairs, 16 December 1911, in Clifton Kroeber, "Introduction to Part One," in K. Kroeber and C. Kroeber, *Ishi in Three Centuries,* 5.

30. T. Kroeber, *Ishi,* 142–44.

31. Ira Jacknis, "Yahi Culture in the Wax Museum: Ishi's Sound Recordings," in K. Kroeber and C. Kroeber, *Ishi in Three Centuries,* 235–74.

32. "Ishi Tells the Story of Wood Duck for 6 Hours," *San Francisco Examiner,* 7 September 1911, in Heizer and Kroeber, *Ishi, the Last Yahi,* 105–6; Jacknis, "Yahi Culture," 252–54; T. Kroeber, *Ishi,* 199–201.

33. *San Francisco Call,* 7 September 1911.

34. T. Kroeber, *Ishi,* 131–32.

35. Pope, "Medical History," 231.

36. A. Kroeber, "Ishi, the Last Aborigine"; A. Kroeber, manuscript of "Ishi, the Last Aborigine," Reel 71, A. L. Kroeber papers, BANC FILM 2049, Bancroft Library.

37. T. Kroeber, *Ishi,* 139.

38. Klehn, *Broncho Billy.*

39. Letter from Herbert Samuels to Theodora Kroeber, n.d. [1962?], Box 10, Folder 11, Theodora Kroeber Papers, BANC MSS 69/145 c, Bancroft Library; Burrill, *Ishi Rediscovered,* 163.

SIX: NATURE WALKS...

1. Letter from Harold French to Alfred Kroeber, 17 February 1912, and letter from Kroeber to French, 20 February 1912, CU-23, Box 21, Anthropological Papers, Bancroft Library.

2. Robert Santos, *The Eucalyptus of California* (Denair, Calif.: Alley Cass, 1997); Carl Nolte, "Sutro Forest Dying," *San Francisco Chronicle,*

20 June 2000; Harold French, "A Mountain Wilderness in the City's Heart," *Overland Monthly* 46 (1911): 136–39.

3. John Muir, *The Story of My Boyhood and Youth* (Boston: Houghton Mifflin, 1916).

4. John Muir, *A Thousand-mile Walk to the Gulf* (Boston: Houghton Mifflin, 1913), xvi; John Muir, *The Yosemite* (New York: Century Company, 1912), 4; Muir, *Story of My Boyhood and Youth*, 343.

5. Muir, *Thousand-mile Walk*, 122.

6. John Muir, *The Mountains of California*, in *Nature Writings* (New York: Library of America, 1997), 372–73; John Muir, "By Ways of Yosemite Travel," *Overland Monthly* 13 (July–December 1874): 272; Spence, *Dispossessing the Wilderness*, 109.

7. Spence, *Dispossessing the Wilderness*, 83.

8. Spence, *Dispossessing the Wilderness*, 83–100.

9. James Welch, *Fools Crow* (New York: Penguin, 1987), 273.

10. Spence, *Dispossessing the Wilderness*, 83.

11. Letter from A. Kroeber to Kelsey, 30 October 1906; Spence, *Dispossessing the Wilderness*, 106–8.

12. T. Kroeber, *Kroeber*, 154, 163; Burrill, *Ishi Rediscovered*, 172.

13. Raymond Clary, *The Making of Golden Gate Park: The Early Years, 1865–1906* (San Francisco: Lexikos, 1988); Isenberg, *Destruction of the Bison*; Jeffrey Ostler, *The Plains Sioux and U.S. Colonialism from Lewis and Clark to Wounded Knee* (New York: Cambridge University Press, 2004), 243–369.

14. Isenberg, *Destruction of the Bison*, 164–92; Pope, "Medical History," 231.

15. Edward Weston, "Ishi, the Archer," *Forest and Stream*, n.d. [reprints Pope's letter to the editor], Reel 87, Robert Fleming Heizer Papers, BANC FILM 2106 (originals: BANC MSS 78/17 c), Bancroft Library; Pope, "Medical History," 231–32; L. G. Moses, *Wild West Shows and the Images of American Indians, 1883–1933* (Albuquerque: University of New Mexico Press, 1996).

16. Saxton Pope. *Hunting with Bow and Arrow* (N.p.: Bibliobazaar, 2007), 33, 36.

17. Weston, "Ishi, the Archer"; Pope, "Yahi Archery," 193; Pope, *Hunting*, 21.

18. Letter from Marcella Healy to Theodora Kroeber, 20 May 1962, Box 10, Theodora Kroeber Papers, BANC MSS 69/145 c, Bancroft Library.

19. Letters from Fred Zumwalt Jr. to Theodora Kroeber, 2 April and 20 May 1962, Box 10, Theodora Kroeber Papers, BANC MSS 69/145 c, Bancroft Library; Philip Deloria, *Playing Indian* (New Haven, Conn.: Yale University Press, 1998).

20. Raymond Clary, *The Making of Golden Gate Park: The Early Years: 1865–1906* (San Francisco: Don't Call it Frisco Press, 1984); "John McLaren," American Academy for Park and Recreation Administration website, www.rpts.tamu.edu/pugsley/McLaren.htm (accessed 6 June 2008).

21. Brechin, *Imperial San Francisco*, 84–89.

22. Terence Young, *Building San Francisco's Parks, 1850–1930* (Baltimore: Johns Hopkins University Press, 2004), 47–57.

23. Frederick Law Olmsted, "Draft of Preliminary Report upon the Yosemite and Big Tree Grove," "Typed Transcription of Draft of Preliminary Report upon the Yosemite and Big Tree Grove," and "Typed Transcription of Letter on the Great American Park of the Yosemite" (1865), in *American Memory: Evolution of the Conservation Movement*, Library of Congress, http://memory.loc.gov/cgi-bin/query/r?ammem/consrvbib:@field(NUMBER+@band(amrvm+vm02)): (accessed 6 June 2008).

24. Young, *Building San Francisco's Parks*, 71–97; Brechin, *Imperial San Francisco*, 84.

25. For the Hetch Hetchy battle, I have drawn on Brechin, *Imperial San Francisco;* Robert Righter, *The Battle over Hetch Hetchy* (New York: Oxford University Press, 2005); and John Simpson, *Dam! Water, Power, and Preservation in Hetch Hetchy and Yosemite National Park* (New York: Random House, 2005).

26. John Muir, *Our National Park* (New York: Houghton Mifflin, 1901), 1.

27. Robert Price, "With the Sierra Club in 1911," *Sierra Club Bulletin* 8, no. 3 (1912).

28. A. Kroeber, "California Place Names of Indian Origin," 42; Philip Kinsley, "Untainted Life Revealed by Aborigine," *San Francisco Examiner*, 6 September 1911.

29. Thorstein Veblen, *Theory of the Leisure Class* (1912; Norwood, Mass.: Macmillan, 1899), 132–35; Rebecca Solnit, *River of Shadows: Eadweard Muybridge and the Technological Wild West* (New York: Penguin, 2003).

30. Muir, *Our National Parks*, 1–2; John Muir, "Hetch Hetchy Damming Scheme," memorandum received 14 May 1908 from J. Horace McFarland, Virtual Museum of San Francisco, www.sfmuseum.net/hetch/hetchy7 .html#muir (accessed 6 June 2008).

31. William Badé, *The Life and Letters of John Muir* (New York: Houghton Mifflin, 1924), 2:76.

32. "Ishi, Last of the Deer Creeks, Yields to Lane," *Fresno Republican,* 7 September 1913; Pope, "Medical History," 225, 234.

33. T. Kroeber, *Kroeber,* 76–80; Henriette Rothschild Kroeber, "Wappo Myths," *Journal of American Folklore* 21, no. 82 (1908): 321–32; A. L. Kroeber, "Catch-Words in American Mythology," *Journal of American Folklore* 21, no. 81 (1908): 222–27.

34. T. Kroeber, *Kroeber,* 80.

35. T. Kroeber, *Ishi,* 84–85.

Seven: The Call of the Wild

1. Jack London, "The Nature Man," in *The Cruise of the Snark* (New York: Macmillan, 1911), 178–97; Starn, *Ishi's Brain*, 145; "'Back to Nature Man' Disappointed in Ish [*sic*]," *Oakland Tribune*, 21 June 1913; "Slit Skirt to Reach V-Neck," *Los Angeles Times*, 3 July 1914.

2. Joseph Knowles, *Alone in the Wilderness* (Boston: Small, Maynard, 1913); "Interesting People," *American Magazine*, January 1921; letters from Waterman to A. Kroeber, 10 and 29 July 1914, Box 85, CU-23, Anthropological Papers, Bancroft Library; T. T. Waterman, "Will Instinct Aid Knowles? Indian Knew; But Will He?," *San Francisco Examiner*, 12 July 1914; *San Francisco Examiner*, 25 July 1914; T. T. Waterman, "Knowles Living Again as Our Ancestors Lived," *San Francisco Examiner*, 4 August 1914; Philip Kinsley, "New Adam Confident of Success," *San Francisco Examiner*, 12 July 1914.

3. Quoted in John Kasson, *Houdini, Tarzan, and the Perfect Man: The White Male Body and the Challenge of Modernity in America* (New York: Hill and Wang, 2002), 159.

4. T. Kroeber, *Ishi,* 207.

5. T. Kroeber, *Ishi,* 206; Starn, *Ishi's Brain,* 232.

6. "Primitive Ishi Guiding Savants," *Oakland Tribune,* 14 May 1914; "To Show Ishi in His Native Haunts," *Oakland Tribune,* 14 June 1914.

7. T. Kroeber, *Ishi,* 209.

8. Burrill, *Ishi Rediscovered,* 185–87.

9. Apperson, *We Knew Ishi;* Burrill, *Ishi Rediscovered,* vi.

10. Burrill, *Ishi Rediscovered,* 178; Adolph Kessler interview.

11. *Chico Record,* 4 June 1914, reprinted in Burrill, *Ishi Rediscovered,* 194–95; Adolph Kessler interview.

12. Hill, "Ishi's Cave"; Pope, *Hunting,* 29.

13. Pope, *Hunting,* 39; Hill, "Ishi's Cave."

14. T. Kroeber, *Ishi,* 207, 211.

15. T. Kroeber, *Ishi,* 211–12.

16. Pope, *Hunting,* 40.

17. Pope, "Yahi Archery," 197.

18. Letter from Saxton Pope Jr. to Theodora Kroeber, undated, Box 10, Theodora Kroeber Papers, Bancroft Library; Marshall Kuhn, *Catalyst and Teacher: San Francisco Jewish and Community Leader, 1934–1978* (Berkeley: Regional Oral History Office, Bancroft Library, 1979), 255.

19. Hill, "Ishi's Cave"; A. Kroeber, Ishi field notes, p. 69, Reel 161, A. L. Kroeber Papers, BANC FILM 2049, Bancroft Library; Sapir and Spier, "Notes on the Culture of the Yana," 247.

20. Letter from Saxton Pope Jr. to Theodora Kroeber, undated, Box 10, Theodora Kroeber Papers, Bancroft Library.

21. Pope, "Medical History," 236; Letter from Saxton Pope Jr. to Theodora Kroeber, undated, Box 10, Theodora Kroeber Papers, Bancroft Library.

22. Pope, "Medical History," 234; "Irish-Indian Is the Latest to Come Out as White Hope," *Sacramento Union,* 3 September 1911.

23. Kasson, *Houdini.*

24. A. Kroeber, Ishi field notes, p. 110, Bancroft Library; letter from Saxton Pope Jr. to Theodora Kroeber, undated, Box 10, Theodora Kroeber Papers, Bancroft Library.

25. Ishi, "Long, Long Ago," 280–91.

26. A. Kroeber, *Handbook*, 344; Hill, "Ishi's Cave."

27. A. Kroeber, Ishi field notes, "Ishi's Map of Deer Creek," and "Explanation of Sketch J", pp. 108–10, Bancroft Library.

28. Letter from A. Kroeber to Edward Sapir, 8 June 1914, in Victor Golla, ed., *The Sapir-Kroeber Correspondence* (Berkeley: Department of Linguistics, University of California, 1984), 141.

29. A. Kroeber, Ishi field notes, p. 69, Bancroft Library; "Old Indian Cave Containing Relics, Plunder and a Human Scalp Is Found on Deer Creek," *Chico Daily Enterprise*, 3 January 1907, reprinted in Burrill, *Ishi Rediscovered*, 36–37.

30. Hill, "Ishi's Cave"; T. Kroeber, *Ishi*, 214–15.

31. A. Kroeber, "Ishi, the Last Aborigine," 119.

32. T. Kroeber, *Ishi*, 214.

33. *Fort Wayne Sentinel*, 10 August 1912.

34. Letter from Saxton Pope Jr. to Theodora Kroeber, undated, Box 10, Theodora Kroeber Papers, Bancroft Library.

35. Apperson, *We Knew Ishi*; T. Kroeber, *Ishi*, 216.

36. A. Kroeber, Ishi field notes, dated June 2, "Obtained near Speegle's house", p. 102, Bancroft Library; letter from Alfred Kroeber to Elsie Parsons, 7 January 1920, quoted in Grace Wilson Buzaljko, "Kroeber, Pope, and Ishi," in K. Kroeber and C. Kroeber, *Ishi in Three Centuries*, 60.

EIGHT: DEATH MASK

1. *San Francisco Examiner*, 9 August 1914.

2. Panama-Pacific International Exposition Brochure, 1915, Virtual Museum of San Francisco, www.sfmuseum.org/hist9/ppietxt1.html (accessed 10 June 2008); "Fair Opening Shatters All Attendance Records," *Los Angeles Times*, 21 February 1915; "President Opens the Fair by Wireless" and "How President Opened the Fair," *New York Times*, 21 February 1915.

3. "Fair Opening"; Juliet James, *Sculpture of the Exposition Palaces and Courts* (San Francisco: H. S. Crocker, 1915).

4. Stella Perry, *A Pictorial Survey of the Art of the Panama-Pacific International Exposition* (San Francisco: Paul Elder, 1915).

5. "Ishi to Be Seen and Heard in Encinal City," *Oakland Tribune*, 15 January 1912.

6. Richard F. Weingroff, "The Lincoln Highway," U.S. Department of Transportation, Federal Highway Administration, www.fhwa.dot.gov/infrastructure/lincoln.htm (accessed 10 June 2008).

7. "Exposition Auto Show the World's Greatest," *Los Angeles Times*, 2 May 1915.

8. Badé, *Life and Letters of John Muir*, 2:378.

9. Carew, "They Learn about Indians from Kroeber."

10. Anna Blake Mezquida, "The Door of Yesterday: An Intimate View of the Vanishing Race at the Panama-Pacific International Exposition," *Overland Monthly* 66 (July 1915): 3–11.

11. Letter from Zumwalt to T. Kroeber, 2 April 1962.

12. Jeanne Redman, "Miracles of Science Tell of World's Wondrous Speed," *Los Angeles Times*, 18 July 1915.

13. Mezquida, "Door of Yesterday."

14. Letter from Alfred Kroeber to Panama Pacific Exposition, 1911, Reel 40, A. L. Kroeber Papers, BANC FILM 2049, Bancroft Library; Triloki Pandey, "Anthropologists at Zuni," *Proceedings of the American Philosophical Society* 116, no. 4 (1972): 330.

15. Alexandra Stern, *Eugenic Nation: Faults and Frontiers of Better Breeding in Modern America* (Berkeley: University of California Press, 2005), 48.

16. Letter from A. Kroeber to David Starr Jordan, 13 March 1915, Reel 5, A. L. Kroeber Papers, BANC FILM 2049, Bancroft Library.

17. "Eugenic Fad Called Joke," *Los Angeles Times*, 27 February 1914.

18. "Eugenic Fad."

19. A. L. Kroeber, "Inheritance by Magic," *American Anthropologist* 18, no. 1 (1916): 19–40; A. L. Kroeber, "Eighteen Professions," *American Anthropologist* 17, no. 2 (1915): 283–88; A. Kroeber, "Superorganic."

20. "Glimpses of San Francisco," *Los Angeles Times*, 8 March 1914; Robert Rydell, *All the World's a Fair: Visions of Empire at American International Expositions, 1876–1916* (Chicago: University of Chicago Press, 1984), 222; A. Kroeber, "Eighteen Professions," 286.

21. Rydell, *All the World's a Fair*, 225.

22. "Eskimo Wedding at Ocean Park," *Los Angeles Times*, 10 August 1915.

23. Alfred Kroeber submitted an article to the San Francisco *Call* titled "The Explorers' Eskimo," apparently published 5 December 1909. Letter from James Barr to Alfred Kroeber, 3 December 1909, Reel 39, A. L. Kroeber Papers, BANC FILM 2049, Bancroft Library.

24. "Why Arctic Explorer Peary's Neglected Eskimo Wants to Shoot Him," *San Francisco Examiner*, 9 May 1909, reprinted in Harper, *Give Me My Father's Body*; Harper, *Give Me My Father's Body*, 145.

25. T. Kroeber, *Kroeber*, 91.

26. Telegram from A. Kroeber to Edward Sapir, 6 September 1911, Reel 4, A. L. Kroeber Papers, BANC FILM 2049, Bancroft Library; letter from A. Kroeber to Sapir, 21 February 1914, Reel 5, A. L. Kroeber Papers, BANC FILM 2049, Bancroft Library.

27. Letter from A. Kroeber to Sapir, 24 November 1914; letter from Sapir to A. Kroeber, 2 December 1914; letter from A. Kroeber to Sapir, 7 December 1914; letter from A. Kroeber to Sapir, 26 April 1915, all in *Sapir-Kroeber Correspondence*, 161–63, 186–87.

28. T. Kroeber, *Kroeber*, 91–92, 96–99; T. Kroeber, *Ishi*, 232; Buzaljko, "Kroeber, Pope and Ishi," 51.

29. T. Kroeber, *Ishi*, 231; Buzaljko, "Kroeber, Pope and Ishi," 49; Edward Sapir, "Terms of Relationship and the Levirate," *American Anthropologist* 18, no. 3 (1916): 330.

30. Letter from Sapir to A. Kroeber, 23 September 1915, in *Sapir-Kroeber Correspondence*, 194–96; letter from A. Kroeber to Sapir, 12 September 1915, Reel 5, A. L. Kroeber Papers, BANC FILM 2049, Bancroft Library.

31. Grant MacCurdy, "Anthropology at the San Francisco Meeting," *Science* 42, no. 1085 (1915): 541–46; letters from Esther Watson to Theodora

Kroeber, 2 September 1962 and n.d., Box 10, File 9, Theodora Kroeber Papers, BANC MSS 69/145 c, Bancroft Library.

32. "Cave Man a Lecturer," *Los Angeles Times*, 5 July 1915.

33. Victor Golla, "Ishi's Language," in K. Kroeber and Kroeber, *Ishi in Three Centuries*, 217; letter from Sapir to A. Kroeber, 23 September 1915; letter from Waterman to A. Kroeber, 7 November 1915, Reel 47, A. L. Kroeber Papers, BANC FILM 2049, Bancroft Library; Buzaljko, "Kroeber, Pope and Ishi," 55.

34. Ishi, "Long, Long Ago," 280–92; Ishi's story "Coyote and his Sister" in Herbert Luthin and Leanne Hinton, "The Days of a Life: What Ishi's Stories Can Tell Us about Ishi," in K. Kroeber and Kroeber, *Ishi in Three Centuries*, 333–43.

35. Saxton Pope, "The Medical History of Ishi," *University of California Publications in American Archeology and Ethnology* 13, no. 5 (1920): 198; letter from A. Kroeber to Gifford, 7 July 1915, in Buzaljko, "Kroeber, Pope and Ishi," 55.

36. Pope, "Medical History of Ishi," 198.

37. Letter from A. Kroeber to Waterman, 28 August 1915, Box 85, CU-23, Anthropological Papers, Bancroft Library.

38. Pope, "Medical History of Ishi," 200, 204.

39. Linda Nash, *Inescapable Ecologies: A History of Environment, Disease, and Knowledge* (Berkeley: University of California Press, 2007); Georgina Felding, *Disease and Class: Tuberculosis and the Shaping of Modern North American Society* (New Brunswick, N.J.: Rutgers University Press, 2005); Gregg Mitman, *Breathing Space: How Allergies Shape Our Lives and Landscapes* (New Haven, Conn.: Yale University Press, 2007). Climate had begun to lose some of its power as both an explanation for and possible cure of disease by the early twentieth century, but vestiges of that belief remained and were particularly strong in the medical profession's treatment of tuberculosis.

40. Letters from Waterman to A. Kroeber, 18 October and 17 November 1915, Box 85, CU-23, Anthropological Papers, Bancroft Library.

41. Letter from A. Kroeber to Waterman, 28 August 1915; Pope, "Medical History of Ishi," 205.

42. H. L. Reider, "Tuberculosis among American Indians of the Contiguous United States," *Public Health Report* 104, no. 6 (1989): 653–57; Felding, *Disease and Class.*

43. Pope, "Medical History of Ishi," 204–6.

44. Pope, "Medical History of Ishi," 178–93.

45. Letter from Waterman to A. Kroeber, 17 November 1915; Pope, "Medical History of Ishi," 204–6; letter from Pope to A. Kroeber, 14 January 1916, Reel 39, A. L. Kroeber Papers, BANC FILM 2049, Bancroft Library.

46. Pope, "Medical History of Ishi," 205; Buzaljko, "Kroeber, Pope and Ishi," 57.

47. Pope, "Medical History of Ishi," 205–8.

48. Letter from Edward Gifford to A. Kroeber, 18 March 1916, Box 60, Records of the Department of Anthropology, CU-23, University Archives, Bancroft Library; letter from A. Kroeber to Gifford, 24 March 1916, in Heizer and Kroeber, *Ishi, the Last Yahi,* 240.

49. Buzaljko, "Kroeber, Pope and Ishi," 55; Pope, "Medical History," in Kroeber and Heizer, *Ishi, the Last Yahi,* 236.

50. Pope, "Medical History of Ishi," 209–12.

51. Pope, "Yahi Archery," 193, 23; Pope, "Medical History of Ishi," 213; Starn, *Ishi's Brain,* 128. Something of the same desire to possess the other is suggested by the view that Pope, who finished second in his class in medical school, married his wife because she finished first (Kuhn, *Catalyst and Teacher,* 253).

52. Ishi, "Journey of the Dead," 278–80.

53. T. Kroeber, *Kroeber,* 92; Starn, *Ishi's Brain,* 160; Julian Steward, *Alfred Kroeber* (New York: Columbia University Press, 1973), 22.

54. Letters from A. Kroeber to Hrdlička, 27 October, 14 December 1916, letters from Hrdlička to A. Kroeber, n.d. and 20 December 1916; letter from Rosenbusch to A. Kroeber, 17 January 1917; letter from A. Kroeber to Rosenbusch, 20 February 1917, all in Box 73, CU-23, Anthropological Papers, Bancroft Library.

55. T. Kroeber, *Kroeber,* 87.

EPILOGUE

1. T. Kroeber, *Kroeber*. 103.

2. Letters from A. Kroeber to Sapir, 7 December 1918, 27 December 1919, 23 January 1920 and 8 February 1920, in *Sapir-Kroeber Correspondence*, 288–334.

3. T. Kroeber, *Kroeber*, 133.

4. Alexander Cockburn, "Kroeber and the California Indians," *Counterpunch*, 26 July 2003, www.counterpunch.org/cockburn07262003. html (accessed 18 June 2008); T. Kroeber, *Kroeber*, 139–42.

5. T. Kroeber, *Kroeber*, 135, 44.

6. A. Kroeber, *Handbook*, 344.

7. T. Kroeber, *Kroeber*, 92–93, 276–86.

8. Theodora Kroeber telegram draft, "UC's Alfred Kroeber Dies," *San Francisco Chronicle*, 6 October 1960; Dornback, "Anthropologist, Educator"; T. Kroeber, *Kroeber*, 223.

9. Starn, *Ishi's Brain*, 59.

10. Kenneth Brower, book review of *Ishi in Two Worlds*, *Sierra Club Bulletin*, November 1962, Box 13, Folder 8, Theodora Kroeber Papers, BANC MSS 69/145 c, Bancroft Library.

11. Leslie Marmon Silko, "Landscape, History and the Pueblo Imagination," in Cheryll Glotfelty and Harold Fromm, eds., *The Ecocriticism Reader* (Athens: University of Georgia Press, 1996), 267.

12. "Ishi Wilderness Proposal," Mother Lode Chapter of the Sierra Club mailing, Box 6, Folder 6, Dorothy Hill Collection, Meriam Library Special Collections, California State University, Chico.

13. Ishi Conference flyer, Box 6, Folder 6, Dorothy Hill Collection; Gary Snyder, "The Woman Who Married a Bear," in *The Practice of the Wild* (New York: North Point Press, 1990), 155–74.

14. Frank Tuttle, "What Wild Indian?," in K. Kroeber and Kroeber, *Ishi in Three Centuries*, 394–95.

15. Mary Curtius, "Group Tries to Rebury Tribe's Last Survivor," *Los Angeles Times*, 8 June 1997.

16. Mary Curtius, "California and the West: Museum Refuses to Give Ishi's Brain to Indians," *Los Angeles Times*, 25 March 1999; Sara-Iarus Tolley, *Quest for Tribal Acknowledgment: California's Honey Lake Maidus* (Norman: University of Oklahoma Press, 2006), 96.

17. Silko, "Landscape," 265.

18. Starn, *Ishi's Brain*, 264–66; Winona LaDuke, "Imperial Anthropology," in *Recovering the Sacred: The Power of Naming and Claiming* (Cambridge, Mass.: South End Press, 2005), 75.

AFTERWORD

1. William Cronon, "A Place for Stories: Nature, History, and Narrative," *Journal of American History* 78 (March 1992): 1347. For the perspective of stories being imposed on the landscape by humans to create "place," see Wallace Stegner, "The Sense of Place," in *Where the Bluebird Sings to the Lemonade Springs: Living and Writing in the West* (New York: Random House, 1992), 199–206. For the idea that stories come out of the land, see Silko, "Landscape."

2. Frederick Jackson Turner, "The Significance of the Frontier in American History" (1893), in John Mack Faragher, ed., *Rereading Frederick Jackson Turner* (New York: Henry Holt, 1994), 31–60.

3. See Patricia Limerick, *The Legacy of Conquest: The Unbroken Past of the American West* (New York: Norton, 1987); Patricia Limerick, Clyde Milner II, and Charles Rankin, eds., *Trails: Toward a New Western History* (Lawrence: University Press of Kansas, 1991); Kerwin Klein, *Frontiers of Historical Imagination: Narrating the European Conquest of Native America, 1890–1990* (Berkeley: University of California Press, 1997).

4. Richard White, *The Middle Ground: Indians, Empires, and Republics in the Great Lakes Region, 1650–1815* (New York: Cambridge University Press, 1991); Deloria, *Indians in Unexpected Places.*

5. Carl Nolte, "Westfield San Francisco Centre," *San Francisco Chronicle*, 24 September 2006.

6. Nolte, "Westfield."

7. William Leach, *Land of Desire: Merchants, Power, and the Rise of a New American Culture* (New York: Pantheon, 1993).

8. T. J. Jackson Lears, *No Place of Grace: Antimodernism and the Transformation of American Culture, 1880–1920* (Chicago: University of Chicago Press, 1983); Berman, *All That Is Solid;* Solnit, *River of Shadows.*

9. Molly Gloss, *Wild Life: A Novel* (New York: Simon and Schuster, 2000), 31.

10. Standing Bear, *Land of the Spotted Eagle,* 38.

11. M. K. Anderson, *Tending the Wild,* 3.

12. Vizenor and Lee, *Postindian Conversations,* 73–74.

13. Jean François Lyotard, *The Postmodern Condition: A Report on Knowledge* (Minneapolis: University of Minnesota Press, 1984).

14. Ursula K. Le Guin, "The Carrier Bag Theory of Fiction," in Glotfelty and Fromm, *Ecocriticism Reader,* 149–54.

15. Santiago and Lowry, *Home to Medicine Mountain;* Judith Lowry, *Illuminations* (Santa Fe, N.M.: Wheelwright Museum of the American Indian, 1999); Darryl Babe Wilson, *The Morning the Sun Went Down* (San Francisco: Heyday Books, 1997); Janice Gould, *Earthquake Weather* (Tucson: University of Arizona Press, 1996).

16. Gould, *Earthquake Weather,* vii–xiii.

17. Gould, *Earthquake Weather,* ix.

18. Greg Sarris, *Mabel McKay;* California Indian Basketmakers Association website, www.ciba.org/about.html#vision (accessed 18 June 2008).

19. Gould, *Earthquake Weather,* 41.

20. Patricia Limerick, *Something in the Soil: Legacies and Reckonings in the New West* (New York: W. W. Norton, 2001), 33; William Cronon, "The Trouble with Wilderness; or, Getting Back to the Wrong Nature," in Cronon, ed., *Uncommon Ground: Toward Reinventing Nature* (New York: W. W. Norton, 1995), 69–90.

INDEX